PHILIPPIAN NOTES

AN INSPIRATIONAL COMMENTARY
ON PAUL'S EPISTLE TO THE PHILIPPIANS

Philippian Notes

*AN INSPIRATIONAL COMMENTARY
ON PAUL'S EPISTLE TO THE PHILIPPIANS*

GREG HINNANT

PhilippianNotes by Greg Hinnant
Published by Creation House
A Charisma Media Company
600 Rinehart Road
Lake Mary, Florida 32746
www.charismamedia.com

This book or parts thereof may not be reproduced in any form, stored in a retrieval system, or transmitted in any form by any means—electronic, mechanical, photocopy, recording, or otherwise—without prior written permission of the publisher, except as provided by United States of America copyright law.

Unless otherwise noted, all Scripture quotations are from *The New Scofield Reference Bible*, King James Version (New York: Oxford University Press, 1967). *The New Scofield Reference Bible* contains introductions, annotations, subject chain references, and some word changes in the King James Version that will help the reader.

Scripture quotations marked amp are from the Amplified Bible. Copyright © 1954, 1958, 1962, 1964, 1965, 1987 by The Lockman Foundation. Used by permission.

Scripture quotations marked esv are from the Holy Bible, English Standard Version. Copyright © 2001 by Crossway Bibles, a division of Good News Publishers. Used by permission.

Scripture quotations marked gw are from God's Word Translation, copyright © 1995 by God's Word to the Nations. Used by permission of Baker Publishing Group.

Scripture quotations marked isv are from the International Standard Version of the Bible. Copyright © 1995–2014 by ISV Foundation. All rights reserved internationally. Used by permission of Davidson Press, LLC.

Scripture quotations marked kjv are from the King James Version of the Bible. Public domain.

Scripture quotations marked MOFFATT are from *The New Testament, a New Translation*, translated by James Moffatt. Copyright © 1950, 1952, 1953, 1954 by James A. R. Moffatt. Used by permission.

Scripture quotations marked NAS are from the New American Standard Bible, copyright © 1960, 1962, 1963, 1968, 1971, 1972, 1973, 1975, 1977, 1995 by The Lockman Foundation. Used by permission. (www.Lockman.org)

Scripture quotations marked NCV are taken from the New Century Version®. Copyright © 2005 by Thomas Nelson. Used by permission. All rights reserved.

Scripture quotations marked NIV are taken from the Holy Bible, New International Version®, NIV®. Copyright © 1973, 1978, 1984, 2011 by Biblica, Inc.™ Used by permission of Zondervan. All rights reserved worldwide. www.zondervan.com The "NIV" and "New International Version" are trademarks registered in the United States Patent and Trademark Office by Biblica, Inc.™

Scripture quotations marked NKJV are taken from the New King James Version®. Copyright © 1982 by Thomas Nelson. Used by permission. All rights reserved.

Scripture quotations marked NLT are from the Holy Bible, New Living Translation, copyright © 1996, 2004, 2007. Used by permission of Tyndale House Publishers, Inc., Wheaton, IL 60189. All rights reserved.

Scripture quotations marked PHILLIPS are from *The New Testament in Modern English*, Revised Edition. Copyright © 1958, 1960, 1972 by J. B. Phillips. Macmillan Publishing Co. Used by permission.

Scripture quotations marked THE MESSAGE are from *The Message: The Bible in Contemporary English*, copyright © 1993, 1994, 1995, 1996, 2000, 2001, 2002. Used by permission of NavPress Publishing Group.

Scripture quotations marked WEY are from the Weymouth New Testament. Public domain.

Scripture quotations marked WUEST are from *The New Testament: An Expanded Translation* by K. S. Wuest, copyright © 1961 by Eerdmans Publishing, Grand Rapids, MI; located in Logos Digital Software.

Scripture quotations marked YLT are from *Young's Literal Translation*. Public domain.

AUTHOR'S NOTE: Some Scripture quotations have specific words and/or phrases that I am emphasizing. I have added italics to these verses to show that emphasis. Also, in some of the Scripture quotations, with the exception of the Amplified Bible, I have inserted in brackets explanatory text to help with the understanding of certain words and phrases.

Design Director: Justin Evans
Cover design by Nathan Morgan

Copyright © 2015 by Greg Hinnant
All rights reserved.

Visit the author's website: www.greghinnantministries.org.

Library of Congress CataloginginPublication Data: 2015909619
International Standard Book Number: 978-1-62998-474-2
E-book International Standard Book Number: 978-1-62998-475-9

While the author has made every effort to provide accurate telephone numbers and Internet addresses at the time of publication, neither the publisher nor the author assumes any responsibility for errors or for changes that occur after publication.

First edition

15 16 17 18 19 — 987654321
Printed in the United States of America

To the late Dr. Judson Cornwall, who encouraged me to persevere in biblical scholarship and ministry...

BIBLE ABBREVIATIONS

AMP: The Amplified Bible

ESV: The English Standard Version

GW: God's Word Translation

ISV: International Standard Version

KJV: The King James (or Authorized) Version

Moffatt: The New Testament: A New Translation, by James A. R. Moffatt

NAS: The New American Standard Version

NCV: The New Century Version

NIV: The New International Version

NKJV: The New King James Version

NLT: The New Living Translation

Phillips: The New Testament in Modern English, Rev. Ed., by J. B. Phillips

The Message: The Message: The Bible in Contemporary English (a paraphrase)

WEY: The Weymouth New Testament

Wuest: The New Testament: An Expanded Translation, by K. S. Wuest

YLT: Young's Literal Translation

CONTENTS

    Preface xiii

    Introduction xv

1 Exploring Paul's Heart 1

2 Jesus' Kenosis—and Ours!. 63

3 Pressing Toward New Goals! 129

4 Standing Fast! 187

    Bibliography. 263

    Contact the Author 267

    Other Books by this Author 269

PREFACE

For many years I've spent considerable time most workdays studying various books of the Bible and preparing in-depth notes. Nearly all my books, courses, sermons, and pieces have come from these studies.

A few years back I wrote my first commentary on the Book of Daniel. With this new work I'm renewing my expositional writing, which, God willing, will be the first of a series of similarly crafted commentaries.

In *PhilippianNotes* I've attempted to explore the Philippian epistle in depth, offering historical and grammatical detail combined with a practical application of the rich spiritual truths it presents. This commentary reflects my method of study, linear and lateral—moving forward systematically verse by verse, yet stopping to explore wonders left and right, in Old and New Testament references and topical links to other sources. My style is noncontroversial and my intent to simply help you understand more fully Paul, his readers, their times, the various points he raised, and what God is saying to us through them today.

Christian scholars will likely find my work moderately technical, yet very sufficiently researched. Laymen will find here not just information but inspiration aplenty, particularly in the personal application paragraphs ending each entry. Pastors and teachers will discover many potential sermons and teachings in not only these entries but also their footnotes. Thus to one and all I urge, *read the footnotes!* If you miss them, you've missed much.

And I pray you won't miss anything! May you derive as much useful information and timely inspiration in studying this commentary as I have in preparing it. *Soli Deo gloria!*

—Greg Hinnant

INTRODUCTION

THE EPISTLE TO the Philippians was written about AD 61–62 from Rome by the Apostle Paul, who was under house arrest awaiting trial before Nero (Acts 28:30–31).

Paul's words should command our attention since they are the inspired insights of Christianity's foremost apostle, evangelist, teacher, theologian, writer, missionary, church planter, overseer, spiritual father, prayer warrior, loving pastor, humble sufferer, and overcomer. Need I say more?

One of Paul's four prison epistles, this message, though neither polemical nor admonitory, contains some very important truths. Most significantly it describes the wondrous humility of Christ in His incarnation and sufferings, reveals Paul's Christlike heart, spotlights his (and our) new goals in life and ministry, and specifies how we can stand fast in Christ whatever our circumstances. It also prominently showcases the extraordinarily faithful charity of the Philippian Christians for our emulation.

That said, this letter, though brief, touches on many other key themes: the mind of Christ, joy, love, unity, contentment,

Jesus' lordship, working out our salvation, spiritual circumcision, spiritual maturity, selflessness in ministry, giving, the passion to know Christ, releasing the past to pursue our new goals, our heavenly citizenship, eagerly looking for Christ's return, right thinking, confidence in Christ's all-sufficient assistance, the assurance of divine provision, and the amazing power of the gospel. Paul's immediate reason for writing was to thank the Philippians for the generous gift they sent him in his distress—revealing their special love for Paul as openly as this letter reveals his for them.

This beloved Philippian church was the first known European church; founded through divine guidance on Paul's second missionary journey; initially headquartered in the home of Lydia, a local businesswoman; witness to Paul's brutal, illegal public beating, jailing, and miraculous deliverance; and by the time of this epistle well established in the city of Philippi.

The "city of Philip" itself was in Macedonia, a Roman colony—and very much a "little Rome" in its government, local culture, and self-view—located on a major Roman road (the Ignatian Way) near a small river (Gangites), and about ten miles west of the Aegean seaport of Neapolis. Since Lydia and a few other Jewish proselytes worshipped outside the city, it appears there was no synagogue there and thus very few Jewish residents. Hosting a medical school, Philippi may have been Luke's hometown or possibly the site where he studied medicine prior to joining Paul on the latter's second missionary journey. These are the facts. More facts and inspiration await.

So explore with me now Paul's inspired letter to this inspiring church in Philippi.

Chapter One

EXPLORING PAUL'S HEART

As Philippians opens, so does Paul's heart. There we find the stuff that made him such an extraordinary Christian and leader: his humble self-description, deep love for Christians, powerful prayer requests, grasp of God's purposes, willingness to suffer, readiness to die, confidence that God turns even persecution for our good, love of fellowship, yearning for unity, shepherdly desires, faithfulness to remind us we too are called to suffer, and so forth. Let's explore Paul's heart and behold the stuff of greatness…

1:1–2 Paul's signature salutation. Paul begins this epistle much like his other twelve. He identifies himself and his companions (here "Timothy"), names his addressees (the Philippian Christians, their leaders[1]), and invokes fresh supplies of divine "grace and peace" upon his readers from the heavenly Father and Son. This is his signature salutation.

---

1. "Bishops" and "deacons" were the elders appointed to oversee the church's spiritual life and business and practical affairs. Today these are usually referred to as "ministers" and "board members."

On this distinctively Pauline form greeting Matthew Henry says, "We must not be shy of forms [set prayers], though we are not to be tied down to them."[2] Jesus gave us a prayer for us to use as both a form prayer and a guideline for prayer (Matt. 6:9–13). He repeated His own prayer in Gethsemane three times (Matt. 26:44), yet typically prayed spontaneous prayers for a ceaseless stream of needy supplicants. So we conclude He didn't order us to never repeat any of our prayers. Instead He forbade us to not do so (a) imagining our "much speaking" will earn God's answers (Matt. 6:7–8; Isa. 1:15–17), or (b) in a doubtful mind as if earlier prayers on the same subject were unheard (Matt. 21:21–22; James1:5–8). Only such meaninglessly repetitive or doubtful prayers are "vain repetitions" (Matt. 6:7). Whether your prayers are set or spontaneous, will you confidently believe God always hears and answers you "when ye pray" (Mark 11:24)?

By addressing "all the saints[3]" in the Philippian church, Paul indirectly requested this letter to be read aloud to the entire assembly, not just the leaders (Col. 4:16). This further shows that Paul believed *all* believers were equal in Christ (James 1:9–10; 2:1) and, by the Spirit's help, equally able to understand God's Word. Thank God the whole Word is for the whole church! Paul's reference to two levels of ministers, "bishops" and "deacons," shows that the church God founded through him a few years earlier (Acts 16) had grown larger, necessitating full ministerial staffing. When God founds churches, they flourish! Are

---

2. Matthew Henry, *Commentary in One Volume* (Grand Rapids, MI; Zondervan Publishing, 1961), 1860.
3. "Saints" (1:1) is translated from the Greek *hagios*, meaning "holy, dedicated," and refers to all who are elected to salvation in Christ, not a special class of exceptionally sanctified believers canonized by Roman, Eastern or other churches.

you preparing to become a wise minister or diligent deacon to help lead your growing church?

On Paul's mention of grace first and then peace, Matthew Henry adds, "[There is] no peace without grace. Inward peace springs from a sense of divine favor."[4] Concerning peace in its fullest sense, one commentator notes:

> Peace in the Bible is more than the absence of conflict. It is complete well-being, involving reconciliation to God and to our fellows (Eph. 2:14–18) and the blessing of inner peace (4:7).[5]

We do well to distinguish between peace with God, peace with people, and inner peace. It's rare that we have peace with all people, though we should earnestly try to think, speak, and act peacefully toward everyone (Rom. 12:18). It's imperative, however, that we maintain peace with God and the peace of God—the inner peace that flows from Him who is "our peace" (Eph. 2:14)—no matter how many adversaries and adversities surround us.

See Romans 1:7; 1 Corinthians 1:3; 2 Corinthians 1:2; Galatians 1:3; Ephesians 1:2; Philippians 1:2; Colossians 1:2; 1 Thessalonians 1:1; 2 Thessalonians 1:2; 1 Timothy 1:2; 2 Timothy 1:2; Titus 1:4; Philemon 3.

1:1 Paul's providential partner. Timothy is with Paul now (1:1) and is no doubt a great comfort to the imprisoned apostle as he faces the unsettling prospect of standing trial before the nefarious, psychotic, and predictably unpredictable emperor Nero.

---

4. Henry, *Commentary in One Volume*, 1860.
5. D. A. Carson, R. T. France, J. A. Motyer, and G. J. Wenham, editors, *New Bible Commentary: 21st Century Edition*, 4th ed. (Leicester, England; Downers Grove, IL: InterVarsity Press, 1994), Phil. 1:2, note.

Here's another instance of the great truth "two are better than one" (Eccles. 4:9–12).

Ecclesiastes 4:9–12 reveals the advantages of two servants of God working in tandem. Such providential pairs enjoy increased resilience; greater warmth of devotion, faith, and love through regular close fellowship; more strength to stand against spiritual attacks; more fruitful labors (due to ministerial synergy); the advantage of correcting and challenging each other; and a greater reward for their service. For these and other reasons, when God initiates ministries and missions, He often calls not one but two (Mark 6:7; Exod. 4:27; Acts 13:2; Hag. 1:1; Ezra 5:1; 6:14; Neh. 8:9; Rev. 11:3–12; 1 Pet. 5:13).

Sometimes these providential pairs are co-ministers from different backgrounds: Barton A. Stone and Alexander Campbell, cofounders of the Disciples of Christ. Sometimes they're husband and wife teams: William and Catherine Booth,[6] or more recently Dick and Rita Bennett, who were influential in the Charismatic Renewal. Sometimes they're father-son teams: of recent note, Pastors John and Matthew Hagee. Sometimes they're brothers: John and Charles Wesley. Sometimes they're two leaders working simultaneously in different countries: John Wesley (England) and George Whitfield (America). Or two leaders working successively in the same movement in different countries: John Wesley (England) and Francis Asbury (America). Sometimes they're two leaders working concurrently (even if not unitedly) in launching significant spiritual movements: William F. Seymour and Charles F. Parham.

---

6. Two other notable husband-wife teams of the nineteenth and twentieth century were Phoebe and Walter Palmer and Oswald and Beatrice Chambers, though in both cases one led in utterance ministry and the other played a key supportive role.

Do we know those with whom God has providentially paired us? Are we building a closer partnership with them or neglecting or even abandoning them?

1:1–2 Paul's signature self-description. As always, Paul refers to himself as one of Christ's "servants"; or more accurately, "bondservants," (NKJV), "slaves," (NLT).[7]

No crowing about his apostolic authority here, just a sober, humble self-view as he taught (Rom. 12:3). Every minister, however anointed, appointed, and endowed with gifts and power, is but another love slave in sweet service of Christ. We're here "not to be ministered unto" with honors and gifts, "but to minister, and to give" our lives for the welfare of Christ's precious people (Matt. 20:28). We have no right to live for our own purposes or pleasures and every obligation to live for Christ's bride. Matthew Henry notes Paul "mentions the church before the ministers, because the ministers are for the church, not the churches for the ministers."[8] Oh, how badly aspiring ministers need to adopt Paul's humble self-view!

Are we seeking to be Christ's humble, faithful servant or a notable religious personality, high officeholder, or materially wealthy minister? Feel you need higher grace to bend lower?

This will help. God's slaves are more important than this world's free men. Craig Keener notes that in the first-century Roman world:

---

7. "Servants" is translated from the Greek *doulos*, meaning "slave." See J. Swanson, *Dictionary of Biblical Languages With Semantic Domains: Greek (New Testament)*, electronic ed. (Oak Harbor: Logos Research Systems, Inc., 1997), s.v. "*doulos.*"
8. Henry, *Commentary in One Volume*, 1860.

Slaves of the emperor and other high officials wielded far more power than independent free persons.[9]

Similarly, the humblest, most selfless servant of heaven's Emperor, Jesus, enjoys more authority, influence, and honor from God's perspective than the proudest, most self-centered, self-serving sinner—or minister! Though they don't know it, the latter are through their feverish self-promotion constantly serving the proud prince of this world, not the Prince of Peace, with slavish submission (Rom. 6:16, 17; 2 Pet. 2:19). Should Christ's ministers facilitate Satan's ambition?

For several years I was blessed to be mentored by the late Dr. Judson Cornwall in things pertaining to the ministry in general and writing in particular. Dr. Cornwall, who is now with the Lord, pastored several churches, authored more than fifty books, held doctoral degrees in theology and divinity, taught on a Bible school faculty, and traveled the world for several decades. Yet one day he felt led of God to renounce his ministerial titles and thereafter be known simply as "Brother Judson." His decision was distinctly Pauline in spirit, and highly recommendable.

Whether in this way or another, why not humble yourself under the Lord's mighty hand so He can raise you in His time and way (1 Pet. 5:6)? When that time arrives, instead of crowing about your authority, position, and achievements, you'll think, feel, and sound Pauline: "I'm Jesus' love slave, here to assist, nurture, serve, and suffer for you, the people He loves." Or in Paul's words, we'll see "ourselves" as "your servants for Jesus' sake" (2 Cor. 4:5).

See Romans 1:1; 1 Corinthians 7:23; Titus 1:1; Galatians 1:10.

---

9. C. S. Keener, *The IVP Bible Background Commentary: New Testament* (Downers Grove, IL: InterVarsity Press, 1993), Phil. 1:1, note.

1:5 How full is your fellowship? Paul said he frequently and joyfully thanked God for the "fellowship" he enjoyed with the Philippians (vv. 3–5). Obviously it was very full and sweet and every thought of it satisfying and sustaining in his present bitter circumstances.

"Fellowship"[10] is friendly company, conversation, and comradeship around a common interest; or simply sharing experiences, activities, or hobbies. We may have fellowship in Christian and many other interests and activities. Paul's fellowship with the Philippians revolved around his ministry to them, friendship with them (1:8), sufferings with them (1:30; Acts 16:40), and their ministry to Him (through prayer and financial partnership, 4:10, 14–16). Are we fellowshipping regularly or rarely?

We may fellowship with other Christians in believing and spreading the gospel (1:5); ministry activities or support (1:5; 2 Cor. 8:1–4), Bible study (Acts 17:11), edifying spiritual conversation (Heb. 3:13; 13:16; Prov. 27:17), praise and worship (Ps. 95:6; Acts 2:46–47), intercessory prayer (Acts 12:5, 12; Eph. 6:18–20), receiving the Holy Spirit (Acts 2:4; 10:44; 11:15–17), gifts of the Spirit (1 Cor. 12), giving or sharing (Phil. 4:15; Acts 2:44–45), obedience to God's Word (1 John 1:7), fellowship meals (Acts 2:46; 1 Cor. 11:33–34), travel (Acts 17:14–15), sacraments (baptism, Acts 19:5; Lord's Supper, 1 Cor. 11:26), suffering (Phil. 3:10; Acts 8:1, 4), enduring tests (Rom. 16:3–4; Rev. 3:10), and watching for Christ (Mark 13:32–37; Luke 21:34–36).

Physical nearness isn't required for meaningful fellowship. We can fellowship with Christians far away (as the Philippians were from Paul) by communications (letters, e-mails, telephone

---

10. Greek *koinōnia*, means "common, [common] association, partnership [sharing], communion, joint participation, [social] intercourse." See J. Strong, *Enhanced Strong's Lexicon* (Bellingham, WA: Logos Bible Software, 2001), s.v. "*koinōnia*."

calls, text messages, Internet conferencing), gifts (Phil. 4:10, 18), and intercessory prayers (Phil. 1:3–4, 8–11). In Paul's case, about a decade had passed since he had last ministered in Philippi.[11]

Whether close or distant, Christian fellowship is not automatic. It's a choice. Sadly some choose not to fellowship, ignoring those who share their Lord and faith (Gal. 2:12; Heb. 10:24–25). Many others, however, choose to fellowship, frequently going "to their own company" to drink from the sweet waters of fellowship in the heat of trial (Acts 4:23). Some begin enjoying fellowship but later stop short.

They don't understand the way of fellowship. Christian fellowship is based on our fellowship with Christ, our universal common interest. Anything that breaks our union with Him also damages our fellowship with other Christians. Therefore our Christian fellowship is broken whenever we depart from the light of Christ's righteousness revealed in God's Word (1 John 1:5–7), whether by personal sins, ignoring divine guidance, divisive thoughts or emotions (judging, envying, holding prejudices, 1 Cor. 3:3–4), offensive behavior (Luke 17:3–4), or by simply selfishly refusing to make the minimal effort required to enjoy the fellowship available to us.

If instead of breaking or ignoring Christian fellowship we indulge it, our fellowship, like that Paul enjoyed with the Philippians, will be sweet, full, and sustaining. It will help keep us full of the Spirit, sweet in disposition, and strong in the Lord in even our bitterest trials. Is your cup of fellowship empty, half full, or brimming over?

---

11. J. F. Walvoord, R. B. Zuck, and Dallas Theological Seminary, *The Bible Knowledge Commentary: An Exposition of the Scriptures* (Wheaton, IL: Victor Books, 1985), Phil. 1:3, note.

Exploring Paul's Heart

1:6 God's—and Paul's—primary post-conversion purpose. God's primary will is that we receive the wondrously gracious salvation He's provided in Christ (John 3:16; 2 Pet. 3:9). But that's not all. He also purposes an ongoing, increasing work of divine grace "in" us (Phil. 1:6).

Paul declares this to the Philippians, assuring them God will "perform [complete, accomplish, perfect]"[12] this work until the day Christ returns (1:6). His use of the words "begun" and "perform [complete]" reveal he's not describing a mere experience (salvation) but rather one that begins a growing work of God's grace that, if we stay faithful, culminates in a spiritually complete (mature) life. Other translations underscore this: God will "bring it to completion" (ESV), or "carry it on to completion" (NIV), or "continue his work until it is finally finished" (NLT). Later Paul charges the Philippians to cooperate with this process, to "work out your own salvation" until it's fully developed (2:12).

So true Christianity is not a once-done experience—though our conversion experience is of enduring effectiveness. Nor is it only two works of grace—though the baptism with the Spirit is a distinct second work of grace. Rather it is a lifelong walk filled with increasing spiritual growth until we become consistently Christlike (complete or spiritually mature) in our thinking and living (Gal. 4:19; Rom. 8:29). This process of working out what God's grace has worked in continues until Jesus appears or we pass away (1 Thess. 4:17; Rev. 19:7–9).

Full of faith in God's faithfulness, Paul is "confident" God will never abandon but ever continue this "good work" in us:

---

12. "Perform" is taken from the Greek *epiteleō*, meaning "to complete, accomplish" and thus perfect. See R. L. Thomas, *New American Standard Hebrew-Aramaic and Greek Dictionaries*, updated edition (Anaheim: Foundation Publications, Inc., 1998), s.v. "*epiteleō.*"

He Who began a good work in you will continue until the day of Jesus Christ [right up to the time of His return] developing [that good work] and perfecting and bringing it to full completion in you.
—Philippians 1:6, AMP

One paraphrase is exceptional:

There has never been the slightest doubt in my mind that the God who started this great work in you would keep at it and bring it to a flourishing finish on the very day Christ Jesus appears.
—The Message

Looking forward, this continuing work of grace is preparing us to escape in the Rapture and live and rule with Christ in the Millennium, and later in New Jerusalem...forever. Thus it's God's kingdom preparation process.

This process aims to make us perfect (consistently Christlike) in heart (2 Chron. 16:9; 19:9), life purpose (Phil. 3:10–14), faith (1 Thess. 3:10), fear of God (Job 1:1, 8), spiritual mindedness (Phil. 3:15), holiness (2 Cor. 7:1), faith (Heb. 12:2), obedience (like Christ, Heb. 5:8–9), peace (Isa. 26:3), patience (James 1:4), speech (James 3:2), ministry (2 Tim. 3:17), love (1 John 2:5; 4:12, 17, 18), Christ's strength and power (2 Cor. 12:9), overcoming or enduring sufferings (1 Pet. 5:10), end-time doctrine (1 Thess. 5:2), good works (Heb. 13:21), fruitfulness (ct. Luke 8:14), unity (1 Cor. 1:10; John 17:23), praise (Matt. 21:16), behavior (Ps. 101:2, 6), and other key areas of thought and conduct. Paul's assertion is not unique.

David and the writer to the Hebrews were also convinced God continues working with us throughout our lives until we're "perfect" (Ps. 138:8; 18:30–32; Heb. 6:1; 12:2). Jesus and Paul challenged us to seek spiritual perfection (Matt. 5:48; 19:21; 2 Cor. 7:1; 13:11; Phil. 3:14–15; Rom. 8:29) and prayed for it (Jn. 17:23; 2 Cor. 13:9). Following Paul's lead, Epaphras prayed persistently for his fellow Colossians to "stand perfect and complete in all the will of God" (Col. 4:12). Paul revealed our individual and corporate spiritual maturity is the goal of the fivefold ministry (Eph. 4:11–13). We must diligently study Scripture if we hope to be "perfect" and thus "thoroughly furnished [prepared] unto all good works" (2 Tim. 2:15; 3:14–17). And if we continue trusting and obeying Christ, He will use everything, even our sufferings,[13] to finish His "good work in you."

God earnestly desires to complete the "good work" of mature Christlikeness He's begun in you. Will you let Him? Even if it means persevering through long seasons of seeking, study, humility, obedience, and suffering?

1:3–7 Marks of great Christian leaders. In these few short verses Paul's words reveal the greatness of his spiritual leadership. While many immature or corrupt leaders sought wealth (1 Tim. 6:3–5; 2 Pet. 2:3), property (Luke 9:57–58), followings (Acts 20:30), power (3 John 9), fame, or other selfish interests in ministry (Phil. 2:21), Paul served only Christ's purposes among Christ's people.

His words reveal:

- He loved the Philippians—"I have you in my heart" (v. 7), or "you have a special place in my heart" (NLT); or, "you are very dear to me" (Phillips); also, "how I long for all of you with

---

13. As a man, even Christ was perfected by His humble, trusting obedience amid sufferings (Heb. 2:10; 5:8–9) and we are called to follow His steps (John 12:26).

the affection of Christ Jesus" (1:8, NIV). Paul took Christ's directive to the first minister, Peter, very seriously (John 21:15–17). Love for Christ's people, springing from love for Christ, drives all true ministry.

- HE THANKED GOD FOR THEM OFTEN—"upon every remembrance" (1:3). Paul was habitually thankful for all his fellow believers and ministers. Henry notes, "Thanksgiving must have a part in every prayer. What we have the comfort of, God must have the glory of."[14] See Philippians 4:6–7; Ephesians 5:20; John 11:41–42.

- HE PRAYED FOR HIS CONGREGANTS OFTEN—"always in every prayer" (1:4). Like his Lord, Paul was an incessant intercessor (Col. 1:3, 9; Heb. 7:25; Luke 22:31–32).

- HE REJOICED IN THEIR "FELLOWSHIP"—which lay "in the gospel" (1:3–5). This Christian camaraderie consisted of the Philippians' (1) long and very faithful financial "partnership in the gospel" (1:5, NIV; see 2 Cor. 8:1–4), and (2) friendly communications in person, by letters, and by messengers. This was very uplifting to Paul, since he was now older, confined, and sometimes lonely (2 Tim. 1:15; 4:16). Thus rejoicing, he lovingly commended them for their faithful fellowship (4:14–16).

---

14. Henry, *Commentary in One Volume*, 1860.

- HE MINISTERED TO THEM JOYFULLY—"With joy" Paul ministered to the Philippians by intercession (1:4). Joy springs from realizing we are pleasing God by fulfilling His purposes. Paul knew he was doing Christ's will daily just as Christ knew He was doing the Father's will (John 8:29; Ps. 40:8). Jesus wants our joy "full" or constant and satisfying (John 15:11; 16:24; 17:13). One commentator notes:

    > The secret of his [Paul's] joy is the *single mind;* he lives for Christ and the Gospel. (Christ is named eighteen times in Philippians 1, and the Gospel is mentioned six times.) "For to me to live is Christ, and to die is gain" (Phil. 1:21). But what really is "the single mind"? It is the attitude that says, "It makes no difference what happens to me, just as long as Christ is glorified and the Gospel shared with others."[15]

    Oswald Chambers said:

    > The joy of a thing lies in fulfilling the purpose of its creation. Jesus Christ's joy is that He fulfilled the design of His Father's will, and my joy is that I fulfill God's design in calling me, viz., to make me a follower of Him.[16]

- HUMBLY HE SAW THEM AS EQUALS—Paul considered the Philippians not subordinates but

---

15. W. W. Wiersbe, *The Bible Exposition Commentary* (Wheaton, IL: Victor Books, 1996), Phil. 1:1–11, note.
16. Harry Verploegh, *Oswald Chambers: The Best from All His Books.* (Nashville: Thomas Nelson Publishers, 1987), 189.

equal partakers in the same "grace" he received and lived in (v.7; see NIV).

- HUMBLY HE WORKED COOPERATIVELY WITH THEM—Paul's words reveal his ministerial manner was not condescending but cooperative. He and the Philippians became joint partners on one ministry team or body (v. 5): "We have worked together for the gospel" (PHILLIPS), in "your partnership" (NIV), and "you have been my partners" (NLT).

- HE UNDERSTOOD GOD'S PURPOSE—Paul knew what Christ wanted to do "in" them—transform them into His image so He could translate them into His presence (v. 6).[17] Thus he prayed, taught, corrected, and counseled the Philippians to help complete this grand divine design.

- HE WAS CONFIDENT GOD WOULD COMPLETE THIS PURPOSE—Remembering his expressly divine call to minister in Philippi (Acts 16:9) and that God's Word never returns void (Isa. 55:9–11), Paul was "confident" Christ would faithfully "perform" the work He began in the Philippians (v. 6), or "bring it to completion" (ESV). What God begins and we continue, God ends!

- HE CONTINUED MINISTERING WHILE SUFFERING—All this pastoral love, faithfulness, and service flowed from Paul not while enjoying inspiring

---

17. Jesus prayed for the church's transformation and translation (John 17:21–23, 24) and Paul described and prophesied their fulfillment (1 Thess. 5:23–24; 4:16–18; 1 Cor. 15:50–53).

success but while enduring undignifying sufferings: "in my bonds" (v. 7).

- HE REPRODUCED HIS OWN KIND—Paul said the Philippians had become "partakers of my grace" (1:7). His true students and partners, they had now become like him by standing by him even when his sufferings persisted in Philippi (Acts 16:16–2), in Jerusalem and Caesarea (Acts 21:27–26:32), and now in Rome (Acts 28:30–31). Henry observes:

  > "You have joined with me in doing and suffering." They were partakers of his affliction by sympathy and concern, and readiness to assist him. Those shall share in the reward who bear their part of the burden.[18]

Thus we see Paul's largeness of heart, his love, faith, humility, prayerfulness, joy, thanksgiving, knowledge of God's purpose, and spiritual reproduction. All these traits marked him as an exceptional Christian leader. How much of his spiritual greatness is in us?

Paul's example gives us a litmus test by which ministers, teachers, and counselors may examine themselves:

- Are my congregants, students, or counselees "in my heart," or is my heart occupied with other loves, ends, or yearnings, perhaps even a desire to

---

18. Henry, *Commentary in One Volume*, 1861.

use my present ministry as a stepping stone to a larger, more prestigious or lucrative ministry?

- Do I spend time praying for my people, or merely teach them about prayer and criticize them for their prayerlessness?

- Do I thank God for them every day just as they are, with all their faults, shortcomings, sins, childishness, and stubbornness, grateful that despite these negatives Christ loves them dearly and is growing in them daily?

- Do I rejoice that they're helping me discharge my commission and deeply appreciate their work, prayers, gifts, and support?

- Do I take time to fellowship with them and share loving, meaningful conversations, or stand apart, aloof and unconcerned?

- Am I humble, realizing they're exactly like me and called and gifted by grace to know and serve Christ just as I am, or am I haughty, imagining myself made of better stuff and possessing better gifts?

- Do I know what God wants to do in those I pastor, or am I full of my own goals, programs, and plans for them?

- Am I "confident" God will finish the good work He's begun in them, or have I lost faith in His power to change their attitudes, habits, sins, and weakness by the power of His Spirit and Word until they're consistently Christlike?

- Will I faithfully persist in these excellent ministerial attitudes and duties while suffering injustices and humiliations for Christ?

- Am I reproducing my own kind, others who walk in the spiritual maturity I teach and practice?

Our honest answers will reveal just how large- or small-hearted a minister we are, how Pauline or petty. Paul's ministerial greatness shows us how to reform our ministerial smallness. Luther launched the church's Reformation nearly five hundred years ago. Let's launch ours today!

1:7 Marks of great Christian followers. While we believe in the priesthood of all believers, it's evident God doesn't call everyone to be a congregational leader. Just as congregants need faithful leaders, leaders need faithful congregants. Like their leaders, these followers' loyalty will be tested.

The Philippians were outstanding followers in many ways. After praising their persisting support through gifts and prayers (1:3–5), Paul now lauds their loyalty. While many Christians distanced themselves from Paul during His Roman detainment (2 Tim. 1:15; 4:16), the Philippians remained loyal to him in his "bonds" (Phil. 1:7). Refusing pride and fear, their love wouldn't let them be "ashamed" of their teacher, even in his dishonorable condition (2 Tim. 1:8, 16–18). Not surprised, Paul said they "always obeyed" his (and God's) teaching (Phil. 2:12). All this confirms the Philippians were outstanding followers of God. And of Paul!

Are we as outstanding? Will we continue supporting leaders whom we know God has called, gifted, and sent when they're falsely accused and widely misjudged? Will we continue loyally supporting them, praying for them, and fellowshipping with them? Cowardly congregants will withdraw in the day of trouble. They follow only popular, powerful, or prosperous leaders. But great followers—overcomers!—continue standing by God's anointed ones no matter what public, and at times church,[19] opinion dictates.

David's six hundred men continued supporting him though Israel's leader, King Saul, denounced and persecuted him and all Israel increasingly lost faith in him. The Apostle John stood by Jesus all the way to the cross, while the others all forsook him and fled (John 19:25–27; Mark 14:50). Many continued standing with John Wycliffe and his Lollards when Pope Gregory XI publicly denounced him as the "master of errors." Many continued reading Martin Luther's books and pamphlets after Pope Leo X denounced Luther as a "wild boar" ravaging the vineyard of the Lord. Chinese congregations stood by their house church leaders while atheistic government officials denounced, prosecuted, and jailed them and many Western churches forgot them.

Such loyalty reveals followers' true motives. If we continue following leaders who are enduring hardship or reproach for Christ's sake, we're not doing so for what we'll get out of it. Rather our actions prove we believe God has called them and that by standing with them we're also standing with God and His kingdom truth and cause. Abandoning embattled leaders

---

19. We include church misjudgment since occasionally leaders of one church, denomination, or theological persuasion turn on those of another (2 Cor. 10:10).

sometimes reveals we had selfish motives in following them all along (John 6:66, 26).

Loyal believers are a tremendous encouragement to suffering leaders. Paul gushed to the Philippians, "I thank my God upon every remembrance of you" (1:3–5; 4:1, 10). Their loyal hearts touch their leaders' hearts: "You have a special place in my heart" (1:7, NLT). Like that of Aaron and Hur, whose support won the day when Moses' strength waned during Israel's conflict with the Amalekites (Exod. 17:8–16), loyal Christians' enduring support makes the difference between their "Pauls" continuing or capitulating, finishing their courses or collapsing short of their finish line!

As Jesus neared His finish line, He lauded His great followers (Luke 22:28) and promised to reward them richly (Luke 22:29–30; 2 Tim. 1:18). Can He do the same for you? What kind of a follower are you? Philippian or non-Philippian? Small-hearted or great?[20]

See Luke 22:28–30; John 19:25–27; 2 Timothy 1:8; 1:16–18; 1 Thessalonians 5:12–13.

1:7 Paul, a suffering minister. "In my bonds"—this is the first of Paul's four references to being a wrongfully accused prisoner in custody of the Roman legal system (1:7, 13, 14, 16). Thus he reveals he's a suffering minister, one who continues loving, seeking, and worshipping God and serving His people with undiminished fervor and energy despite having his blessings stripped away for a season. While writing this letter, Paul was

---

20. Such loyalty does not mean becoming blind, spineless "yes" men, who refuse to speak out when their leaders fall into sin, heresy, or folly. Under such circumstances truly loyal followers will respectfully but firmly protest as did Joab and the priests of Uzziah's day, though not always successfully (2 Sam. 18:33–19:8; 1 Chron. 21:1–4; 2 Chron. 26:16–18).

confined, maligned, and faced with the prospect of execution—but still ministering!

His condition seems strange to twenty-first-century American Christians. How many of our ministers have written us from prison? Yet Paul's reference to his "bonds" didn't shock the Philippians. Why?

They remembered well the terrible ordeal Paul endured while planting their church (Acts 16:14–39, 40). They watched in horror as he suffered false accusation, public humiliation, unjust sentencing, illegal scourging, and cruel imprisonment. But they also remembered the glorious outcome of that brutal conflict with Satan's dark forces. God honored Jesus' power over that of occultists, miraculously delivered Paul and Silas from prison, converted their jailer and his family (thereby growing the Philippian church), and humbled the arrogant city magistrates who had ruled against Paul illegally.[21] News of this impressive divine intervention surely intimidated any who were considering opposing the Philippian Christians. Thus God used Satan's attempt to uproot the Philippian church and prevent its fruitfulness to do the opposite: root it deeply and produce its first sprout of new growth. Why?

In part because its leaders were willing to suffer persecution for Christ's sake.[22] Suffering fully accepted and endured well for Christ's sake is part of our Christian calling (Phil. 1:29) and a

---

21. Paul was a Roman citizen (Acts 21:39; 25:11), and citizens were never to be (a) condemned without having a chance to defend themselves before their accusers, or (b) scourged. Paul suffered both injustices from the Philippian magistrates (Acts 16:19–24).

22. Christian leaders in many countries exemplify this in our day. Many Chinese house church leaders and members have suffered long imprisonments, hostile interrogations, and other abuses and emerged uncompromised, more fruitful, and willing, if necessary, to suffer again to continue fulfilling their divine calling.

mark of spiritual greatness (Acts 15:25–26). Great leaders suffer to bless their congregations and great Christians suffer to help their afflicted leaders—and God blesses both in His time and way (Acts 16:25–26).

Are you a self-centered or suffering minister? Ready to sacrifice your comfort to bless others (Matt. 20:28) or serving only to be served and comforted by others?

1:7 Paul the apologist and teacher. Paul said the Philippians partnered with him not only in his general ministry and sufferings but also in his apologetic teaching, or "defense and confirmation of the gospel" (1:7).

Paul's ministry often involved defending the truth about Messiah Jesus from a plethora of Jewish lies that in turn fostered many Roman misunderstandings (Acts 24:5–6). He also defended Christianity against the scandalous rumors the Romans themselves generated against the growing sect.[23] Furthermore, Paul assured open-minded Jews that Jesus was indeed their Messiah by teaching in their synagogues the Old Testament prophecies concerning Messiah's sufferings and describing how Jesus fulfilled them (Acts 17:2–3), as did Peter, Apollos, and later church fathers (Acts 2:22–36; 18:27–28). (These Messianic proof texts were probably first identified and expounded by Christ Himself after His resurrection; see Luke 24:27; Acts 1:2–3.)

Paul's reference to his defense and explanation of the faith to the wider public explains why he asked Christians to pray for him for boldness (Eph. 6:19). It's easy to expound Christ's teachings to hungry Christian disciples who hang on our words.

---

23. The primitive church was grossly misunderstood by the average Roman citizen, who misjudged them as being cannibalistic, incestuous, unpatriotic, anti-social, anti-family, atheistic, ignorant, and the cause of natural disasters.

But it's very challenging to open them to unbelievers whose minds are filled with suspicion, misjudgment, and hatred before you've said hello—and want to hang you for your words! Despite two thousand years of church and academic teaching about Jesus, Satan's relentless misinformation campaign has left much of the secular and ecclesiastical public misinformed and prejudiced against His nature, faith, will, and way of life. We still need apologists; will you be one?

Peter ordered us to "be ready always to give an answer to every man that asketh you a reason of the hope that is in you, with meekness and fear [of God]" (1 Pet. 3:15). Are you ready, when asked, to explain Christ and His salvation to unbelievers? Or to teach key biblical doctrines to other Christians who, despite sharing your general faith and devotion, hold strong misconceptions against your particular beliefs or practices? Diligently "study to show thyself approved unto God" (2 Tim. 2:15) and pray for sufficient boldness and wisdom to help you excel at "defending and confirming the truth of the Good News" (Phil. 1:7, NLT).

1:8 The Record Keeper. Paul says God is his "record," or record keeper (1:8). Various translations render this: "God is my witness" (NAS, ESV), "God can testify" (NIV), "God knows" (NLT, NCV). Thus Paul asserts God had witnessed the genuineness of his love for the Philippians and, knowing it to be true, could bear witness.

God often testifies of His people's true condition in Scripture. For instance, He faithfully witnesses to our righteousness (Job 1:8; 2:3), disobedience (1 Sam. 15:10–11), wickedness (Exod. 32:7–9; 1 Sam. 3:13), faithfulness (John 1:47–48), endurance (Rev. 3:10), self-deception (Rev. 3:17), good works (Rev.

2:2–3), obedience (Rev. 3:8), suffering (Rev. 2:9–10, 13), and error (Rev. 2:15). Such abundant testimony proves He keeps excellent records on His elect. In keeping with this biblical tradition, Paul says, "God keeps my records too." How? God's angels, specifically His "watchers" (Dan. 4:13, 17, 23), observe His people and write inspired histories of our lives, interactions, and ministries (Mal. 3:16). Why is this important?

Down through the centuries human records—religious, legal, and social—have often described God's servants and others inaccurately.

For instance, Jewish records still show Jesus of Nazareth was a messianic pretender whose apostles staged His purported resurrection. But we know Jesus was the Messiah and His resurrection real. According to Roman records, Jesus, Peter, and Paul were put to death, and John banished, for treason. Yet we know none rebelled against Roman authority. Catholic records describe many nonconformist groups as heretical. But scholars note that since the church often distorted their critics' teachings or destroyed their writings, some of these groups may have advocated not error but truth. Papal decrees condemned Wycliffe, Hus, Luther, and other Reformers as being deluded, rebellious, and worthy of excommunication and execution. We know them, however, to be enlightened, submissive, brave leaders whom God approved and personally empowered to reprove erring popes and councils.

While our courts often produce justice, they sometimes err. Thus criminal records may be criminally wrong. Recently in America, DNA evidence has proven innocent many previously convicted by shoddy investigations or unethical prosecutions. Conversely, some have walked free who were guilty only because their guilt couldn't be proven beyond the shadow of a doubt. In some "he said, she said" lawsuits or divorce actions the right side gets the wrong judgment.

In the unofficial court of public opinion Christians are sometimes grossly misunderstood, misjudged, and denounced when they're innocent or only partly to blame for their fiascos. Our adversaries launch slander campaigns against us (Ps. 62:4), believing God will never call them to account (Ps. 10:11). Today slander can circle the globe instantly, as distorted, defamatory rumors are posted to the Internet—the new universal vault of public records.

When in religious, legal, or social spheres we're misjudged, let's remember "God is my record keeper," rest in His accurate heavenly record, commit our troubled circumstances to Him (Ps. 37:5), believe He'll ultimately set the earthly record straight, and meanwhile "rejoice" that we're counted worthy to suffer for Him (Luke 6:22–23). In His time and way, the Record Keeper will vindicate us (Ps. 37:6; Luke 18:1–8) and humble our accusers (Esther 7:5–6; Acts 18:12–17).

1:8 Paul's powerful, pining love! "God is my witness, how greatly I long after you all," Paul assured the Philippians (1:8). Since longing demands a strong emotional commitment, we don't "long" for much, perhaps one or two things in our lifetime. Thus longing describes no mild wish but rather an intense, yearning passion.

Paul's word choice reflects this. "Long after" is taken from the Greek *epipotheō*, meaning "to yearn, deeply desire, (intensely) crave."[24] This was nothing less than the love of God, Christ's own compassionate, yearning love manifesting in Paul toward

---

24. Thomas, *New American Standard Hebrew-Aramaic and Greek Dictionaries*, updated edition, s.v. "*epipotheō*."

the Philippians, "the tender mercies of Jesus Christ" (1:8). Thus Paul was motivated by the same compassion that "moved" Jesus to pursue His amazing Galilean ministry of teaching, healing, guiding, praying, and feeding God's people.[25] This is the great motive for true ministry. Without it all knowledge, gifts, and service will ultimately prove worthless (1 Cor. 13:1–8). But let's see something else.

Paul seemed to love the Philippians even more than other churches: *"How greatly* I long after you all" (1:8). This is very strong language reflective of exceptional love. Note the context shows Paul's great longing for the Philippians prompted intercession for them: "And this I pray…" (1:9–11). Christ's great longing for His disciples also prompted His intercessions for them (Mark 6:45–46).

Is this powerful, pining divine love for our fellow believers regularly manifesting in us? Is it leading us to minister, share, teach, guide, provide, and especially intercede daily? Or is our love weak and apathetic and our ministry sporadic?

1:9–11 Paul's powerful prayer. Paul's powerful love moved him to pray powerfully for the Philippians: "And this I pray…" (1:9). Specifically he asked the Lord to:

- INCREASE THEIR LOVE (1:9)—until they "abound" (Gk. *perisseuō*, "overabundant, excessive"[26]) in love, or overflow with love for God, His people, His will, and all souls.

---

25. See Matthew 9:36; 14:14; 15:32; 20:34; Mark 1:41; 9:22–23.
26. G. Kittel, G. Friedrich, and G. W. Bromiley, *Theological Dictionary of the New Testament*, electronic ed. (Grand Rapids, MI: W.B. Eerdmans, 1985), s.v. "*perisseuō*."

PhilippianNotes

- Increase their knowledge (1:9)—until they "abound...in knowledge," or overflow with the knowledge of God, academic (2 Tim. 2:15) and experiential (Phil. 3:10; Mark 3:14), thus becoming God's intimate "friends" (John 15:14–15; Gen. 18:17–18; Exod. 33:11; Num. 12:6–8; 2 Chron. 20:7; Isa. 41:8; James 2:23); and that they overflow with other worthy, relevant knowledge (Phil. 4:8).

- Increase their spiritual perception (1:9)—until they "abound...in all judgment [Gk. *aesthesis*, 'perception' by senses or mind[27]]," or overflow with discernment—the full range of spiritual vision including insight, discernment, and judgment. Thus they would grasp truths and issues clearly and assess the correctness of teachings (Acts 15:1–2), prophecies (1 Thess. 5:20–21; 1 Cor. 14:29), and conduct (1 Cor. 5:1–3; 6:2–5; 1 Kings 2:20–22).

- Give them a love of excellence (1:10)—or a passion for perfection, or "what is best" (niv), as Paul had (Phil. 3:12–15), in their relationship with Jesus (John 8:29) and in every human endeavor (Phil. 4:8; Col. 3:23).

- Make them pure-hearted (1:10)—or deeply "sincere" (Gk. *elikrinēs*, "tested by the light of the sun," suggesting something "carefully examined by looking through it in sunlight [thus 'sun

---

27. Ibid., s.v. "*aesthesis*."

judged']"[28] to assure it is pure, without mixture, spotless). Figuratively, this alludes to someone pure in motives and honest in dealings. Such Christians are "Son-judged"—thoroughly examined, convicted, and changed by cooperation with Christ's patient, thorough correction process (Matt. 3:11–12; Mal. 3:1–3) until they're without dishonesty, deceitfulness, and hypocrisy (Matt. 6:1–8, 16–18; Eph. 4:25; Gal. 2:11–14).

- HELP THEM NEVER GIVE OR TAKE OFFENSE (1:10)—or live "without offense," neither stumbling nor causing others to stumble. For this they must diligently forgive offenders (Mark 11:25–26), refuse to hold offenses (Luke 7:23), go extra miles with difficult people (Matt. 5:41), in honor prefer and defer to one another (Rom. 12:10), be all things to all men (1 Cor. 9:22), and be spiritually minded toward adversaries and adversities (Rom. 8:6; 1 Thess. 5:18).

- FILL THEM WITH "FRUITS OF RIGHTEOUSNESS" (1:11)—or the works and character of God's righteous Son (see NLT). This "fruit of righteousness"—or outgrowth of the Righteous One's presence—is synonymous with the "fruit of the Spirit" (Gal. 5:22–23). "Fruits of righteousness" include all the attitudes, words, and deeds God and just men consider to be right, commendable, and winsome (Matt. 5:16; 26:10; John 10:32; Acts 9:36, 39; Rom. 13:3; 2 Cor. 9:7–10; Col. 1:10;

---

28. Finnis Jennings Dake, *Dake's Annotated Reference Bible* (Lawrenceville, Ga: Dake Bible Sales, Inc., 1963), Phil. 1:10, note "v," 215.

1 Tim. 2:9–10; 1 Tim. 3:1; 5:10; 5:24–25; 6:18; 2 Tim. 2:21; 3:17; Titus 2:6–7; 2:14; 3:1; 3:8, 14; Heb. 10:24; 13:21; 1 Pet. 2:12–15). They manifest regularly only "by Jesus Christ" (1:11), or "through Jesus Christ" (NIV)—as we abide in close fellowship with the righteous One, Jesus, through devotion, trust, and obedience (John 15:1–8).

- HELP THEM BRING HIM "GLORY AND PRAISE" (1:11)—thus fulfilling their destiny to glorify God (John 17:1). They (and we) were born to find God and reborn to fully know, enjoy, serve, and glorify Him forever—and help others do the same! Is there any possible better end to a prayer?

This is Paul's powerful prayer for the Philippians—and us. Its inclusion in Scripture confirms that it is inspired and therefore not just Paul's but also the Spirit's petitions for us. Are our petitions for ourselves or others? Prayer is our surest, most available means of helping others, even those whom we can't presently evangelize or counsel. Let's pray this powerful prayer and trust God's Spirit to powerfully fulfill it.

1:12 Turned for good—again! This verse reveals yet another example of two monumental biblical truths:

> We know that God causes all things to work together for good to those who love God, to those who are called according to His purpose.
> —ROMANS 8:28, NAS

> As for you, ye thought evil against me; but God meant it unto good…
> —GENESIS 50:20

Exploring Paul's Heart

By trying to stop the foremost messenger of the gospel, the Jews only spread the good news further! This turning of adversity into advantage has been a hallmark of God's favor upon His people and their works from time immemorial. It persists today in the lives and works of faithful Christians, churches, and ministries.

God turned Paul's cruel injustice during his first visit to Philippi (Acts 16:12–40) to favor the Christians' cause there by (1) spreading the news of God's awesome intervention, which both the jailer and other prisoners personally witnessed (16:25), and (2) intimidating would-be enemies of the faith when they heard how the powerful city magistrates made a hasty, humiliating retreat before the newly delivered apostles (16:35–39). After that, who would want to defy Paul's God? And who would lightly dismiss the Christians' message about Jesus of Nazareth as a mere Jewish myth or the ignorant ravings of uneducated Galileans?

Now, in Rome, God again turned circumstances to serve His good purposes. It seems He appointed Paul's guards as unofficial local missionaries. Paul's imprisonment for his faith was known "in all the palace [lit. *praetorium*]" (Phil. 1:13), or among the "whole imperial guard" (AMP). This implies the soldiers guarding him, probably in four six-hour shifts, were members of the imperial Praetorian Guard (Acts 28:16). One commentator notes:

> No army was allowed in Italy, but the Praetorian Guard consisted of about thirteen to fourteen thousand free Italian soldiers. They were the emperor's elite bodyguard under the praetorian prefect. Viewed as clients of the emperor (thus part of his household), they were kept loyal with the highest pay in the Roman military;

they were also kept loyal by the leadership of a prefect who could never legally become emperor (being a knight rather than a senator).[29]

Chained to Paul daily, these elite guards became well soaked in the gospel waters of Paul's teaching.[30] One paraphrase conjectures:

> All the soldiers here, and everyone else, too, found out that I'm in jail because of this Messiah. That piqued their curiosity, and now they've learned all about him.
> —PHILIPPIANS 1:13, THE MESSAGE

If correct, the Praetorian guards apparently shared with others what they were hearing from Paul's ongoing, prolific, and Spirit-empowered message about Jesus (Acts 28:30–31). Both his message and manner—joyfully accepting unjust incarceration and continuing his work unabated—must have impressed and won them, much as Christ's gracious non-resistance on the cross and perseverance in ministering to those around Him (Luke 23:42–43; John 19:25–27) won the centurion standing by (Mark 15:39). Their "gospel" then reached "the palace" and "all other places" (Phil. 1:13) in Rome, implying Caesar's family, bodyguards, and servants;

---

29. Keener, *The IVP Bible Background Commentary: New Testament*, Phil. 1:13, note.
30. These guards were chained to Paul as he "prayed without ceasing" (1 Thess. 5:17) for others (and them!); witnessed to visitors about Christ, judgment, and salvation (cf. Acts 24:24–25); taught Bible studies to Roman Christians; preached the gospel to various groups who, hearing of his incarceration and message, came to his house (Acts 28:30–31); and dictated Spirit-inspired letters to the Ephesians, Philippians, Colossians, Philemon, and many other Christian leaders and groups around the Mediterranean. Sitting by such a constantly flowing fountainhead of Christian truth, surely some, perhaps many of Paul's guards were saved by his prayers, words, and example. See Wiersbe, *The Bible Exposition Commentary*, Phil. 1:12–14, note.

Exploring Paul's Heart

the Roman Christians; and even the general public became aware of Paul's predicament, message, and Messiah.[31] So though the messenger was bound, his message was loose and running swiftly throughout Rome's highest circles of influence (2 Tim. 2:9)![32] God used the Jews' narrow hatred to open a wide door for Paul in the world's capital! And He wasn't finished.

Paul's two-year detention (c. AD 61–63) became a much-needed sabbatical, similar to the three months he had recently spent on Malta (Acts 28:1–11). Despite it beginning with a harrowing shipwreck, the timing of Paul's visit to Malta (winter) ensured he would have three months of comparatively easy ministry without the threat of further persecution (28:11). Now, in Rome, Paul enjoyed another Sabbath for "two whole years" (Acts 28:30). His physical stress was reduced. He had no long pedestrian travels, stormy voyages, or steep mountain roads to climb as on earlier missions (Acts 13:6; 13:14). He had no stress from impending death threats or plots. In Roman custody he was safe from Jewish assassins. Presumably well fed, Paul's health would have been replenished also, with no periods of temporary privation as he sometimes suffered during his challenging travels (2 Cor. 11:25, 27; Phil. 4:11–12). Most importantly, for these two years Paul had much more time for

---

31. In his taped message "When the Boat Sinks," the late David Wilkerson suggested that news of Paul and his God was "seeded" throughout Rome by the 275 passengers who, sailing with him, had witnessed his courageous leadership in the storm, fulfilled prophecies about their voyage, miraculous recovery from a deadly snake bite, compassionate ministry to Publius' father, and three-month healing campaign on Malta (Acts 27:1–28:11).
32. Today this would be equal to having influence with the Secret Service's presidential detail, or other persons close to the president, such as the aides to the Joint Chiefs of Staff or the various members of the president's Cabinet. Through their high-level contacts, these could easily spread news around the nation's capital and beyond.

PhilippianNotes

study of God's Word[33] and prayer, thus refilling his inner spiritual reserves. Thus Paul's time in Rome was a vital "pit stop," refitting him spiritually, emotionally, and physically for the remaining five-year[34] leg of his epic "course" (2 Tim. 4:6–7).

The Bible showcases this divine turning in many lives. God used Balaam's attempted curse as a blessing upon Israel. He used the low envy of Joseph's brothers to propel Joseph toward his predestined high service. He used Haman's hatred of the Jews to free them from all their enemies. He used the first great Jewish persecution to launch the first great Christian missions to Samaria, Antioch, and beyond. He used the Apostle John's banishment on Patmos to give him a perfectly quiet setting in which to record the greatest prophecy ever given. So God turns every attack upon His people and message into something that advances them! Please reflect on your past.

Has God turned your adversities into advantages? Praise Him for it, and encourage other believers to do so by faith, before they see His turning. And the next time you experience injustice, hindrance, or rejection for Jesus' sake, confess confidently, "Lord, I believe to see You turn *this* situation for good!"

See Exodus 1:12; Deuteronomy 23:3–5; Acts 8:1–4; 8:5–13; 11:19–21.

1:13 A small window well used. Comparing Acts 28:30–31, we see that during these two years in Rome (c. AD 61–63), Paul enjoyed amazing liberty in preaching Christ as Savior, Lord, and Son of God despite his "bonds" (Phil. 1:13). That

---

[33]. Provided, of course, local Christians or Jews shared copies of Old Testament books and gospel texts ("recollections of the apostles") that may have been available (Acts 28:15, 17, 24).
[34]. If Paul was released in AD 63, he had five years of ministry remaining before his execution in AD 68.

Exploring Paul's Heart

he did so under the nose of Nero's bodyguards, with news of his gospel message spreading daily among Nero's Praetorian guards, palace servants, (possibly) family members, and many other Christians and pagans in "all other places" (1:13) in Rome is remarkable. Anyone, especially his guards, could have lodged new insurrection charges against him for preaching an illegal religion, namely, that Jesus (not Caesar) was "Lord." This would have confirmed the Jews' allegations and ensured Paul's execution. But God restrained them. So Paul made the most of his window of opportunity. Luke says he preached with "all confidence, no man forbidding him" (Acts 28:31). But Paul's liberty would soon end.

Shortly after Paul's release in AD 63, trouble struck the Roman Christian community. In AD 64 Rome burned, triggering the first brutal Roman persecution. Because Christianity was considered a dangerous "superstition" (unauthorized religion) and Christians were suspected of many forms of bad behavior, Nero successfully blamed them for the devastating conflagration. Knowing this was coming, the Spirit urged Paul to make the most of his small window of opportunity in Rome, and he complied, receiving "all that came in unto him, preaching the kingdom of God, and teaching those things which concern the Lord" (Acts 28:30–31). Are we doing the same?

When we have even the smallest, seemingly most unpromising opportunities to share Jesus or Scripture with others, are we taking them? Nero reportedly fiddled while Rome burned. Are we fiddling away our present ministry opportunities through apathy, indolence, or worldly entanglements? History often repeats itself.

The Roman Christians certainly didn't expect the fiery trial that engulfed them. We too may experience an unexpected conflagration (Prov. 27:1). The atmosphere in our city, province, nation, or world may suddenly turn radically against our Messiah and message. Russia could turn hard against Russian believers and churches. China's government could again crack down on its unregistered house churches. Fanatical Muslims (jihadists) could take power in sub-Saharan African countries and brutally suppress Christians.[35] An election or crisis could cause the American government to turn hard against Christ's faith and followers. These are real possibilities, though we can't be sure they'll happen.

But we are sure the church's "window" will close at the Rapture (and Israel's will open, Rev. 7:1–17), and everywhere signs of the times shout, "Christ is coming soon!" So let's follow Paul's example in our "Rome." Small or large, let's use our windows of opportunity well.

1:14 The paradox of persecution. Paul describes a wonder: news of his persecution made other Christians bolder! We would assume the opposite, that hearing of other Christians suffering, especially prominent ministers, would intimidate: "If this can happen to *Paul*, we may be next!"

But the Spirit planted other thoughts in these early Christians' minds. "If God's grace can keep Paul peaceful, strong, and ministering daily in such injustice, He can keep us too!" Thus, paradoxically, fearful news prompted new faith. Let's probe deeper.

---

35. As I write (April 2014), the brutal terrorist group ISIS is rampaging through Syria and Iraq, pillaging, raping, and killing Christians, Muslims, atheists, and anyone else refusing to convert to their brand of Islam.

Exploring Paul's Heart

We fear most the adversities we've never experienced. Deliverance from these fears of the unknown comes by (1) facing our fears of adversity and (2) taking steps to overcome them by trusting and obeying God when adversity comes. As we successfully endure our fearful situations, our fears of the unknown dissipate because we now realize that by God's help we've endured the thing we dreaded. Thus we're girded by a proven faith in God's unfailing faithfulness—the Lord who saw me through will see me through again! "The LORD who delivered me out of the paw of the lion, and...the bear, he will deliver me out of the hand of this Philistine" (1 Sam. 17:37). But God did something even greater with Paul.

He made Paul a surrogate sufferer for his inexperienced brethren. When they saw him overcoming their worst fears with Christ's help (Phil. 4:11–13), they believed they could also, even though they hadn't yet suffered for Christ! Thus Satan couldn't use his fearful lies—"When you're persecuted, you'll fail and deny Christ!"—to torment them any longer. Instead they were freshly reenergized in their witness, or "much more bold to speak the word without fear" (1:14), or "with more freedom and indifference to the consequences" (AMP). This is very relevant.

Christians everywhere constantly face the prospect of opposition, sometimes severe, for Christ's sake. Every faithful Christian will experience rejection or trouble for Christ, His Word, or His calling (2 Tim. 3:12). Before experiencing opposition, we're confronted by intimidating fears of the unknown. "Will I stand or flee? Can I take the pressures? Will I endure false accusation, misrepresentation, ostracism, or loneliness and peacefully walk on with Christ, carrying my cross without rebellion or discouragement? Will I joyfully suffer the loss of possessions, relationships, or hopes? Or will I succumb to the pressure to compromise my beliefs or calling to gain relief?" Such questions haunt those who've never suffered.

But when "tribulation or persecution...because of the word" (Matt. 13:21) visits faithful Christians whom we know and identify with, and they stand unmoved, faithful, and even joyful, it's a watershed moment. We realize if by God's grace they can be strong, steady, and fruitful in trouble, we can too. Thus, paradoxically, we grow not weaker but stronger, not cowardly but confident, not confused but clear-minded—and energized to rise above our present challenges and challengers. Soon, like Paul, we've become surrogate sufferers and our example is emboldening others. Why is this important?

Christian suffering will increase in these last days,[36] and God needs many surrogate sufferers. Ponder the paradox of persecution, and "when thou art converted" by proving your willingness to suffer and confidence in God's faithfulness, "strengthen thy brethren" (Luke 22:32).

1:15 Paul's other enemies. Other New Testament references reveal Paul was opposed by the Judaizers,[37] but here he refers to other antagonistic ministers. Why did they oppose him?

---

36. "Severe episodes of martyrdom are found throughout church history, but there has been an increase in such incidents and in the number of Christians killed since 1900." See Christof, Sauer, and Thomas Schirrmacher, "Father, Forgive Them," *Christian History Magazine*, issue 109: Eyewitness to the Modern Age of Persecution, 4. Worchester, PA: Christian History Institute, 2014.

37. Judaizers were Jewish Christian teachers who insisted erroneously that Gentiles had to become Jewish converts before they could be saved (thus Judah-izing—or making Jews of—them by conforming them to the Torah-keeping ways of the people of Judah [Jews]). Paul first encountered them at Antioch (Acts 15:1–2), and they subsequently tried to replace Paul's teaching with theirs wherever they went.

We don't know the whole story, but we have some key facts. First, Paul says they envied him or his ministry (1:15). A companion sin of pride, envy drives religious imitation and rivalry (one-upmanship, Acts 19:11–12; 19:13–17) and, if it persists, deadly persecution (Matt. 27:18). This alone would move them to speak or work against Paul, hoping to rival or replace his prominent ministry (3 John 9–11).[38] Second, they hoped to "add" to his pain, apparently by reminding him that their ministries were thriving and his was, by all appearances, stalled (Phil. 1:16). Thus, they wanted to vex him by provoking him to envy, just as the Pharisees tried unsuccessfully to do to John the Baptist (John 3:26–30). But they failed. Their envy blinded them to God's higher purposes in Paul's incarceration and to the fact that spiritually minded men like Paul would never surrender to envy. Who were they?

We don't know. Perhaps they were new Roman converts with excessive religious ambition and deficient grace and knowledge.[39] Maybe they were Christian elders who knew and opposed Paul's teaching before he came to Rome (Acts 20:30). By exposing their envy, he implies he's had a history with them and thus has derived his opinion from personal experience, not imaginations. Yet we must assume they presented the basic doctrines of the faith correctly and were therefore not Judaizers. Why?

The Judaizers taught fundamental error, namely, a works-based salvation claiming Gentiles must first become Jews to be saved (Acts 15:1). Paul called their message "another gospel,"

---

38. Of Paul's amazing humility and utter lack of religious rivalry Henry notes, "Paul was so far from envying those who had liberty to preach the gospel that he rejoiced in the preaching of it even by those who do it in pretence, and not in truth." See Henry, *Commentary in One Volume*, 1862.
39. Like Ahimaaz, who was too eager to "run" as the king's messenger, even when told his message ("tidings") wasn't yet complete (2 Sam. 18:19, 22).

proclaimed it inadequate to save, anathematized its proponents (Gal. 1:6–9), and warned the Philippians and others to avoid them (Gal. 1:6–9; 5:1; Phil. 3:2–3). Paul couldn't rejoice at anyone preaching the Judaizers' gospel; it was heresy, and he loved truth![40] So apparently those he speaks of in this text envied his ministry, specifically his powerful evangelism, numerous church plants, apostolic authority, heavenly revelations, vast scriptural knowledge, amazing miracles, Word-rich teaching, respect among ministers, and exceptional writings that even Peter praised for their obvious inspiration (2 Pet. 3:15–16). Yet, gifted at seeing God's goodness in men's meanness, Paul chose to rejoice that, despite their motives, their message was blessing others.

Have we made the choice to be spiritually minded toward our antagonists? Are we seeking God's purposes in their pettiness? If so, we'll discover that whenever they attempt evil against us, God always overrules it for good (Gen. 50:20).

1:15–18 Set to do God's will. Trained to "give thanks in all circumstances" because they are in some way "God's will for you" (1 Thess. 5:18, NIV), Paul accepted his involuntary sojourn in Rome (Acts 28:30–31) as part of God's plan. With acceptance came insight.

Paul soon perceived multiple advantages in his adversity. In Roman custody he was protected from Jewish attacks, fed by the Romans, favored to live in a house rather than a cell, free to receive whomever visited, permitted to preach Christ as Lord, relieved of the hardships of incessant travel, at liberty to write

---
40. The equivalent today would be anyone preaching a false Christianity (e.g., Mormonism or Jehovah's Witnesses) that denies Christ's deity or salvation by grace alone and instead advocates a grace-plus-works salvation. No truth-loving Christian, however broadminded, can rejoice when such heresy is taught (1 Cor. 13:6).

and receive personal letters, and able to send edifying epistles to Christians and churches everywhere without censure. So he relished in the revelation that God was causing "all things," even the worst scenarios, to work for His good purpose. And what was that?

Primarily God's plan was to use the Jews' unjust legal action to place Paul before Caesar so he could give an inspired defense of the faith. This was a key part of Paul's destiny. God assured Ananias Paul would "bear my name before Gentiles, and kings" (Acts 9:15). Thus Paul saw God in his grief and divine purpose in the Jews' diabolical plan. Instead of crying "Persecution!" he exclaimed, "Providence!" Many Roman Christians also understood he was imprisoned in Rome not for misbehavior but for ministry—to complete his divine mission: *"For they know I am here to defend the gospel"* (Phil. 1:17, PHILLIPS). Once convinced of God's purpose, Paul determined to accomplish it.

He vowed to the Philippians, "I am set ['appointed' (NKJV), 'put here' (1:16, ESV), or divinely led here] for the defense of the gospel" (1:17). Or, paraphrasing:

> God sovereignly led me to this low point to serve His high goal of introducing Jesus, explaining His way, and offering His salvation to the world's ruler, court, and capital citizenry. I've forgotten my injustices and fixed my heart on this goal.

So God "set" Paul in Rome, and Paul "set" himself to do God's will. Determined in heart and supported by God, nothing and no one could stop him (Phil. 3:12–14; 4:13; Acts 20:23–24; 21:13–14)! Though Nero and most Romans rejected Christianity, Paul's presentation wasn't wasted. It was a necessary witness to which all its recipients, including Nero, will give account at the judgment. Additionally we may infer many Romans, hearing Paul's gospel, received his Lord.

Are we following Paul's lead? If we continue seeking God in our adversities as Paul did, God will faithfully reveal His wise plan in our adverse situation. We'll see God in our grief and purpose in our pain and, forgetting our adversaries, set our hearts to do God's will.

See Romans 8:6; 1 Thessalonians 5:18; 1 Corinthians 2:9–3:1; 2 Samuel 16:5–14.

1:19–26 Exploring Paul's heart. These verses allow us to examine the thoughts and motives of Paul's heart. They reveal his confidence, earnest expectation, dilemma, liberty, criterion, hope—and Christlikeness.

A man of constant prayer, Paul was confident the Philippians' prayers[41] would bring the "help" of the Spirit's inspiration and intervention (1:19, ISV), thus prompting his release by acquittal or execution (1:20). His earnest expectation was that God's grace would enable him to remain courageous and bold throughout his detention and hearing whatever their outcome (1:20). His dilemma was the conflict between his personal desires and the church's best interests, yet he acknowledges it was a win-win situation (1:21). He wanted to go home, knowing promotion into God's presence was incomparably better (1:23), yet knew by remaining he would produce more fruitful kingdom labors and joyful spiritual growth in Christians (1:22–25). His liberty was that he had become so intimate with Christ that He apparently let Paul choose whether to end or extend his ministry:

---

41. "The prayers of the people may bring a supply of the Spirit to their ministers, to support them in suffering, as well as in preaching the gospel." (Henry, *Commentary in One Volume*, 1862.) See also 2 Corinthians 1:11; Ephesians 6:19–20; Acts 12:5.

"What I shall choose I know not" (1:22). There's more here than we fully understand, something very personal between Savior and servant.[42] Paul's criterion, or standard of judgment, was simple: regardless of his personal preference, he chose what was best for the church (1:24), the people whom Christ so passionately loves and yearns for us to help and protect (John 21:15–17). Matthew Henry wrote:

> His strait was between serving Christ in this world and enjoying him in another. To advance the interest of Christ and his church, he chose rather to tarry here where he met with oppositions and difficulties, and to deny himself for awhile the satisfaction of his reward.[43]

This standard guided all Paul's decisions (Acts 14:21–22; 21:20–24). He hoped that after his release he would continue ministering to the churches, increasing their faith and joy, and would again visit and rejoice with the Philippians. By so informing them (1:26), he immediately lifted their spirits "in the hope of seeing him and enjoying his further labors among them."[44] All these thoughts and motives were in Paul's heart and prayers in Rome. Really, they are hard evidence of a redemptive miracle: Christ's heart had been fully formed in Paul's heart.

Want this heart? Think like Paul! Confidently believe the prayers of God's people will strengthen you to courageously fulfill God's will. Acknowledge your "self's vs. Savior's will"

---

42. This doesn't deny Christ's sovereignty over us His servants. If in His great love He asks us what we want, we serve His sovereign will by choosing what we want. We normally ask, and correctly, "What wilt thou have me to do?" (Acts 9:6), but it sometimes pleases Christ to defer to our wishes as a loving husband would his wife's: "What wilt thou that I should do unto thee?" (Mark 10:51; cf. Esther 8:7–8; John 14:14).
43. Henry, *Commentary in One Volume*, 1862.
44. Ibid., 1862.

dilemmas, and always choose what's best for His people and kingdom. Then you'll be buoyed by the irrepressible hope that He will increasingly bless you and His people as you grow and rejoice together—and form Christ's heart! Paul prayed laboriously for this: "Oh, my dear children! I feel as if I'm going through labor pains for you again, and they will continue until Christ is fully developed in your lives" (Gal. 4:19, NLT). Let his prayer be answered in you.

1:21 A far better life. "For to me to live is Christ, and to die is gain" (1:21). Or, "Living means living for Christ; dying is even better" (NLT). Better? Is this a mistranslation?

Not at all. Paul joyfully affirms that for Christians, dying is even better than living. Why? For one great reason: we "depart...to be with Christ," and that is "far better" than the most desirable life in this world (1:23).

The word *depart* (Gk. *analyō*) means "to unloose, undo, or break up [for departure]."[45] One commentator notes:

> This word was used by the soldiers; it meant *"to take down your tent and move on."* What a picture of Christian death! The "tent" we live in is taken down at death, and the spirit goes home to be with Christ in heaven. (Read 2 Cor. 5:1–8.)
>
> The sailors also used this word; it meant *"to loosen a ship and set sail."* Lord Tennyson used this figure of death in his famous poem "Crossing the Bar."
>
> But departure was also a political term; it described *the setting free of a prisoner* [loosening the bonds of our physical body]. God's people are in bondage because of the limitations of the body and the temptations of the

---

45. Strong, *Enhanced Strong's Lexicon*, s.v. "*analyō*."

flesh, but death will free them. Or they will be freed at the return of Christ (Rom. 8:18–23) if that should come first.

Finally, departure was a word used by the farmers; it meant *"to unyoke the oxen."* Paul had taken Christ's yoke, which is an easy yoke to bear (Matt. 11:28–30), but how many burdens he carried in his ministry! (Read 2 Cor. 11:22–12:10.) To depart to be with Christ would mean laying aside the burdens, his earthly work completed.[46]

All these aspects of Christian death—(1) taking down tent stakes and moving on, (2) loosening a ship's anchor and setting sail, (3) loosening a prisoner from his chains, (4) unyoking and thus unburdening oxen—are positive. So, like Paul, we can be positive even when facing death, "confident" that to be "absent from the body" is to be "present with the Lord" (2 Cor. 5:6–8; Phil. 1:23) in heaven and fully conscious.[47] The contrast between the two realms is stark.

In this world there is darkness, deception, and sin; in Christ's presence there's light, truth, and obedience to God's will. In this world we experience pain, grief, and tears; in God's presence we'll have no pain, grief, or tears (Rev. 7:17; 21:4). In this world we have sickness, weakness, and death; in His presence we'll enjoy health, strength, and immortality. In this world we have a sin nature; in His presence we'll be free of sin forever. In this world there is strife, unrest, and war; in His presence we'll experience sweet unity, tranquility, and peace between

---

46. Wiersbe, *The Bible Exposition Commentary*, Phil. 1:20, note.
47. "Be with Christ" (Phil. 1:23) implies that deceased Christians are not unconscious or asleep, since Christ is not. Rather they're wide awake, active and worshipping, walking, and working "with the Lord" in heaven (2 Cor. 5:8). When used to describe them, "sleep" (1 Cor. 11:30; 15:51; 1 Thess. 4:14; 5:10) refers only to their appearance at death, not unconsciousness after death.

all people and nations. In this world God is misrepresented, rejected, and denied His right to rule; in His presence all will know Him, worship Him, and serve His will joyfully. In this world we suffer for our faith (1:29); in heaven we'll be honored for it. In this world we labor diligently to earn rewards for building Christ's kingdom; in God's presence we'll enjoy our rewards eternally.

In this world we have limited knowledge of the beginning, end, and spiritual world; in God's presence we'll enjoy access to omniscience, knowing all things as fully as we are known. In this world we typically draw near to enjoy Jesus' peaceful presence briefly every day; in the next we'll abide in the unabated glow of His presence (Rev. 22:3–5). In this world we toil to obtain our food and drink; in eternity we'll eat and drink with Christ freely without stressful labor. In this world millions starve; in the new earth everyone will feast on fresh fruits and grains harvested monthly year round (Rev. 22:2; Amos 9:13). In this world we're subject to Satan's temptations, harassments, and deceptions daily; in eternity neither he nor his demons will tempt or trouble us. In this world prejudice, envy, and ambition separate us; in the next we'll flow together in a river of pure, uninterrupted cooperation. In this world the creation is tainted by sin's corruptive effects; in the next land, sea, air, and space will be gloriously pristine, beautiful, and ours to revel in (Ps. 37:11; Rom. 8:19–21, NLT; Rev. 21:5). In this world nature is subject to catastrophic astrological, meteorological, geological, and oceanographic events; in the next earth's systems will be as undisturbed as its inhabitants. In this world leaders often rule selfishly, unjustly, and to our harm; in the next Christ will rule with perfect fairness and love, always serving our highest good.

So who would dare disagree with Paul? Truly, the next life is incomparably better for believers. Whenever we or our loved ones face death, let's remember that living here vs. dying is a "good-better" situation: "Life versus even more life! I can't lose" (1:21, THE MESSAGE). We don't cease existing, fall asleep, or hang in limbo. We simply "depart"—pulling up one tent and moving into another, weighing anchor and embarking on an eternal voyage, laying aside the chains of our bodily limitations, and removing the yoke of our Christian labors—bound not for perdition, purgatory, or perplexity but a far better life "in His presence."[48]

1:27 What good shepherds desire. Paul asked the Philippians to so conduct themselves in godliness and unity that the next report he heard on earth or in heaven would be that they were perfectly unified—having "one spirit," not many; "one mind," not a host of carnal attitudes; ardently "striving together," not against each other; all "for the faith," not indulging the sin, strife, or heresy that works against it (2 Tim. 2:14). He makes the same plea for deep, loving unity twice more in this epistle (Phil. 2:2; 4:2). Wise, devoted undershepherds want this because it's the central passion of the Chief Shepherd and thus the primary work of the Executor of His will, the Holy Spirit (John 17:21–23). This passion reveals Paul had a pastor's heart.

Every good undershepherd wants to hear that those he (or she) is pastoring are walking in true Christian unity. News of schisms is always unpleasant. Paul describes with heaviness his hearing of divisions in the Corinthian church (1 Cor. 1:10–11; 3:1–4). Division is acceptable only where it's necessary to

---

48. When Oswald Chambers passed unexpectedly at age forty-three, his wife telegraphed his family and friends: "Oswald, in His presence." See http://www.oswaldchambers.co.uk/bio/ (accessed March 31, 2015).

preserve the holiness of the church from the corrupting influences of impenitent sinners or heretics (1 Cor. 5:1–13; 11:18–19; 2 Cor. 6:14–18). If we remain faithful during such periods of necessary division, God will ultimately restore our unity and growth (2 Cor. 2:5–8).

Pastor, elder, deacon, spiritual leader, do you desire unity passionately, yet also have the discernment to recognize when godly separation is necessary?

See Ephesians 4:1–3, 4–6; 4:13; Philippians 4:1–2; John 10:16; 17:21, 22, 23; Psalm 133:1–3; Isaiah 11:13–14; Jeremiah 32:37–39; Ezekiel 34:23; Zephaniah 3:9; Acts 1:14; 2:1; 2:44–45; 4:24; 4:32; 5:12; 8:6–8; 15:25; (ct. 15:39); Romans 12:16; 15:5–6; 1 Corinthians 12:12–13; 2 Corinthians 13:11–12; Galatians 3:26–28; 1 Peter 3:8; 4:9; 5:10.

1:27 Becoming conduct. Paul exhorts the Philippians to not only learn but also live the gospel: "Let your conversation be as it becometh the gospel" (1:27).

> The old English word *conversation*, of course, means *walk* and not *talk*.... The most important weapon against the enemy is not a stirring sermon or a powerful book; it is the consistent life of believers.[49]

Our regular conduct as Christians either promotes or undermines the influence of the gospel message. We're all walking advertisements, continuing testimonies, human billboards, personified blogs and social media posts, telling others constantly (though unconsciously) they should or should not come to our Lord. Or, to change the symbol, our everyday

---

49. Wiersbe, *The Bible Exposition Commentary*, Phil. 1:27, note.

life is writing not Matthew's, Mark's, Luke's, or John's, but The Gospel According to Us!

> You are writing a Gospel,
> A chapter each day,
> By the deeds that you do,
> And the words that you say.
> Men read what you write,
> Whether faithful or true:
> Just what is the Gospel
> According to you?
>
> —ANONYMOUS

Thus Paul tells us to "behave what we believe."[50] Or, "Make sure that your everyday life is worthy of the Gospel" (PHILLIPS).

This contrasts sharply with first century Greco-Roman religions, which typically emphasized participation in cult worship without requiring lifestyle changes. To pagans, behavior was beside the point; to Christians, conduct is the point. It doesn't save, but it does show our faith in Christ is genuine (James 2:14–26)! Furthermore, every believer who diligently obeys his pastor's teaching is a "living epistle" of his pastoral ministry for all to read (2 Cor. 3:1–3). Is conduct really this important?

It is to the United States military forces. Article 133 of the Uniform Code of Military Justice states that for "conduct unbecoming an officer and a gentleman" commissioned military officers are subject to whatever punishment a court martial shall deem appropriate—for instance, confinement, loss of salary or privileges, or dishonorable discharge. Conduct should also be an important issue to every "soldier of Jesus Christ" (2 Tim. 2:3). Why? We will one day stand before the General

---

50. Ibid., Phil. 1:27a, note.

of heaven's armies, Jesus Christ, in heaven's court for an official review of our life works, the judgment seat of Christ (2 Cor. 5:10). How will He assess our "everyday life"? We're determining that daily.

Is your behavior becoming or unbecoming of Christ? Is it making His gospel more or less "attractive" to unbelievers (Titus 2:10, NIV)? Are you recommending or reproaching your pastor's teaching?[51]

See 1 Timothy 4:12; 3:2; Titus 2:9–10; Ephesians 4:1–3.

1:27 As citizens of heaven! The word "conversation" (KJV) has further implications. It is translated from the Greek *politeuomai*, which means "to be a citizen; be or act or behave as a citizen."[52] Thus it urges not merely good conduct but specifically that of good Roman citizens. As always, Paul's word choice was on target.

Since Philippi was a Roman colony, many of the Philippian Christians were Roman citizens. Roman citizenship gave one enviable rights and privileges and was therefore highly valued (Acts 22:27–28). Citizenship carried with it the responsibility to behave legally if not honorably. The noble Roman hoped to avoid reproach, as this would shame not only his name and family but also his empire and emperor. Mindful of this Paul writes, "Only let your conversation [life as a citizen] be as it becometh the gospel."

---

51. Often we excuse our bad conduct because others with whom we interact, even Christians, are behaving badly. Two wrongs don't make a right. Christ is looking for responsible believers who will see to it that, regardless of what others do, they conduct themselves according to His teaching and guidance.
52. Kittel, Friedrich, and Bromiley, *Theological Dictionary of the New Testament*, s.v. "*politeuomai*."

Understanding Paul's use of *politeuomai*, the Philippians probably took him to say:

> You have always behaved as Roman citizens, honoring the empire and emperor. Be sure that you do no less for Christ. Live here and now as heaven's citizens (Phil. 3:20–21; Eph. 2:19) to honor your new kingdom, King, and His gospel.
> —Author's paraphrase

This implies living not just according to Caesar's edicts but also Christ's sayings, especially the Sermon on the Mount (Matt. 5–7). It assumes the Philippians acknowledge their dual citizenship as Christians and Romans (Phil. 3:20–21), yet see their abiding capital as not Rome but New Jerusalem—that glorious, divinely prepared, God-inhabited city-state awaiting Christians on the new earth (John 14:2–3; Rev. 21:1–2). And if pressed, they should confess, "Christ is my king and heaven my home" (Heb. 11:13–16).

Like the Philippians, all Christians are heaven's citizens with obligations as well as rights and privileges. What are ours?

Some of our obligations are: to live by faith in our King; spend time with Him daily (Mark 3:14); thank and praise Him often (Eph. 5:18–20; Heb. 13:15); study and obey His Word (imperial decrees); genuinely love one another, as He desires (John 13:34–35); assist one another in need (Acts 4:34–35; 11:27–30; Gal. 2:10); bear witness to our King's deity, Saviorship, and truth (Acts 1:8); serve Him faithfully in whatever vocation or ministry He appoints (1 Cor. 4:2); use the natural and spiritual gifts He's given us for His honor (Matt. 25:20–21); seek and follow His guidance (Rom. 8:14); put His interests "first" every day and in every decision (Matt. 6:33); not seek friendship

PhilippianNotes

with those who hate Him (James 4:4); intercede faithfully for all leaders and people (1 Tim. 2:1–4; 2 Pet. 3:9); examine ourselves regularly, quickly confessing all sins (1 John 1:9); maintain strong faith in our King (John 6:28–29; 2 Cor. 13:5); when necessary, suffer willingly for Him (Phil. 1:29; Luke 14:26–27; Col. 1:10–12); financially support His work (Phil. 4:10, 14–19; 1 Cor. 9:7–14); and strive together to purge heresy and preserve sound teaching in our churches (Phil. 1:27; Jude 3; Gal. 2:4–5).

Some of our enviable privileges are: peace with God (Rom. 5:1); the peace of God (Phil. 4:7; Col. 3:15); remission of past sins (Acts 10:43); provision for present cleansing (1 John 1:9; Prov. 28:13); access to our King's presence (Heb. 10:19–20); the rest and joy He gives (Matt. 11:28–30; Ps. 16:11); membership in God's family (Eph. 2:19; 3:15); growing biblical insight (Matt. 13:11, 18–23; Mark 4:34); our King's personal counsel and assistance for every earthly need (Phil. 4:6–7); the companionship of His divine Associate, the Holy Spirit, to comfort us and teach us "all truth" (John 14:26); His ministers to teach, counsel, and guide us into spiritual unity (Eph. 4:11–13; 1 Pet. 5:1–3); His Spirit's gifts for supplemental help, especially in adversity (1 Cor. 12:1–31); His unfailing material provision (Phil. 4:19); an appointment as His ambassadors (2 Cor. 5:18–20); sweet fellowship with other kingdom citizens (1 John 1:7); prophetic insights (John 16:13); the hope of resurrection (1 Thess. 4:13–16; 2 Cor. 5:1–6); the hope of our King returning for us (John 14:1–3; 1 Thess. 5:9–10; Titus 2:13); confidence that an immortal body awaits us (1 Cor. 15:49–53; 1 John 3:2; 2 Cor. 5:1); and a clarifying, comforting revelation of things to come (Rev. 4:1–22:21).

To thus live as heaven's citizens requires scriptural thinking. Scripture tells us we're here not for the glory of our "Rome" (nation) or "Caesar" (head of state) but to promote our soon-returning King and solicit souls to seek and serve Him. Concern for our present nation's reformation is admirable, but we should be more zealous to build our King's coming realm; to hope in our "better country" (Heb. 11:13–16), not this imperfect one. Just remembering that, by God's grace, we're honored citizens of New Jerusalem (Rev. 21:1–22:5) inspires us to live obediently and joyfully in this secular world.

Are you a good citizen of Christ's kingdom? Remembering and treasuring your new citizenship? Inspired by the hope that New Jerusalem awaits?[53] Joyfully fulfilling your kingdom obligations and enjoying your kingdom privileges?

1:27 Fighting together. Paul pleads with the Philippians to strive not against but with each another for the attainment of God's ends and against everything detrimental to His people and plan: "Standing together...fighting together" (NLT); "fighting side by side like one man for the faith" (MOFFATT).[54] It's time we exhibit flawless teamwork.

"Striving together" is translated from the Greek *sunathleō*, which describes "striving together as athletes."[55] This implies

---

53. As Zionism's influence grew, many Diaspora Jews said when parting, "Next year in Jerusalem," hoping Israel would soon, perhaps in the next year, be reestablished in Palestine with Jerusalem as its capital. Even today, after Israel's reestablishment, many Jews end their Seder praying, "Next year in Jerusalem," some adding, "the rebuilt." These ardently hope very soon in Jerusalem the temple will be rebuilt, its worship restored, and Messiah enthroned—making it the world's worship center. Shouldn't Christians yearn for Christ's appearing and New Jerusalem with equal passion? Say with me, "Next year with the Lord, then Jerusalem, and New Jerusalem!" See 1 Thessalonians 4:13–18; Rev. 20:1–4; 21:1–22:5.
54. Scripture often describes God's people fighting together to receive God's spiritual and natural blessings (Jer. 31:10–12), against common enemies (Phil. 1:27–28; Isa. 11:12–14; Acts 18:26–28), against unnecessary divisions (1 Cor. 3:5–8), against heresy (Acts 15:24–25), with co-laborers in ministry (Phil. 4:3).
55. Wiersbe, *The Bible Exposition Commentary*, Phil. 1:27b, note.

every church (and ministry) is a spiritual team and should therefore assume a team mentality. That means not individual but team (church) interests always come first; everyone does their part without pride, envy, discontent, or grumbling; honors go first to the team, not individuals; everyone must be humble, work hard, practice their gifts and jobs, and stay focused and disciplined (avoiding overindulgence and distractions); we must learn the "rules" of our holy game and not break them (2 Tim. 2:5); we must not quit until our contests (tests, challenges) are over; we must practice obedience, service, and worship until we work together in perfect unison; we must neither fear nor mock our adversaries but study and defeat their strategies; and when exhausted, we must overcome by sheer will to win for Christ and kingdom. Such thoughts possess and drive excellent teams—and churches and ministries!

It's time Christians come together around our common Lord, salvation, Word, Spirit, and destiny and "fight side by side like one man for the faith" against all the forces that would keep souls from the Savior or stunt the spiritual growth and ministry of those He's saved. Real, deep, spiritual unity is Christ's passion for His people, and His final prayer reveals whenever it manifests, it converts unbelievers in every nation (John 17:21–23). Thus the Spirit has made genuine unity His top priority; everything He's doing in our individual attitudes and lives is to help us better worship and serve Christ alongside other Christians. Thus Paul's emphasis on unity in this letter (1:27; 2:2–3; 4:2). The pride, envy, prejudice, and unforgiveness of our flesh make this goal elusive, but if we'll cooperate, God will train us in perfect unity.

If all else should fail—biblical appeals to love, humility, reason, Christ's high priestly prayer, and usefulness—perhaps

Exploring Paul's Heart

persecution, brought on by a truly heaven-sent revival, will at last drive us together. Like a strife-torn family, nation, or military unit coming together when attacked by outsiders, so it may be with the church. If God does this, we'll be shocked to find how much we have in common with Christians we've misjudged or even worked against. One way or another God will get His team ready to fight "together" and win for His kingdom.

Will you pray with Paul, "Lord, do whatever it takes to end our infighting and motivate us to 'strive together' for the faith"?

1:28 Intrepid! Paul urged the Philippians to be intrepid: "In nothing terrified by your adversaries" (1:28). This fearlessness speaks of Christians who are embodiments of 2 Timothy 1:6–7, stirring and strengthening themselves in the Spirit daily, unmoved by their enemies' accusations, and ready for new challenges (Acts 4:12–13; 4:17–20; 5:27–29).

Implied is that they are so deeply rooted in eternal truth and thoroughly tested by stressful storms that they're fully established in God-confidence. Nothing and no one can shake their conviction in the veracity of God's Word, the immutability of His ways, the power of His Spirit, the wisdom of His guidance, the predestination of their call, and the error of those who reject Christ or oppose His truth, churches, ministers, or their ministries. Established in spiritual maturity, these have become like the Old and New Testament overcomers: Jesus (John 7:25–26; 18:4–8), Paul (Acts 14:3, 21; 19:26–27; Eph. 6:19–20), the (other) apostles (Acts 4:29–31; 5:40–42), Elijah (1 Kings 18), Daniel (Dan. 6:10), Daniel's three friends (Dan. 3:10–12), Stephen and the original martyrs (Acts 6:8–7:60; 8:1–4), and many others (Heb. 13:6).

Are you faithless or fearless, intimidated or intrepid, before your enemies? Relive the Philippians' intrepidness!

1:28 An "evident token." Paul describes two opposing religious groups, each utterly convinced that they are right and their opponents wrong.

The Philippian Christians' unflinching fearlessness in the face of pagan and Jewish resistance[56] seemed an "evident token," or "clear sign" (ESV), to their persecutors that the Christians were utterly deluded and hopelessly headed for damnation (as Israel's leaders considered Jesus' followers, John 7:47–49). Conversely, the Philippian Christians felt that their persecutors' dogged opposition was "plain proof" (PHILLIPS) that they themselves—the bearers of the true salvation message—were heaven bound: "…while the fact that you have such men as enemies is plain proof that you yourselves are being saved by God" (1:28, PHILLIPS). The principle here?

We can often locate people by the kind of enemies they make. Luther's position was confirmed by the fact that Pope Leo X, an utterly corrupt man, adamantly denounced and opposed him. The best entry on Elijah's résumé stated he was for years viciously hated and harried by Jezebel. John the Baptist's anointing was corroborated by the insatiable hatred directed at him by wicked, unscrupulous Herodias. Jesus' divine calling was confirmed when He was persecuted and mischaracterized as an insane demoniac by corrupt religious leaders (whom He accurately characterized as "whited sepulchers," "blind guides," "serpents," and hell bound; Matt. 23:16, 27–28, 33; Mark 3:22).

---

56. The Greeks thought Jesus' resurrection incredible and the Jews staunchly maintained Jesus was a false prophet and messianic pretender.

Exploring Paul's Heart

Thus Paul warned the Philippians that their fearlessness in serving God in the face of adamantly contradictory opposition (1:28–30) would be misinterpreted by their enemies as being proof they were hopelessly lost. Yet this very senseless, relentless opposition would be one of God's ways of confirming they were indeed His servants and wonderfully saved. Are we interpreting these signs of spiritual warfare in our conflicts?

If so, instead of cowing before our condemners, we'll "rejoice and be exceedingly glad" when they misread and malign us—and we'll correctly interpret their adamant denunciations as "evident tokens" we're on the right side, serving the right master, and bound for the right kingdom.

1:29 An unpopular but undeniable truth. Paul asserts we're called to not only believe Christ but also suffer for Him. We prefer to do the believing and let others do the suffering, but Paul will have none of it. He has suffered for Christ, and so must the Philippians—and all of us!

Paul assures us that all the trouble and suffering righteousness brings is a core component of biblical Christianity (1:29). Jesus agreed (Matt. 5:10–12; 13:21), and the apostles embraced this (Acts 5:41). Thus Paul bids the Philippians and us to "recognize and accept that true faith in Jesus Christ will involve suffering for His sake."[57] We'll discover this as we learn to walk and work with Christ by faith in a faithless world (and sometimes church):

---

57. Jack W. Hayford, general editor, *The Spirit-Filled Life Bible* (Nashville: Thomas Nelson Publishers, 1991), 1808.

> There's far more to this life than trusting in Christ. There's also suffering for him. And the suffering is as much a gift as the trusting.
>
> —The Message

Like faith, suffering is "given" to us by God's grace: "For unto you it is *given*...to suffer" implies suffering, and the ability to endure it, is a gift of God's grace (1:29). Thus the same grace that gives us faith, the Spirit, ministry gifts, spiritual gifts and the fruit of the Spirit also gives us the strength to suffer faithfully for Christ. Suffering to help bring in Christ's eternal kingdom is, though painful, a great honor: "You are given the privilege...of suffering for his sake" (1:29, Phillips). We call ourselves "believers"; why not "sufferers"?

Early Christians who endured Jewish persecution and later sporadic Roman persecution were more likely to recognize suffering for Christ as a privilege. In the first three centuries two distinctive titles developed for those who suffered for Christ's sake: "martyrs" and "confessors." Martyrs suffered death for their faithful witness for Christ, while confessors suffered torture (and often loss of property, imprisonment, or enslavement) but not death. Like every other part of the Christian life, suffering serves good purposes (Rom. 8:28).

Some benefits of Christian suffering are:

- It corrects our faults (if caused by sin or disobedience).

- It confirms our obedience (if caused by faithfulness to God's Word, call, guidance).

Exploring Paul's Heart

- It purifies us, by forcing us to examine ourselves more efficiently so we can peacefully endure the increased pressures in our life.

- It inspires and emboldens other Christians, who see us suffer willingly and with grace (Phil. 1:12–14).

- It's an "evident token" or clear sign confirming we are saved (Phil. 1:28).

- It prepares us to feel "worthy," or fully at home, in God's kingdom, where all will have suffered for Christ (2 Thess. 1:4–5).[58]

- It purges our churches of "chaff" and "mixed multitudes," false or carnal believers who won't suffer for Christ (2 Tim. 4:10).

- It honors Christ by disproving Satan's standing accusation that Christians only serve God for temporal benefits (Job 1:9–10).

- It purifies our faith of selfish motives and visions which wither as, while suffering, we continue pursuing Christ's goals and serving His people.

- It strengthens our faith, as we endure long, baffling contradictions and adversities, yet continue trusting in God's love, power, and promises (John 11:15; Rom. 4:18–21).

---

58. Thus we'll enter the "fellowship of his sufferings [and sufferers]" (Phil. 3:10), or heaven's VSW (Veterans of Spiritual Warfare), along with confessors, martyrs, and Christians of every era who have suffered for Christ's sake.

- It proves our loyalty, as we lovingly hold fast to Jesus, His Word, and calling no matter how painful our lot or losses (Dan. 3:17–18; Ps. 91:14).

- It conforms us to Christ's character image, since He too was "a man of sorrows, and acquainted with grief" (Isa. 53:3; 1 Pet. 2:19–23).

- It wins sinners, who contrast our generous faith, loyalty to Jesus, willingness to suffer, and unselfish service to others with their typically selfish lives[59] (Acts 16:27–30).

- It wins us sweet personal rewards in this life and the next, including the right to rule with Christ in His kingdom (Heb. 11:6; Ps. 37:4; 2 Tim. 2:12; Rev. 2:26–27; 3:12, 21).

- It causes rejoicing among heaven's "witnesses" who observe and cheer our spiritual victories in conflicts similar to their own (Heb. 12:1–3).

- It increases our ministerial capacity, or ability to comfort others who suffer by sharing the truths and ways of God that have sustained us (2 Cor. 1:3–4).

- It increases our spiritual discernment, giving us deeper insight into God's Word, quicker detection of Satan's deceptive agents and works, and a clearer grasp of God's master plan (Heb. 5:14; Phil. 1:9–10).

---

59. Many Romans, witnessing the extraordinary grace of Christian confessors and martyrs during the first three centuries, converted to the faith. Others, hardened in sin, mocked them as foolishly deluded.

- It frees us from the fear of suffering, as while suffering we discover for ourselves God's grace is sufficient to endure all the adversities we used to dread (2 Cor. 12:7–10).[60]

- It helps us see what matters most—knowing God, pleasing Him, finishing His will, helping His people, building His kingdom—as our tests repeatedly force us to choose between worldly and heavenly values (Col. 3:1–4; 1 John 2:15–17).

- It helps qualify us for translation (Rapture), since Jesus explicitly promised deliverance "from" the world's final "hour of temptation" only to those who patiently endure adversities for His sake (Rev. 3:8–10).

Thus, though unpopular, it is undeniable: we're called to suffer for Christ! You believe; will you also suffer?

Are you suffering misunderstanding, misrepresentation, mistreatment, or other forms of rejection from unbelievers, carnal Christians, or hardened apostates? Don't lose heart; take heart! Ponder the benefits of Christian suffering and joyfully embrace your part of "the sufferings of Christ that continue for his body, the church" (Col. 1:24, NLT). Confess your confidence that they are developing, not defeating you, taking you "from strength to [greater] strength" in Christ (Ps. 84:7).

---

60. Before we suffer, dread of failing God (or God failing us) in hard trials lingers in our minds; after suffering, however, we're no longer easily intimidated since we know experientially God can and will keep us no matter how hard or long our challenges (1 Sam. 17:37).

1:30 The same conflict. Paul told the Philippians to expect "the same conflict [lit. contest, contention, struggle, fight, race[61]]" they witnessed him suffer in the past and heard of him suffering at present (1:30). Thus he put them on notice: "Expect to be treated as I have been." Or, "Prepare to face 'the same kind of struggle you saw me go through' (THE MESSAGE)."

"Which ye saw in me" (1:30) refers to the injustice, abuse, and indignities Paul and Silas had endured in Philippi (Acts 16:16–40). "And now hear to be in me" (1:30) refers to the humiliating, prolonged injustice Paul was presently suffering as a prisoner in Rome (Acts 28:30–31). Combining these episodes, he suffered slander, injustice, and abuse from persistent, bitter enemies.

And these enemies were not merely flesh and blood but also demonic, the "rulers of darkness of this world...spiritual wickedness [wicked spirits] in high [heavenly] places" (Eph. 6:12). Why were these demons and enemies after Paul? Two reasons are apparent. First, he was a light-bearer, persistently spreading the light of God's Word—news of Jesus, His saving cross, His New Testament teachings, and key illuminations from Old Testament Scriptures—everywhere he went. Second, he wouldn't forsake this work or compromise his message however much it cost him. The man was abandoned, utterly and irreversibly committed to spreading the light. And he wanted the Philippians to be equally committed and prepared. Thus he warned them. He wasn't the first to do so.

Jesus also warned His disciples to expect the same conflict He faced (Matt. 10:24–25, 34–39; John 15:18–21). Peter told his readers to expect the same conflicts he faced, or "fiery trial[s]" (1 Pet. 4:12). Faithful ministers have warned the Christian remnant down through the centuries that they too

---

61. Strong, *Enhanced Strong's Lexicon*, s.v. "*agōn*."

would suffer the same conflicts that they faced. Are we continuing this message?

Are we warning new disciples and ministers that, if they persist in learning, living, and spreading the light in this dark world, they'll face "the same conflict"—persisting rejection, slander, abuse, and injustice from bitter human and demonic enemies? Ultimately we'll either face the same conflict Paul faced or, to avoid it, fall into the same compromise the Laodiceans chose. And we know how Jesus felt about them (Rev. 3:16).

Which will you choose, the same conflict or the same compromise?

Chapter Two

JESUS' KENOSIS— AND OURS!

Philippians 2 discloses this epistles' greatest truth: the Kenosis or self-emptying of Christ! In consummate humility Jesus set aside His divine glory to come down and save us. As wondrous as this is, the implications are equally arresting: Christ's self-emptying is an example we all should follow! While many Christians in Paul's day, even ministers, wouldn't "work out" Christ's humble mind and ministry, Timothy did. So did Epaphroditus. Will you? Will I? Let's consider Jesus' kenosis—and ours...

2:1–4 Fulfill Jesus' joy! Paul affirmed the Philippians would "fulfill" his joy if they lived regularly in love, humility, and unity with their fellow Christians, putting their needs before their own (2:1–4). But there's more here.

Since Paul was utterly identified with Christ, his joy reflected Christ's.[1] Christ repeatedly declared His passion to see

---
1. For example, the Apostle John's joy also reflects Christ's (2 John 4–5; 3 John 4, 5–6).

Christians live, work, minister, and worship together in perfect loving unity (John 13:34–35; 17:21–23). This is a much-needed reminder. If nothing else, Paul's plea will move us to pursue loving unity with all believers, including those who try us. If we won't humbly love them for their sake, may Paul's words prod us to do so for Christ's sake (John 21:15–17). Remember, there's no third option: we either please or grieve Christ.

And too many have already disappointed Him. Many of Jesus' disciples spoiled His joy when they "went back" after He began teaching hard sayings (John 6:66). Mary and Martha grieved and saddened Jesus by doubting His goodness when He didn't quickly heal their brother (John 11:20–21, 32). Peter disappointed Jesus by doubting His word and power while walking on water to go to Jesus (Matt. 14:28–31). Peter troubled Jesus again by denying Him at the high priest's court (Luke 22:55–62). Judas deeply wounded Jesus by betraying Him for thirty pieces of silver (Luke 22:47–48). Millions since have inflicted similar griefs on our Savior. What about us? Will we re-inflict these psychological wounds on Jesus or relieve Him?

Why not respond to Paul's and Christ's heartfelt plea? "Fulfill ye my joy" by walking in humble loving unity with all Christians, but especially those in your church (as Paul here exhorts). You want Christ to fulfill your desires, so "your joy may be full" (John 16:24). Why not fulfill His!

See Ephesians 4:1–3; 4:30–5:2.

2:1 And help yourself! Paul's conjunction "therefore" (2:1) refers the Philippians to his previous assertion that suffering was part of their calling (1:29–30). His following exhortation to brotherly love (2:1–4) implies loving fellowship and sweet unity will help them endure their sufferings (1:29–30). Or:

> In light of your ongoing Christian sufferings, be sure to give and receive the comforting consolations of Christian fellowship and unity. Walk in love by humbly putting the needs of your fellow sufferers before your own.
>
> —Author's paraphrase

If pursued, sweet friendship and harmonious teamwork with believers would counterbalance the adversarial treatment and dysfunctional relationships they often encountered among unbelievers. Paul knew that to survive the bitter, we need the sweet.

And the bitterer our troubles for Christ's sake, the more sweet fellowship we need. When rebuked and threatened by the powerful Sanhedrin, the Apostles Peter and John "went unto their own company" for timely consolation and group prayer—through which they received a reinvigorating refilling of the Spirit and His boldness (Acts 4:23–31). When driven out into the wilderness by King Saul's sudden persecution, David drew comfort from Jonathan's supportive fellowship. And when Paul was dictating this letter, he had just received deep comfort and joy from the Philippians' timely gift and the loving concern it represented (Phil. 4:10, 14–18). What if these had been out of fellowship with their believing friends?

Truly the "consolations," "comforts of love," and "tender mercies" (Phil. 2:1) of our friends in Christ will heal every wound our foes inflict (1:29–30). We begin receiving this curative sweetness the moment we start giving it to others: "Give, and it shall be given unto you" (Luke 6:38). So help yourself! Start loving the Christians around you, including those you've disliked, avoided, or resented. Especially reach out to them when they're suffering rejection, trouble, or grief, "having [now] the same love, being of one accord, of one mind," considering and serving their needs "better" than yours (Phil. 2:2–4). Then expect to reap what you're sowing—sweet fellowship and support from others when you "suffer for His sake" (1:29).

2:1–4 Pass on the love. The second of three strong appeals for humble, loving unity to prevail in the Philippian church (see 1:27; 4:1–2), this appeal is based on what the Philippians had received "in Christ" and "of [or in] the Holy Spirit" (2:1). If God's love is in fact real in them, he pleads, they should show it by sharing the manifold love—"consolation, comfort, fellowship, tender mercies, and compassions" (2:1–2)—they've experienced and enjoyed since becoming Christians ["in Christ," born "of the Holy Spirit"].

The Phillips translation is excellent:

> Now if you have known anything of Christ's encouragement and of his reassuring love; if you have known something of the fellowship of his Spirit, and of compassion and deep sympathy, do make my joy complete—live together in harmony, live together in love, as though you had only one mind and one spirit between you.
>
> Never act from motives of rivalry or personal vanity, but in humility think more of each other than you do of yourselves. None of you should think only of his own affairs, but consider other people's interests also.
> —PHILIPPIANS 2:1–4, PHILLIPS

Or, paraphrasing, Paul's thought seems to be:

> If you have received and experienced firsthand Christ's personal encouragement and "reassuring love"

(PHILLIPS); if you have also received and experienced the Holy Spirit's tender mercies and compassions, don't let the love stop with you. *Pass it on to others, especially believers,* by living together with them in patient love and humble harmony.

Never speak or act adversarially[2] or divisively, to enviously compete (imitation, one-upmanship) or to show off.[3] Instead be thoughtfully considerate, regularly thinking of others' needs, desires, feelings, and welfare as you do your own…

—AUTHOR'S PARAPHRASE

Thus as we've received the "stimulus" of Christ's love (2:1, MOFFATT), let's stimulate others with love. Is all the love Christ and the Holy Spirit are showing you daily—their mercies, forgiveness, understanding, patience, support, encouragement, assistance, favor—stopping with you? Don't be like the Dead Sea, always receiving but never releasing. Pass on the love![4] "Freely ye have received, freely give" (Matt. 10:8).

See John 13:34–35; 15:12, 17; Romans 13:8; 1 Thessalonians 4:9–10; 1 Peter 1:22; 1 John 3:10–12; 3:21–23; 4:11–12.

2:3–4 How to love others. As stated above, J. B. Phillips translates the words for "esteem" (2:3) and "look on" (2:4) as referring to our thoughts. "*Think* more of each other" (2:3)

---

2. "Christ came to slay all enmities; therefore let there not be among Christians a spirit of opposition." (Henry, *Commentary in One Volume*, 1863.)
3. "Christ came to humble us, and therefore let there not be among us a spirit of pride." (Ibid.).
4. God's love is without prejudice (Acts 10:34; John 4:9; James 2:1–4), forgets others' sins once confessed (Acts 9:10–17), prefers giving to receiving (Acts 20:35), builds and perfects unity (Eph. 4:13, 15–16; 1 Cor. 8:1), brings or "commands" outpourings of the Spirit (Ps. 133:1–3; Acts 1:14; 2:1–4), and causes others to respond in love—thus the epigram, "Love, and you shall be loved." (Ibid.) Also see Luke 6:38; Galatians 6:7.

and "none of you should *think* only of his own affairs" (2:4, Phillips), but should *"consider* others' interests also" (2:4). This illuminates a key truth.

Love begins in our thoughts! We must think lovingly if we aspire to behave lovingly. We'll never flow in love with people as long as we harbor unkind thoughts toward them. First we must correct our thought patterns by rejecting unloving thoughts—apathy, envy, prejudice, condemnation, anger, unforgiveness, mockery, superiority—and choosing to let only kind thoughts remain in our minds. Like the God of love, we must have His goodwill toward all (2 Pet. 3:9), including those who hold ill will toward us. Then we can make loving choices and naturally and freely manifest love in kind words, beneficial acts, and gracious responses (Prov. 15:1; Rom. 12:17–21). Nothing theoretical here, this is practical instruction. It's "how to" time.

Ready to think love? If you're having difficulty thinking kindly toward someone, ask God for more grace. The grace of Him who is "kind unto the unthankful and to the evil" is richly "sufficient" to help you love the lovable and the unlovable (Luke 6:35; 2 Cor. 12:9). So diligently "guard your heart" and let only loving thoughts remain (Prov. 4:23; 2 Cor. 10:3–5). Then you'll pass on the love you're receiving from Christ to whomever you meet—sinner, saint, relative, neighbor, or enemy.[5]

2:1–5 The humility of love. These verses intentionally blend loving unity with humility, since they introduce this epistles' most important message—Paul's description of Jesus' *kenosis*, or His humble, self-emptying transition from divine to human

---

5. One sure sign of spiritual maturity and true Christlikeness is consistently walking in love toward our enemies. That's why Jesus' "love your enemies" talk climaxed with His charge, "Be ye, therefore, perfect [spiritually mature], even as your Father, who is in heaven, is perfect" (Matt. 5:38–48).

form to lovingly visit and save us (2:5–11). One commentator adds Paul thus "urges humility on the Philippians as the only way to secure unity."[6]

Philippians highlights the subject of humility and God's call for us to humble ourselves. It showcases the humility of love in:

- Jesus' humility, especially His self-sacrificing submission to the Father's will (2:5–11)

- Paul's humility, specifically his selflessness (1:7, 15–18, 24–25), sober self-view (3:7–9, 13), and contentment (4:11–12)

- The Philippians' humility, seen particularly in their consistent obedience (2:12–16)

- Timothy's humility, revealed in his unselfish ministry to God's people and assistance of Paul (2:19–21)

- Epaphroditus' humility, displayed in his self-sacrificing service in labor, prayer, and travel to relieve Paul's and the Philippians' suffering, respectively (2:25–30)

Have you realized love is humble and humility is loving, that both are essential to Christian unity and Christlikeness, and that both reside in Christ in you? If you've realized it, reveal it to others! Philippians showcases the humility of love; go show it!

---

6. A. Robertson, *Word Pictures in the New Testament* (Nashville: Broadman Press, 1933), Phil. 2:5, note.

2:5 Think like Jesus! Paul urges us to think like Jesus, to share His heavenly viewpoint and attitudes, especially His humility (2:6–8).[7] "Let your attitude to life be that of Christ Jesus himself" (2:5, PHILLIPS). Real Christlikeness begins with a humble—*Christ's* humble—viewpoint.

Without it we'll never be like Jesus, no matter how numerous, philanthropic, or sacrificial our good works. Nor will we please Him, because everything we do will serve our proud self-will or self-promotion (our "pride of life" desiring to be seen and praised by men; Matt. 23:5; John 12:42–43), without any real regard for what pleases Christ (Col. 3:23). Our humble Lord sought only His Father's favor (John 8:29). Truly humble Christians seek only His favor! Always they aim to be seen and approved of Him (Gal. 1:10; Col. 3:24; 2 Tim. 2:15; Matt. 25:21, 23).

Obeying this charge to think like Jesus involves more than trying to be a little less full of ourselves. It requires that we commit ourselves to receive, revere, review, and respond to Jesus.

We receive Christ in the new birth experience, when we receive the gospel of salvation through His cross and grace alone (John 1:12–13). We revere Christ by thereafter living in the fear of God—deep respect for His awesome power and authority and the utter truthfulness of His every Word (1 Pet. 2:17). We review Christ by committing ourselves to a quest to know Him—prayerfully studying the biblical record, noting Christ's values, decisions, spiritual disciplines, doctrines, works (in life, ministry), goals, and attitudes (especially His humility, Phil. 2:5–8). We add experiential knowledge by pondering

---

7. "He was eminently humble, and this is what we are peculiarly to learn of him." (Henry, *Commentary in One Volume*, 1863.)

how He responds to us today in our lives by encouraging, instructing, correcting, disciplining, and blessing us. Studying Christian history and biographies further reveals how Christ worked in and through Christians in earlier times and is thus likely to do again (Heb. 13:8). We then respond to Christ by personal obedience, by diligently practicing the biblical truths we're learning in our ongoing review of Christ and by receiving His correction, whether prompted by the Spirit's conviction or elders' counsels. This response—"working out" our salvation "with fear and trembling" in our daily life-tests (2:12)—is crucial. It alone enables the Holy Spirit to finish humbling us and give us spiritual insight to know Jesus and think like Him. As we continue revering, reviewing, and responding to Jesus, our minds become increasingly "renewed" and humble, until we're consistently "spiritually minded" (Rom. 12:1–2; 8:6).

When "this mind" (Phil. 2:5) is in us, we'll live like Jesus, humbling ourselves easily and often (2:5–8); love like Him (2:1–4); obey the Father's will consistently, as He did (2:8, 12); minister like Him, always looking to give and serve (Phil. 1:24–25; Matt. 20:28); suffer like Him (1:28–30; 2:8); reflect His character, accurately and winsomely representing what He's like (Phil. 2:15–16; John 17:21, 23); and be raised like Him, honored and rewarded in God's time and way, as He was (Phil. 2:9; 1 Sam. 2:30; Luke 14:10–11; Acts 28:10). Are we there yet?

Are we as individuals and churches ready to be "spiritually minded" (Rom. 8:6), or wholly conformed to God's viewpoint?[8] Ready to be as meekly sober-minded as Jesus of Nazareth was?

See Matthew 23:12; Romans 12:3; Matthew 18:1–4.

---

8. The context, in which Paul appeals for loving unity among the Philippians, proves his address was not only to individuals but also to the whole church: "Have this mind among yourselves" (2:5, ESV).

PhilippianNotes

2:5 Equal with God. Paul asserts that before His incarnation Jesus was "equal with God" (2:6), "possessing the fullness of the attributes which make God God" (AMP). Therefore, being immutable (Heb. 13:8), Jesus was, is, and will forever be "equal with God." Thus any doctrine denying His absolute, immutable, and unending deity is false. Those teachings that state Jesus is a created being, and thus not eternally preexisting in the Godhead (Col. 2:9), also deny His divinity.

Jesus revealed His deity in several ways. He declared His equality with the Father to the Jews (John 10:30–33) and their highest council (Luke 22:66–71). He also asserted His eternal preexistence to the Jews (subtly identifying Himself as the I AM of the Exodus, John 8:58; Exod. 3:14) and again in His high priestly prayer (John 17:24). Furthermore He received worship (Matt. 15:25; 20:20; 28:9, 17), something no mere righteous man would dare do. Scripture consistently forbids glorying in, much less worshipping flesh (1 Cor. 1:29–31) or angels (Col. 2:18), and shows holy men and angels vigorously rejecting worship offered them by overexcited individuals and redirecting it to God: "See thou do it not!...Worship God [alone]" (Rev. 19:10; 22:8–9; Acts 10:25–26).[9] Scripture also describes Jesus appearing in His visible divine glory during His lifetime (Mark 9:2–3), after His resurrection (Acts 26:13–15; Rev. 1:10–18), and receiving worship in heaven along with the Father (Rev. 5:8–14). Paul further asserted "in him dwelleth all the fullness of the Godhead bodily" (Col. 2:9). Peter famously exclaimed Jesus' deity by the Spirit's personal

---

9. This vigorous rejection of misdirected worship is prompted by God's prime commandment (Exod. 20:3, 4–5). It's no wonder, therefore, that the persisting quest of God's nemesis, Satan, has been this very thing: to usurp the worship that is due God alone. This explains his motive for inspiring the world to worship his "trinity"—the dragon, beast, and false prophet—in the Great Tribulation (Rev. 13:2, 4, 11–15; 16:13).

revelation to his heart (Matt. 16:15–17). Even the demons acknowledged Jesus as God's Son and thus divine (Luke 4:33–34).

Do we fully respect the deity of Christ? Are we obeying His sayings and worshipping Him as God? Is there any misdirected worship in our hearts, excessive praise for men, or insufficient thanksgiving to Christ from whom, along with the Father and Spirit, all blessings flow?

2:6–8 The Kenosis: God came down. "But [Jesus] made himself of no reputation"—with these words Paul unveils one of the greatest New Testament revelations, the *kenosis*, or self-emptying of Christ (2:7).[10] Jesus divested Himself of all His divine glory and divine prerogatives, voluntarily stripping away all the divine honors, powers, and position that were His from eternity past. Thus He "did not cling to his privileges as God's equal" (2:7, Phillips), but willingly "stripped Himself [of all privileges and rightful dignity]" (amp). Why?

His Father asked Him to do so. For what purpose? It was necessary for Jesus to become a fit substitutionary sacrifice for the fallen human race whom the Father, in His passionate love, desired to redeem from the destructive control of sin and Satan (2 Cor. 5:19). To die as our surrogate Sufferer, Jesus had to truly be one of us—a human being in a human body—and live under the law, discharging its righteous commands without sin, and then die in His body on the cross (Gal. 4:4–5; Heb. 10:5; 9:14). If not, He couldn't be "the Lamb of God, who taketh away the sin of the world" (John 1:29, 36). So it was love, Christ's love for His Father and His Father's redemptive love for mankind,

---

10. Paul actually used the Greek verb *kenoō*, meaning "to make empty," rather than the noun *kénōsis*, which means "emptiness." See Kittel, Friedrich, and Bromiley, *Theological Dictionary of the New Testament*, s.v. "*kenoō*."

that inspired God's Son to accept our human limitations: the immortal God in a mortal body, subject to time and space, with limited strength and knowledge.[11]

To describe Jesus' amazing change from divine to human form, Paul uses three terms: "form" (2:6, 7), "likeness" (2:7), and "fashion" (2:8). The Greek words he used (*morphē, homoiōma, schēma*) have virtually the same meaning. All speak of "outward form, shape, or appearance."[12] Thus Jesus didn't relinquish His divine nature and person but merely "changed clothes," laying aside His spectacularly regal and scintillating divine wardrobe (Shekinah glory) as part of the Godhead to assume the inglorious, humble clothing of a mortal human body.[13]

Thus in the kenosis Jesus changed "form" but not His essence. He exchanged the "form of God" for the "likeness of men" (2:6–7) yet remained fully undiminished as God. However, while appearing in the "likeness of men," or like any other ordinary man (Isa. 53:2), He was far from ordinary. He was a unique God-man—fully divine and fully human.

To further clarify, Christ's humanity was not procreated by His supposed father, Joseph, but was directly created by an act of God's Spirit in Mary's womb (Luke 1:35). Therefore, like Adam in the beginning, the man Jesus (the second or "last

---

11. Though Jesus was thus limited as a man, the fullness of the Holy Spirit and His power expanded Jesus' capabilities as a minister (Luke 4:14; Acts 10:38). When necessary to bless others, the Spirit enabled Jesus of Nazareth to have and use divine knowledge (John 1:48), power (Mark 4:39, 41; John 18:4–9), and even, on one occasion only, visually unveil His divine glory (Matt. 17:1–2).
12. Kittel, Friedrich, and Bromiley, *Theological Dictionary of the New Testament*, s.v. "*morphē*," "*homoiōma*," and "*schēma*."
13. On this point Gnosticism erred, claiming Jesus of Nazareth was not truly a human with a real material body but was only a spirit person appearing to be but not really being incarnate. The apostle John vigorously rejected their claims (1 John 4:3).

Adam," 1 Cor. 15:45; 15:22) was pure, having no sin nature (Heb. 4:15). And though He completely veiled His divine glory, except during the transfiguration (Mark 9:1–8), He was, at least by age twelve, fully aware of His deity and essential redemptive mission (John 8:58; Luke 2:49).

> The Lord of all things made Himself
> Naked of glory for His mortal change.[14]
> —Tennyson, "The Holy Grail"

But by becoming human, Jesus wasn't yet finished coming down. His complete descent involved two further steps to distinctly lower conditions—as a servant and an apparent criminal.

CHRIST THE OBEDIENT SERVANT. "As a man," rather than walk in proud, Cain-like, self-serving independence, Jesus consistently chose to humbly assume the "form of a servant" (2:7–8). His servantship was twofold:

1. He humbly served His heavenly Father's will, obeying His law and living unobtrusively in Nazareth thirty years (Luke 2:49, 51–53; John 8:29).

2. For His heavenly Father's sake He humbly served human authorities: Joseph, Mary, local rabbis, rulers of synagogues, the chief priests who ruled the temple (Matt. 17:24–27), and Roman authorities (Luke 2:51–52; 4:16; Matt. 22:15–21).

---

14. Richard F. Weymouth, *New Testament in Modern Speech* (Grand Rapids, MI: Kregel Publications, 1978), Phil. 2:7, note #3, 532.

And His obedient service was not partial, as was the case with King Saul (1 Sam. 15:1–11), but full, without reserve. Paul asserts it was this obedience that rendered Jesus a man truly humble (2:8). The further Jesus went in obedience, the further He grew in humility:

- He "humbled himself, *and* became obedient" (2:8).

- Or, He "humbled himself *as* He became obedient."

- Or, He humbled Himself *as far as* He became obedient."

How far did Jesus go in obeying His Father? "Unto death"—the termination of the control of His self-will and ultimately of His bodily life.

CHRIST THE APPARENT CRIMINAL. The death the Father ordained for Christ to suffer was of the lowest kind, that of a common criminal. Crucifixion was the most shameful form of Roman execution and was reserved for those the Romans considered the scum of the earth—slaves, insurrectionists, and other capital offenders.[15] Roman law forbade the crucifixion of Roman citizens.[16] By submitting to die "even the death of the cross" (2:8), Jesus finished His downward

---

[15]. For example, Crassus crucified six thousand survivors from Spartacus' failed slave revolt in 71 BC, their bodies lining the Appian Way from Capua to Rome. From the perspective of Roman law the notorious prisoner Barabbas, truly an insurrectionist guilty of criminal activity, should have been crucified, not Christ, a peace-loving, anti-insurrectionist Rabbi (Matt. 27:16; John 18:40; 6:15; 18:36).

[16]. This explains why according to tradition Nero had Paul, a Roman citizen, beheaded, while ordering Peter, a non-citizen, crucified—though upside down at Peter's request.

journey into total humility. "As a man" He could go no lower. It was this extreme obedience that qualified Him for singular exaltation (Phil. 2:9–11).

His three-stage descent—to humanity, servantship, and criminal execution—is a profound lesson to us. As Jesus came down, so must we.

His long, voluntary descent into the valley of humility blazes a spiritual trail we will follow if we're fully committed to the Father's will. Our outward likeness will not change. Humanity we are and humanity we will remain. But our worldly status and proud reputation, in others' eyes and our own, will diminish. As we pursue the Father's will, "holding forth the word of life" (Phil. 2:16), we'll be misunderstood, rejected, and figuratively crucified. Thorny enemies, nail-like accusations, scourging condemnations, and other humiliating hardships will come our way.

If we rebel, abandoning our calling, we'll remain proud, unchanged, and useless to God. But if, for love of our Savior, we follow His humble way and come down to a life of humble trust and obedience in our "Nazareth," "Gethsemane," or "Golgotha," we'll be changed into Christ's image and ready to fellowship with Him more deeply and serve Him more fruitfully.

So finish your kenosis. For love of Christ, empty your pride and complete your obedience unto the death of your self-will.

2:7 A nobody! Jesus "made himself of no reputation" (2:7), or "made himself nothing" (NIV). Amazing! He who was everything became "nothing." Or, a nobody! Unnoticed, unappreciated, not sought, without honorable reputation, that's a nobody—and what our glorious Lord became!

Isaiah wrote:

> He grew up like a small plant before the LORD, like a root growing in a dry land. He had no special beauty or form to make us notice him; there was nothing in his appearance to make us desire him.
> —ISAIAH 53:2, NCV

So Isaiah saw Messiah as: (1) a "small" plant, not a mighty Lebanon cedar in the religious, political, or academic world; and (2) a root growing in "a dry land," Galilee if you will, not a spiritually fruitful atmosphere like Jerusalem, well watered with the inspired homilies of rabbis and prophets. Thus he described a man so ordinary there was nothing about Him that would impress or attract. The four Gospels confirm Isaiah's vision of Jesus of Nazareth.

He was born among a despised people (Jews), in a poor family (Luke 2:24; Lev. 12:8), of a questionable birth (Matt. 1:18; John 8:41), and in a lowly stable. He grew up in a small, out of the way village far from His nation's worship center and undistinguished for producing rulers, prophets, or scholars. He enjoyed no formal education or tutelage, though He attended synagogue worship regularly, gleaning what He could from rabbis' homilies and Torah readings (Luke 4:16–20). For many years He was a common laborer working for low wages. He never married, and so had no children to carry on His name. He never owned a home or donkey, but rented both when He needed them (Luke 9:58). His typical mode of transportation was His sandal-clad feet. His clothes were ordinary, except for a seamless garment that was ultimately stolen. Without land, He had no clout or influence in His community. Unaffiliated with religious sects or political parties, He was overlooked, held suspect, or summarily rejected by their members. He never rose to a higher socioeconomic class, though His amazing ministry brought meteoric popularity—and undying scandal! When His time came, He took the world's lowest exit: public crucifixion! If not for His heavenly preaching and powers, no one outside of Nazareth would have ever heard the name Jesus of Nazareth.

Thus Jesus lived in the world's "basement." Not merely nobody, He was a nobody's nobody. While billions have since lived socially, economically, vocationally, or educationally low lives, none have lived lower—or more honorably in God's sight, because Jesus lived in extraordinarily close, loving union with His Father and chose always to do His will (John 8:29).

Is God honoring you by letting you go Christ's way? In the drama of life, has He cast you in the role of a nobody? Take heart; remember you're following the footsteps of a Somebody! Worship Him and live honorably in your "basement," remembering, "Them who honor me I will honor" (1 Sam. 2:30).

2:8 Obeying to die—and dying to obey! Paul's phrase "obedient unto death" is profound. Let's go deeper.

Every time Jesus obeyed His Father's word or will, though He had no sin nature, He yet died to sin, specifically to the *possibility* of sinning by acting independent of His Father.[17] Thus by every act of submissive obedience to His Father Jesus became more dependent upon Him and desirous to please Him (John 8:29). His joy in obedience grew until He "delight[ed]" to do the Father's will (Ps. 40:8). Or, as some might say, He was just "dying," or strongly desiring, to obey!

---

17. This was a very real possibility, or else Satan's temptation of Christ (the second or "last" Adam, 1 Cor. 15:45), and Christ's resultant choices to remain obedient, would have been a worthless mockery.

Unlike Jesus, we have a sin nature. Every time we obey God's Word, Spirit, call, or correction, we die further to the actual influence of our sin and self. They control us less and God controls more, until He becomes the unchallenged actual Ruler of our lives and sin and self's control is dead—obeyed to death by our consistent choices to obey God's will rather than their impulses and suggestions. This describes the simplest, most effective way to "mortify"[18] our old nature: obey God! The further we go in obedience, the further we go in death to sin and self and the more Jesus' life in us is released to increasingly manifest His delight in obedience...until we too are dying to obey.

Among their many virtues the Philippians, by Paul's own testimony, were "always" obedient to God and His ministers (2:12). Like their Lord, they obeyed to die and were just dying to obey. Are we?

2:8 The humility process. As God, Jesus didn't need to humble Himself. "As a man," however, He chose to do so as an example for us. How did He do so?

By obedience to the Father's will! As stated earlier, Paul taught Jesus "humbled himself, and [or as, or as far as, He] became obedient" to the Father. It's the same for us. "Let Him be your example in humility" (2:5, AMP).

Every time we obey the Father's will, we humble ourselves, and our humility grows as far as our obedience goes. We can stop short at any point, as King Saul did, but to be Christlike we must complete our obedience. This passage reveals various stages of the humility process in Jesus' life, stages we must experience if we want His humility in our lives. They are:

---

18. See Romans 8:13; Colossians 3:5.

- ACCEPTING A LOWER POSITION (2:6–7). Jesus came down from deity to humanity, the "likeness of men." We must accept the lower stations in life God assigns us and be content as long as He leaves us there (4:11–12; Prov. 15:33; Luke 14:10–11).

- ABANDONING REPUTATION OR TITLE (2:6–7). While on earth Jesus was not regularly addressed as God. Furthermore His reputation as a man was grossly maligned by His enemies (Mark 3:22; John 8:48; 10:20). We must learn to be content without honorable appellations and with dishonorable mischaracterizations (Acts 24:5–6; Phil. 4:11–12).

- ADOPTING SERVANTHOOD (2:7). Jesus became a servant of God and of men. Thus He learned how to submit to His authorities and serve others' needs and desires with joy, not anger or resentment. We must learn to serve our superiors' and others' needs "heartily, as to the Lord, and not [merely] unto men" (Col. 3:23).

- OBEDIENCE TO GOD (2:8). Jesus focused on obeying His Father's will: "I do always those things that please him" (John 8:29). We must focus on obedience if our ministry or counsel is to inspire the same in others. Consider these kinds of obedience:
    - FULL OBEDIENCE. Jesus never stopped short, turned back, or compromised, obeying fully, "unto death." Thus leaving

nothing undone, He ultimately "finished" His life course (John 17:4; 19:30). We must finish our life course if we want our disciples to leave nothing undone.

- SUFFERING OBEDIENCE. Jesus' obedience was of the extreme or radical kind—even while being slandered, betrayed, whipped, and publicly stripped and nailed to a cross (Heb. 5:8; Isa. 50:5–7). We must remain faithful while suffering if we hope to lead and encourage others to overcome their sufferings "with joyfulness; giving thanks" for Christ's sake (Col. 1:11–12).

If with God's grace we embrace and endure these stages of humility, one day we'll emerge thoroughly, peacefully, contentedly, and fruitfully humble—like Jesus! And ready for God to raise and use us without our failing due to pride or self-will. Do we want Jesus' humility?

The way there is challenging but clear: submit to His humility process!

2:9–11 Highly exalted. Paul recounts how God raised Jesus from great humiliation to great honor. Thus Jesus' personal experience exemplifies the principle He frequently taught: "Whosoever shall exalt himself shall be abased; and he that shall humble himself shall be exalted" (Matt. 23:12; Luke 14:11; 18:14).[19] Isaiah also foresaw Jesus' stunning humiliation leading to His lofty exaltation (Isa. 52:13; 53:10–12). Two truths stand out here.

---

19. The references given describe not one but three separate instances in Jesus' ministry recorded in the Gospels. Thus we conclude this principle of God honoring the humble and humbling the proud was a recurring, and thus important, theme in His teaching. See 1 Samuel 2:30.

1. God honors all who humble themselves (and humbles all who honor themselves).

2. The degree of our humility determines the degree of our honors.

Combined, these tell us God honors most the meekest and raises highest the humblest. Because Jesus submitted to the most rigorous humility training ("Because He stooped so low," Phil. 2:9, AMP), the Father gave Him the most regal rewards: an exalted position, a name of distinction, and supreme authority, all to bring the Father more honor: "to the glory of God, the Father" (2:11).

Jesus' position is now the "highest place" (2:9, NIV), or at the Father's right hand. Because He was gazed upon in horror on the cross, all will gaze upon Him in honor on His Father's throne (Rev. 3:21). His name is the most distinguished, or "above every name" in heaven and earth (Phil. 2:9). Souls are converted, healings occur, miracles are wrought, demons flee, and the Spirit is given, all by prayer in the name of "Jesus"—and there is salvation in no other (Acts 4:10–12). Also, Jesus' authority, or honorable influence, is the greatest. Ultimately "every knee" will "bow," or yield, to His will (2:10) and "every tongue" will "confess," or fully acknowledge, His legitimate lordship (2:11).[20]

Joseph foreshadowed Jesus' experience perfectly. He was deeply humbled by not one but two seasons of mortifying defeat: one

---

[20]. Before engaging in combat in the Coliseum, Roman gladiators would parade and then, standing before the emperor's box, shout, *"Ave Caesar! Morituri te salutant!"* ("Hail Caesar! Those who are about to die salute you!"). If even Caesar was hailed by the condemned before they died, how much more will Christ, who shed His blood for all, be hailed by those about to enter the second death (Josh. 7:19–26; Phil. 2:10–11)? On quote, see: Nigel Rogers, *Roman Empire* (New York: Metro Books, 2011), 436.

of family rejection and foreign slavery (Gen. 37) and another involving false accusation and prolonged, unjust incarceration (Gen. 39–40).[21] Once he was thoroughly humbled, God raised him to a high position, conferred upon him an exalted name, and gave him great authority:

- GENESIS 41:40–44—Joseph was raised to (installed in) the highest position in Egypt, Pharaoh's right hand, authorized to rule in his name throughout Egypt. This represents Jesus' glorification, when He assumed the highest position in His Father's kingdom, at His right hand (Acts 2:33; Ps. 110:1; Matt. 28:18; Dan. 7:13–14).

- GENESIS 41:45—Pharaoh gave Joseph a most honorable name that described his saving work in Egypt. *Zaphenath-paneah* means, "the giver of the nourishment of the land,"[22] or "giver of the nourishment of life."[23] This symbolizes the most honorable name of "Jesus" (Greek, *Iēsous*, "Yahweh saves"; or Hebrew, *Jehoshua*, "Jehovah saves"), which describes His saving works of regenerating us and feeding us spiritual nourishment from the Scriptures through His

---

21. It has been said, "For every Genesis 40, there's a Genesis 41 that follows"—or, for every long, low, humbling season of trial, there is an uplifting, joyful season of fruitful service that follows.
22. Charles F. Pfeiffer, Howard F. Vos, and John Rea, *The Wycliffe Bible Encyclopedia*, vol. 2 (Chicago: Moody Press, 1975), 1833.
23. S. Smith and J. Cornwall, *The Exhaustive Dictionary of Bible Names* (North Brunswick, NJ: Bridge-Logos Publishers, 1998), s.v. "Zaphenath-paneah."

appointed ministers in this world (Eph. 4:11–13; 1 Cor. 3:5).[24]

- GENESIS 42:10—All the Egyptians, foreigners, and even Joseph's brothers addressed him as "lord." (See Genesis 44:16, 18, 19, 20, 22; 45:8–9.) This foreshadows the whole world, including Jesus' brothers (the Jews), eventually acknowledging He is not merely a great teacher, prophet, or miracle worker but "Lord" ("supreme authority" or "supernatural master over all," and thus Deity).[25] See Romans 10:9; 1 Corinthians 12:3; John 13:13; Romans 14:9, 11.

- GENESIS 42:6—Everyone bowed down to Joseph, signifying their willingness to respect and yield to his honorable political authority (Gen. 37:5–11; 43:26, 28). This represents Jews and Gentiles worshipping and yielding to Jesus' authority, in His church now and kingdom later (Rev. 3:9). See Isaiah 45:23; Romans 14:11.

---

24. For thirty-three years Jesus "made himself of no reputation" by living a totally anonymous life in Nazareth. Then He endured three and a half years of relentless reputation assassination as His religious enemies hurled every epithet imaginable at Him: "deceiver," "demonic," "[messianic] pretender," "false prophet," "Samaritan," even "carpenter" (mocking His lack of rabbinic training); "born of fornication" (mocking the supposed shameful circumstances of His conception, Matt. 1:18–19; John 8:41). For enduring these pejoratives, the Father gave Jesus many new precious names above all others: Christ (the Anointed One or Messiah), Lord of lords, King of kings, Prince of Peace, King of Glory, Morning Star, Chief Shepherd, Wonderful Counselor, light of the world, and others.

25. In lesser applications *kyrios* means "ruler" or "landowner" or merely "sir" as one would respectfully address any elder or authority (or in ancient times one's husband, 1 Pet. 3:6). See Swanson, *Dictionary of Biblical Languages with Semantic Domains: Greek (New Testament)*, s.v. "*kyrios.*"

As we see with Joseph and Jesus, God brings very low those whom He's preparing for very high honors. Moses, David, Job, and Daniel were also the humblest before they were the highest; "last," who became "first" (Mark 10:31); most rejected "stones" in God's temple who became most respected (Acts 4:11)—and all "to the glory of God, the Father" who sustained and raised them (Phil. 2:11)! Perhaps this speaks to your condition today.

Are you low? Very low? Last? A rejected stone longing for more acceptance and loving appreciation? Ponder where Jesus' and Joseph's long walks through the valleys of life ended—in fruitfulness, not failure!—and patiently finish your appointed course of humbling trials. Be confident that in His time and way your Father will raise you to a higher position of service, an honorable name, and increased authority, all so your life also will be "to the glory of God, the Father."[26]

2:9 The name above every name. Jesus' name is second or subordinate to none. One author notes this humorous anecdote:

> Some years ago, Dr. Henrietta Mears visited the Taj Mahal in India. The famed structure is noted for its unusual acoustical qualities. Standing in the center of the white marble mausoleum, the guide said loudly, "There is no God but Allah and Mohammed is the prophet!" His voice reverberated through all the chambers and corridors of the tomb.
>
> Dr. Mears asked, "May I say something, too?" The guide courteously replied, "Certainly." In a clear, distinct voice, Dr. Mears said, "Jesus Christ, Son of God, is Lord over all!" Her voice too reverberated from

---

26. See Proverbs 15:33; John 17:1.

wall to wall and through the corridors of the minareted shrine, saying, "Lord over all...over all...over all...over all!"[27]

Hers was a bold witness and so necessary today! With Mears' words reverberating in our hearts, may we too be "much more bold to speak" (Phil. 1:14) of the living and written Word as we have opportunities daily!

2:9 The coming imitator. "Highly exalted" means literally, "to lift up over" all other positions.[28] Ever driven by his prideful envy of God, Satan will imitate His Son's worthy exaltation in the person of his unworthy "son," Antichrist, who will lift himself "above all that is called God, or that is worshiped" (2 Thess. 2:4). But his self-exaltation won't last long (Rev. 13:5; Prov. 18:12). In His time, according to His humble Son's teaching, the heavenly Father will "abase" Satan's proud son (Matt. 23:12; Dan. 9:27, NIV; Rev. 19:19–20). Ready to apply this?

When you see sinners or apostates arrogantly exalting themselves, wronging others, and seemingly getting away with it, don't be afraid or offended with God. Whoever "highly exalts" himself has a divine appointment with abasement. When God's time comes, they will go the way of the coming imitator...down! Willing to apply this further?

While they walk in pride, do your duty: pray they'll humble themselves and repent. Impossible? Read about King Manasseh or King Nebuchadnezzar lately (2 Chron. 33:1–16; Dan. 4:28–37)?

---

27. P. L. Tan, *Encyclopedia of 7700 Illustrations: Signs of the Times*, electronic ed. (Garland, TX: Bible Communications, Inc., 1996).
28. Hayford, *The Spirit Filled Life Bible*, 1804.

PHILIPPIANNOTES

2:12 Consistently obedient. Aside from the Philippians' other Christlike qualities, such as their charity (stewardship, 4:10, 14–16), helps (1:7), and willingness to suffer for Christ's sake (1:29–30), they were consistently obedient.

Paul testifies when he was "present" with them he found they "always obeyed" (2:12) his biblical teaching and Spirit-led counsel, which was actually God's Word and guidance coming through him: "You have always obeyed God when I was with you" (NCV). Thus his exhortation to "work out" their salvation is really a call for them to continue what they were already doing well: "Continue to work out your salvation with fear and trembling" (NIV).

This Pauline compliment, which we should holily covet, indicates a high degree of spiritual excellence present in the Philippian church. Like Paul, they were zealously seeking to become spiritually "perfect" (3:15)—fully developed; spiritually mature; spiritually adult; consistently trusting and obedient; or whole, without consistent, besetting sins or weakness.[29]

Here is another instance of disciples becoming as their teacher (Matt. 10:24–25). The Philippians had become as obedient as the great apostle God used to found and instruct their church and model Christianity for them. He reproduced his own kind as they not only listened to his teachings but also followed "my ways which are in Christ" (1 Cor. 4:16–17). You study Paul's doctrine and life story. Will you also follow his "ways"?

Do you want Paul's compliment to the Philippians for yourself? Strongly enough to "always obey" God? Today? In your current tests?

---

29. See Matthew 5:48.

Jesus' Kenosis—and Ours!

2:12–16 Paul's practical point to the Philippians. Paul digs down to spiritual bedrock in these verses and urges the Philippians to build a house of Christlike obedience on it (Matt. 7:24–25). His charge?

Focus on "working out" what God has worked in—His grace-given, blood-bought "salvation" (2:12). It's imperative we understand Paul is *not* teaching we should attempt to work for (or earn) our salvation, as many vainly attempt. He taught us salvation by grace alone through faith alone, and "not of works" (Eph. 2:8–9). Rather Paul charges us to "work out"—manifest, demonstrate, exhibit, or express through consistent obedience—our salvation in a spirit of the worshipful awe of God, so we become radiant living demonstrations of the greatness of our Savior and salvation (2:15–16; Rom. 12:1–2).

Warren Wiersbe writes:

> The verb "work out" carries the meaning of "work to full completion"....In Paul's day it was also used for "working a mine," that is, getting out of the mine all the valuable ore possible; or "working a field" so as to get the greatest harvest possible.... Our lives have tremendous potential, like a mine or a field, and He wants to help us fulfill that potential.[30]

So we should "fully work" our personal salvation mine and field—consistently obeying Christ's nature, Word, and Spirit within until our lives bring forth the full spiritual wealth and fruitfulness Jesus has put in us for His honor. That priceless fortune or bumper crop is us "conformed to the image of his

---

30. Wiersbe, *The Bible Exposition Commentary*, Phil. 2:12–16, note.

Son" (Rom. 8:29).[31] For this full development, full cooperation is required.

Paul understood the mature Christian life is a Savior-saint collaboration. God's inworking of grace prompts, but does not compel, our outworking in obedience. Having emphasized God's part in the Philippians' spiritual growth co-op—"he who hath begun a good work in you" (1:6)—Paul now emphasized their part: "Work out your own salvation" (2:12), or "Take up your responsibility and discharge your duty so the Savior's presence, grace, power, and fruit will be conveyed through your lives" (author's paraphrase). To encourage them, he reminds them God is still present working in them, "For it is God who worketh in you" (2:13), adding two faith-building facts. God's grace will help them "to will and to do" His will. He'll infuse their volition with desire to please Him and their minds and bodies with the wisdom and energy to do it well. How much more could they ask! God is commanding and assisting, "giving you the desire and the power to do what pleases Him" (NLT). What a co-op!

Paul clarifies, "Work out *your own* salvation" (2:12). They should focus on their individual responsibility to obey, not others'! The lust to judge others is a huge issue, and Christ pointedly addressed it (Matt. 7:1–5). Our pride prefers to perfect other peoples' salvation and leave ours quite imperfect, to get everyone else right while we stay wrong. We can't concentrate on two things simultaneously; while examining others' faults, we're not correcting our own. Henry states, "It is not

---

31. Wuest translates, "Work out your own salvation," as, "Carry to its ultimate conclusion [likeness to the Lord Jesus]." See K. S. Wuest, *The New Testament: An Expanded Translation* (Grand Rapids, MI: Eerdmans, 1961), Phil. 2:12.

for us to judge other people; we have enough to do to look to ourselves."[32]

There is also a secondary application here. Paul's phrase "your own" addresses not only the individuals but also the whole assembly. One commentator notes:

> "Work hard to show the results of your salvation," in light of the preceding exhortation to unity, may mean that the entire church was to work together to rid themselves of divisions and discord.[33]

Indeed, Paul's repeated and pointed pleas for unity (2:1–4; 4:1–3) prove he wanted them to conscientiously "work out" their corporate obedience issues until every relationship was right, every conversation loving, every disagreement settled quickly, no resentment was present, no cliques were thriving, every meeting was joyful, everyone worked well together, and they worshipped in one accord consistently.

Paul further charges, "Do all things without murmurings and disputings" (2:14); or "without complaining and arguing" (NLT). Complaining grieves God, hinders Christlikeness, and, if continued, prompts divine chastening (1 Cor. 10:10). Arguing against the duties or paths God assigns us is futile and sure to leave us confused and unfit for God's use. To truly do "all things" without complaining and arguing we must greet them with quiet surrender and thanksgiving to God (1 Thess. 5:18), trusting He will cause them to work for our good (Rom. 8:28) and reward our efforts (Heb. 11:6; Col. 3:23–24).

---

32. Henry, *Commentary in One Volume*, Phil. 2:12, note, 1863.
33. *Life Application Study Bible* (Wheaton, IL: Tyndale House, 2004), Phil. 2:12, note, 2018.

Doing so steadily will make the Philippians "blameless and harmless," not mischievous but good "children of God" (2:15). They'll neither harm others nor be deserving of any blame directed their way. Thus they'll be "without rebuke" (2:15), or "irreproachable" (Wey), though occasionally rebuked or reproached by spiteful adversaries.[34] Disobedient Christians, however, do harm others by unrighteous words, acts, or reactions and, barring repentance, will be justly charged and deprived of rewards at Christ's judgment (2 John 8).

If compliant, the Philippians' Christlike lives will "shine as [spiritual] lights" in the dark Roman "world" (2:15). Their good attitude and works will reveal, or "hold forth" to others by public example and message, the light of the living Word and His hope-giving words and works, thus illuminating for them a clear path out of their spiritual darkness and into a joyful, purposeful walk with God.

Paul says this shining and holding forth occurs not in a perfect Christian kingdom but a spiritually dark, sin-twisted culture, or "crooked and perverse nation" (2:15). This underscores the church's essential calling: to be Christ's *ekklesia*, or loyal believers called out and distinctly different from the society in which they live; not isolated, but dispersed throughout it; not ruling but coexisting and suffering rejection for their witness until Christ returns. In that day, Paul says he'll "rejoice" because all his hard work and prayers paid off: the Philippians worked out their own salvation

---

34. Being irreproachable doesn't mean we'll never be reproached. The Apostle Paul, who authored this verse, was accused of every evil and crime possible by his lying enemies, but wasn't guilty (Acts 16:20; 17:6–7; 21:20–21, 27–28; 24:5–6). Thus, though reproached, he remained irreproachable.

(2:16)!³⁵ What you experience in that day depends on what you're doing in this day.

Has Paul's practical point to the Philippians struck home? Are you focusing on your personal responsibility to cooperate with Christ so His salvation's full value and harvest will be realized in and through your life? Fully cooperating with others in your church? Living harmlessly and blamelessly, consistently thankful and unspoiled by complaining and arguing? Letting the light in you shine through your lifestyle and testimony? If so, keep up the good work—working out in obedience everything God's grace works in.

2:12 In our leaders' absence. Paul urged the Philippians to continue obeying "in my absence" as they had "in my presence" (2:12). Thus he distinguishes between Christians obeying when their leaders are present and when they aren't.

Our leaders are spiritual shepherds and thus obligated to watch over their flocks. When they're with us, we're aware of their oversight and more inclined to obey God, because: (1) they'll know it if we don't; (2) we may lose their approval for further service; and (3) we don't want them to correct us! So there's a subtle holy pressure to walk the straight and narrow when "Paul" is around.

But when mature shepherds leave, immature sheep roam. Like children left at home alone, they abandon their spiritual disciplines, stop examining themselves, and grow lax in devotion and duty. The Corinthians never would have indulged

---

35. Here's biblical food for thought. Ministers who don't teach their people Paul's charge to "work out" their salvation, and congregants who refuse to obey it, won't—they can't—share Paul's rejoicing in the day of Christ. It will be too late. But it's not too late today—if we'll remember Paul's charge daily and diligently fulfill it.

in petty strife, permitted immorality, or behaved badly at Communion if Paul had been present, but they did so when their ministerial parent (1 Cor. 4:15) was away! Diotrephes would never have slandered the honorable Apostle John or usurped his authority in his church if John had been in town. And the Israelites would never have worshipped a golden calf or indulged in unholy behavior if Moses hadn't been away on a Sinai sabbatical. But when God's leaders are away, His people play. Why?

Immature, they forget Christ's omnipresence and omniscience: "The Lord is watching everywhere" (Prov. 15:3, NLT); or, "the Lord's eyes see everything" (NCV). He's the real Watchman and Chief Shepherd.[36] Without His help, pastors wouldn't discern the wolf's work in our lives or churches. So the wise learn to fear God and live every moment under His all-seeing eye, or "with fear and trembling" (Phil. 2:12). They realize God constantly watches His vineyard (church) and branches (believers) even when His vineyard keepers (pastors, elders) are away (Isa. 27:2–3). There's another lesson here.

When leaders are with us, we understandably lean on them for help. But sometimes we go too far, hoping they'll handle situations we should address ourselves. (Wise leaders, discerning this, will insist we assume our responsibilities.) But when "Elijah's" gone, it's a different matter. "Elisha" must step up and smite the waters of trouble with his own mantle of prayer and faith, doing himself what he's often seen Elijah do. Thus he rises to a new level of experience and maturity. The pressure of Elijah's absence has forced him to summon

---

36. Christ's complete awareness of His people's condition is emphasized in His letters to the churches of Asia. In each letter Jesus says, "I know thy works," and then describes their condition in minute detail (Rev. 2:2, 9, 13, 19; 3:1, 8, 15).

everything he's learned and, leaning on Christ alone, test it in his own life. Consequently he's become stronger, wiser, more confident of God's help, and more like his earthly mentor—and heavenly Master! I'm sure Timothy and Titus each experienced this when Paul left them to lead churches in Ephesus and Crete respectively. Isn't this what discipling and ministerial mentoring is all about? So new Christians and junior ministers grow to live and serve as their teachers? Or even better![37]

Thus Paul urged his Philippian students to rise to their life challenges without him—yet still having Christ's all-sufficient grace at their disposal (2 Cor. 12:9). "Those things which ye have both learned, and received, and heard, and seen in me, do, and the God of peace shall be with you" (Phil. 4:9; Matt. 28:20b). Only by doing so could they finish growing into the character image of their undershepherd and the Great Shepherd.

Has your "Paul" left for other fields of ministry? Has the Lord taken your "Elijah" from you to higher service? Listen, as He challenges you through Paul's words: "You've always obeyed 'in my presence.' Now rise, obey God, be faithful, and overcome 'in my absence'"!

2:12 A serious matter. Paul urged the Philippians to work out their salvation "with fear and trembling" (2:12). Why was he so serious?

While salvation is given us by grace, Christian fulfillment—spiritual maturity and Christlikeness—is not. It's the result of a life of sustained, humble trust and obedience. Much hangs in

---

37. Elisha was a great learner. A comparison of his success under great pressure (2 Kings 6:24–7:20, esp. 6:32) and Elijah's infamous failure under similar pressure (1 Kings 19:1–3) suggests Elisha learned from not only his mentor's teachings and triumphs but also his failures—and passed that on to his "elders" (2 Kings 6:32). May we all learn as excellently from our teachers.

the balance: God's delight in us, our fellowship with Him, our usefulness to Him, our influence on others, and our place and service in God's kingdom *eternally*. These are serious matters. "With fear and trembling" means that, once saved, we should be focused, not flippant. Rather than live self-centered, self-serving lives, we should pursue walking obediently with God "with a proper sense of awe and responsibility" (2:12, Phillips), or with the utmost seriousness and attentiveness. Why?

The alternative—living for self or sin—is catastrophic. Consider these consequences of practicing sin in the believer's life. Sin:

- Disqualifies us for higher service

- Quenches the Spirit's work in us, slowing our spiritual growth and, if continued, stopping it

- Hinders our prayers (Ps. 66:18; Isa. 1:15; John 15:7)

- Hinders or, if continued, halts our effectiveness in God's service

- Wastes precious and irrecoverable time

- Harms the church, Christ's holy body, and distorts its witness to the world

- Must be punished by God, who is holy and impartial in judgment

- If persisted in, leads to death, spiritual or physical (James 1:15)

- Unfits us for readiness for the Rapture

- Causes losses, griefs, and reproach in this life
- Causes loss of rewards in the next life

But some may ask, "Isn't sin forgivable"? Absolutely! But God can't be gamed. "Be not deceived; God is not mocked: for whatsoever a man soweth, that shall he also reap" (Gal. 6:7). When Christians take sin lightly they do so at their peril. All the above adversities visit, and soon their life becomes heavy with the oppressive consequences of sin. Then they get serious! Paul would have us be serious now. His counsel is urgent, true, compelling: "Fear God! Get serious about working out your obedience!" He's got my attention.

Show me a failed Christian, and I'll show you someone who doesn't take his Christian walk seriously. Show me a mature Christian, and I'll show you one who stands in awe of God, believes all His Word, and by consistent, trusting obedience lovingly seeks His approval for more fellowship and usefulness daily. Serious yet?

2:13 He helps us obey! Paul asserts God doesn't stand by idly but actively steps into our lives to help us obey. His is an ongoing work: "It is God Who is all the while effectually at work in you [energizing and creating in you the power and desire]" to do His good pleasure (2:13, AMP). How?

He grants us the "power and desire" to obey Him through His Word. Reading of others' faith and obedience in the Bible inspires our imitation. His Spirit assists us. The ever-present *parakletos* quietly brings to mind Bible verses or passages that perfectly fit our situation (John 14:26) and gives us an inner prompting or sympathetic feeling to comply. Leaders often point us in the right direction and urge us to take it. Fellow believers do the same, sometimes offering their assistance. Frequently Bible teachings we hear or read stir our righteous desires, bending us toward obedience and filling us with the wisdom and strength to obey. Occasionally testimonies provide us with examples of other believers' courageous faith and obedience and arouse us to do no less. Even divine chastening fills us with new resolve to not turn again to the disobedience that brought it. Conversely, the blessings of God's approval inspire us to continue the obedience that brought them (2 Chron. 17:6). In these and other ways God helps us run the race set before us.

But He doesn't run it for us. That would make our obedience meritless. He does everything but make us yield and take right action with the right attitude. That we must do. One commentator notes well, "Both divine enablement and human responsibility are involved in getting God's work done."[38]

Truly, grace enables; we enact. Grace softens and inclines our mind to see the wisdom of obeying God in the matter before us, but we must yield to that inclination and not to our contrary desires and prompts. Thus the willingness is given, but we must grasp it. God provides the grace, but we perform it. God illuminates, we initiate—then He provides all the strength, wisdom, assistance, and resources we need to finish the task with excellence. Thus Paul concludes we can do "all things" through Christ (Phil. 4:13). And in the day Christ rewards us for our responses, we'll praise Him for His help, casting our crowns before Him (Rev. 4:10–11; 5:8–14).

With all this help available, no Christian will ever justify disobeying God. All claims of inability will fall on deaf divine ears (Matt. 25:24–30). Don't let Paul's teaching fall on deaf

---

38. Walvoord and Zuck, *The Bible Knowledge Commentary: An Exposition of the Scriptures*, Phil. 2:12–13, note, quoting from Lightner, *Philippians*.

ears. Hear what the Spirit is saying to you through him: God will help you do His will!

2:13, 16 Working in, working through. The order of Paul's instructions is inspired: First, he tells the Philippians God is "working in you" (2:13; 1:6). Second, he says they'll "shine as lights...holding forth the word of life" (2:15–16). So God must "work in" them before He would "shine" through them. Warren Weirsbe points out:

> The principle Paul lays down is this: God must work *in* us before He can work *through* us. This principle is seen at work throughout the Bible in the lives of men like Moses, David, the Apostles, and others...
>
> It took God forty years to bring Moses to the place where He could use him to lead the people of Israel. As Moses tended sheep during those forty years, God was working in him so that one day He might work through him. *God is more interested in the workman than in the work.* If the workman is what he ought to be, the work will be what it ought to be.[39]

Is God's work of preparation in your life expanding to Moses-like dimensions? Years? Decades? Don't be dismayed. God always seems late, yet never is. Let Him have His way in you today with abandoned trust, obedience, service, and contentment; and trust Him for tomorrow. After God worked deeply in Paul a decade in Tarsus, He began working widely through him in Antioch—then all over the Mediterranean and finally all over the world down through the centuries through his epistles and exemplary biography in Acts. I wonder how

---

39. Wiersbe, *The Bible Exposition Commentary*, Phil 2:13, note.

widely He may work through you and me if we let Him finish His work in us?

2:16 The Word of life. Here the Spirit impresses Paul to describe God's Word as not religious doctrine, philosophical truth, literary gems, political ideology, or historical facts, but rather the "word of life" (2:16). This emphasizes that whatever else God's Word may be or do, its chief blessing is that, as a living book, it offers *life*, specifically eternal life, to all people—a way of rebirth into spiritual life for the lost and a means of increasing, richer, and sweeter spiritual life to the saved (John 6:63, 68; Acts 5:20).

The Holy Spirit "inspired," or breathed life into, all God's Words (2 Tim. 3:16–17). Therefore Scripture is "alive and active" (Heb. 4:12, NIV), penetrating, quickening, and reviving. When we read or study it meditatively with faith, it reanimates, refreshes, and re-empowers us for our day. That's why we feel better, stronger, and more prepared for living and testing after every session of prayerful Bible study or devotional readings.

It's also why Paul charged the Philippians to "hold forth," or freely recommend to others, this "word of life"—the divine message that, when received, imparts eternal life, or an ever-growing, rich, powerful, and unending personal relationship with Jesus Christ (John 17:3). To hold forth God's Word, they had to first hold on to it: "Holding fast the faithful word" (Titus 1:9). This meant coming to their Bibles daily to prayerfully seek not more doctrine, philosophy, ideology, history, or facts for debate, but more life![40] The Philippians complied, studying,

---

40. When believed and obeyed, God's Word imparts not only spiritual life (John 6:68; Acts 5:20) but also physical, mental, and emotional vitality (Prov. 4:20–22, AMP, NIV, ESV).

receiving, and obeying the word of life and recommending it freely to their generation.

May Christ help us do no less.

2:15–16 Bright lights in dark nations. Paul envisions Christians and churches shining as "lights" in dark nations. Very dark nations.

Specifically, "crooked and perverse" is the phrase Paul used (2:15); or, "perverse and distorted" (WUEST); or, "a warped and diseased age" (PHILLIPS). Such a people are inwardly bent or twisted and no longer conforming to a right standard of conduct. The Macedonian and Greco-Roman cultures in which the Philippians lived fit this description, and it was in just such a spiritually and morally depraved culture that they were to shine as spiritual torches in the dark night or "stars in the sky" (2:15, NIV). "Provide people with a glimpse of good living and of the living God. Carry the light-giving Message into the night" (THE MESSAGE).

This reminds us that darkness is the perfect, really the only, backdrop for light. In broad daylight stars are not visible to the naked eye. In a fully lit theatre, the brightest spotlight has little effect. Similarly Christians (spiritual light-bearers) need darkness, a "warped and diseased age" in which to hold forth our gospel truth—and the darker the better!

There are many dark nations, and America is becoming darker daily. Though sad, this is no cause for dismay. It's our necessary contrast, a divinely permitted stage. Only on such a backdrop can we "let [our] light so shine before men" (Matt. 5:16) and "hold forth" the enduring truths and standards of God's Word (Phil. 2:16). Jeremiah's light shined brightly in the dark night of Judah's apostasy. Moses' ministry was a torch that lit the Hebrews in the darkness of oppression in Egypt. Daniel's light was a lodestar guiding Israel through its long night of captivity. The early church's—and the Philippians'—gospel light projected far and wide in the theater of the dark Roman world, drawing many to it. Now it's our time to shine.

Let's work out our salvation as "heavenly lights" (2:15, WEY) in these dark days so the Light of this world can draw, save, and disciple many before He returns. Today be a bright light in your dark nation.

2:17–18 Gladly poured out for Christ. Alluding again to his possible execution, Paul says if God takes him, he'll gladly be "poured out" (Phil. 2:17, NKJV) as a libation for Christ's will and work.

Libations were drink offerings (of wine, water, honey, Num. 15:1–10; or in pagan worship, blood, Ps. 16:4) poured out to one's deity and were common in Paul's day. Since fluids are necessary to life, to pour out one's drink to one's deity indicates he is more important than life itself (Ps. 63:3), or that He alone, not the worshipper, is worthy of a blessing or benefit the worshipper has received (Gen. 35:14; 2 Sam. 23:13–17), that as its gracious giver, it rightfully belongs to Him (as symbolized by the wave and heave offerings, Exod. 29:26; 29:27–28). Every Jewish libation typified Christ, who "poured out" His life to redeem us (Ps. 22:14).

While libations were sometimes offered alone (Gen. 35:14), Jewish libations were usually offered with animal or meal offerings.

> Libations were, along with livestock, grain, and oil, part of the regular offerings of the various classes of

food products made by the Israelites every day and in larger quantities on feast days (Num. 28–29).

Libations were the normal accompaniment of any offering of animals or grain (Num. 6:15, 17; 1 Chr. 29:21; 2 Chr. 29:35; Ezra 7:17); the quantity was in proportion to the size of the animal offered (Num. 28:14).[41]

Libations were typically poured over sacrifices after they were placed on altars (2 Kings 16:13). Fittingly Paul described the Philippians' obedience to God as a "living sacrifice" (Rom. 12:1) laid on heaven's altar: "The sacrifice and service of [or springing from] your faith" (Phil. 2:17) or "your faithful service is an offering to God" (NLT).[42] Daily they were yielding themselves to the Lord, increasingly dying to sin and self every time they "always obeyed" and did "all things without murmurings and disputing" (2:12, 14). If God permitted his execution, Paul was ready to be "offered" (2:17, Greek *spendō*, "poured out like a drink offering"[43]) upon their service. Their sacrificial obedience "unto death" (2:8) was the meat and meal, his execution was the wine, and their respective altars were Philippi and Rome. And he was joyful about it.

Paul offered himself not apathetically or reluctantly but gladly: "I joy, and rejoice" (2:17). He urged the Philippians to rejoice with him over his offering and promised to do the same over their sacrifice: "I want all of you to share that joy...and I will share your joy" (2:17–18, NLT). As always, Paul sets the bar high.

---

41. A. C. Myers, *The Eerdmans Bible Dictionary* (Grand Rapids, MI: Eerdmans, 1987), s.v. "Libation," 665.
42. He called the timely financial offering they sent him for Christ's work "a sweet smell, a sacrifice acceptable, well-pleasing to God" (Phil. 4:18).
43. Swanson, *Dictionary of Biblical Languages with Semantic Domains: Greek (New Testament)*, s.v. "*spendō*."

PHILIPPIANNOTES

Are you becoming a "living sacrifice," growing more "obedient unto death" daily like the Philippians? With thanksgiving, without complaining, fully surrendered to Christ's will? Are you like Paul "pouring out" yourself daily in devotion, intercession, praise, duty, Bible study, giving, work, ministry, and love? Or are you holding back, compromised, uncommitted, unenthusiastic?

Athletes speak of "leaving it all on the field," or pouring out their maximum effort in a contest. Paul was ready to "leave it all" on Nero's execution grounds. Reach for the bar he set. Throw off all remnants of self-centeredness, tip over the libation bowl of your heart, and pour yourself out as described above for love of Jesus, His people, and His kingdom. And be joyful about it![44] Show Jesus He's better than life itself, the Giver of all your blessings, and the only worthy One—who poured Himself out to save you.

2:19–23 About Timothy. Paul speaks here of Timothy, an outstanding Christian and minister, and Paul's best aide, coworker, and friend.

"Timothy" is the English form of "Timotheus," meaning "honoring God, zealous; or honored of God."[45] This implies Timothy was zealous (burning in devotion) toward God and, in Paul's words, a "vessel unto honor" (2 Tim. 2:21). The biblical record confirms Timothy's name accurately reflected his true character.

---

44. Is anyone or anything more worthy of our enthusiasm (Col. 3:23; Eccles. 9:10)?
45. Smith and Cornwall, *The Exhaustive Dictionary of Bible Names*, s.v. "Timothy."

Timothy's life confirmed God's universal promise, "Them who honor me I will honor" (1 Sam. 2:30).[46] Because Timothy honored God in his faith, living, ministry, and sufferings, God honored him by:

- Letting him be closely associated with and personally tutored by the greatest apostle, Paul (Acts 16:1–3)

- Permitting him to play a key role in the growth of the early church

- Moving Paul to record glowing commendations of Timothy as a servant of God in this epistle (Phil. 2:19–23) and others (1 Cor. 4:17; 16:10; 1 Thess. 3:2)

- Ordaining that two books of the Bible bear Timothy's name

- Prompting Paul to address his final letter, or apostolic valedictory, to him (2 Timothy)

- Having Timothy mentioned favorably in numerous other biblical references[47]

Timothy was born of a religiously mixed marriage, his mother being Jewish and father Greek (Acts 16:1, 3). At the time Paul called Timothy to serve (during Paul's second mission), Timothy was already a Christian, approved by his church,

---

46. For other expressions or examples of this promise, see Genesis 41:39–44; Esther 6:6–7, 9, 11; Daniel 2:46–49; 3:29–30; 5:29; 6:1–3, 25–28; John 12:26; Acts 28:9–10.

47. See Acts 17:14–15; 19:22; Romans 16:21; 1 Corinthians 16:10–11; 2 Corinthians 1:1, 19; Colossians 1:1; 2 Thessalonians 1:1; Philemon 1; Hebrews 13:23.

and living in Lystra (Acts 16:1–3).[48] His mother (Eunice) and grandmother (Lois) were women of strong faith and both helped nurture the same in him (2 Tim. 1:5). Timothy's submission to be circumcised as an adult at Paul's request (to avoid offending the sensibilities of devout local Jews they hoped to evangelize, Acts 16:3) shows his complete commitment to Christ and His call through Paul.[49] Paul spoke more glowingly of him than of any other minister (Phil. 2:19–22), no small fact considering Paul's wide circle of ministerial contacts and habit of commending exemplary Christians (Phil. 2:25–30; Rom. 16:3–4; 2 Tim. 1:16–18; Philemon 4–7, 21).

Timothy's association with Paul was long, close, productive, and joyful. He was present and no doubt contributing by prayer or perhaps consultation when Paul wrote many of his epistles (Rom. 16:21; Phil. 1:1; Col. 1:1; 1 Thess. 1:1; 2 Thess. 1:1). Does this suggest Timothy sometimes served as Paul's secretarial assistant as Mark presumably served Peter? Though apparently sometimes hindered by timidity (2 Tim. 1:6–7, 8) and a sensitive stomach (1 Tim. 5:23), Timothy's calling to and excellence in ministry was abundantly proven by prophetic utterances (1 Tim. 1:18; 4:14); elders' approval (4:14); his successful assistant, interim, and long-term pastorates (in Corinth, Berea, and Ephesus); and multiple apostolic commendations (Phil. 2:19–22). He often served as Paul's trusted messenger and informant, reporting to Paul on the churches' many needs and problems and delivering Paul's responses (Phil. 2:19, 20; 1 Cor. 4:17; 1 Thess. 3:5–6). Paul urged the Christians to respect Timothy and his work among them, and not discount him due to his youth or occasional lack

---

48. It's unclear if Paul evangelized Timothy on one of his first two visits to Lystra (Acts 14:8–20; 14:21–22), but clear that he called him to serve during his third visit (and second apostolic mission) (Acts 16:2–3).
49. *Life Application Study Bible*, 2059.

of boldness (1 Cor. 16:10–11). Like a faithful and enduring son (Phil. 2:22), Timothy accompanied and assisted Paul on his second and third apostolic missions, including his final trip to Jerusalem (Acts 20:4). When Timothy later became the leading elder of the large Ephesian church (succeeding Paul and preceding John), Paul's two letters to him (1, 2 Timothy) encapsulated the apostle's primary teaching on matters pertaining to the ministry. Pauline in purpose, teaching, and living, Timothy, like his mentor, suffered for Christ's sake. He was imprisoned, probably by Nero, and released after the latter's death in AD 68 (Heb. 13:23). That Paul's last letter, written when he knew his end was near (2 Tim. 4:6–8, c. AD 68), was addressed to Timothy and requested a final visit from him (4:9) shows just how warm, close, and strong was their bond.

Chiefly our text (Phil. 2:19–23) reveals Timothy was "genuinely concerned" (2:20, ESV) for the Philippians. Because ministers are expected to care for their people (John 21:15–17), those who don't often pretend concern. Not Timothy! His ministerial compassion was a fact, not an act. When Timothy seemed concerned, he was—not to be "seen of men" (Matt. 6:5, 2, 16; 23:5) but to be seen of and to please the Chief Shepherd, Christ. Paul must have observed this humble desire to emulate Christ's selfless service in Timothy repeatedly through the years, in public and private ministry, for him to give him such a powerful endorsement—which, sadly, he couldn't give to any other minister (probably in Rome; perhaps anywhere!): "I have no [other] man likeminded, who will naturally care for your state. For all seek their own, not the things which are Jesus Christ's" (2:20–21). So Timothy was a rare model minister: an unselfish servant of Christ among many selfish ones.

Are you following his example? Honoring God...zealously? Pauline in thought, deed, and teaching? Serving faithfully, excellently, enduringly, in Christ's unselfish love, in whatever duty or ministry Christ assigns you? "Steadfast, unmovable, always abounding in the work of the Lord" (1 Cor. 15:58), even when less committed Christians prosper and you suffer or serve without recognition? Then don't stop! Keep following Timothy as he followed Paul and Christ: honor God so He can honor you—for His honor!

2:19 Substitute ministers. "But I trust in the Lord Jesus to send Timothy shortly unto you" (2:19). Since Paul was in Roman custody, and thus unable to visit the Philippians, he sent Timothy as his substitute. This wasn't the first time.

Paul's original appointment of Timothy to help in his ministry was also a ministerial substitution. Timothy assumed the position (as Paul's aide) that Mark had vacated on Paul's first mission. So twice we see Timothy appointed as a substitute minister, one appointed to serve in the place, office, or duties of another unable or unwilling to fulfill a work for Christ. The Bible repeatedly shows God calling substitute ministers.

Samuel replaced Eli, David replaced King Saul, Elisha replaced Elijah, and Paul replaced Judas.[50] God's servants even substituted for unredeemed government ministers and royals. Joseph, Daniel, Daniel's three friends, and Mordecai replaced secular state officials or counselors who could or would not give their monarchs sufficiently wise, benevolent, or unbiased assistance, and in each case served God's higher purposes. When

---

50. Acts shows that while God permitted the apostles to tap Matthias as Judas' initial replacement, Paul was God's lasting choice (Acts 1:24–26; 9:15, NIV). As an interim apostle, Matthias filled Judas' office; Paul, however, fulfilled his ministry.

the Persian queen Vashti fell from Xerxes' favor, he replaced her with the Jewish maiden Esther, who subsequently served her people's welfare. What qualified these and other divinely appointed substitutes for their appointments?

What qualified Timothy? His successful résumé was his excellent character: he was faithful, loyal, genuinely concerned for others' (especially Christians') welfare (2:19–20), not distracted or entangled by his personal interests (2:21), proven in ministry (2:22), respected by his home church (Acts 16:2), and heartily endorsed by godly elder ministers. Ministers of all types and ages—from young university, Bible school, or seminary students to older retired ministers—should stay spiritually fit and ready, so the Lord may providentially appoint them as He did Timothy to fulfill whatever missions, ministries, pastorates, or assistantships may come open.

Are you growing in Timothy's character traits? Ready to answer God's call to be a substitute minister? To serve His purposes and people in sacred or secular service?

See 1 Samuel 2:34–35; 13:14; 15:28; Esther 8:2; 10:3.

2:19–20 Comforting good shepherds' hearts. Paul hastened to send Timothy to the Philippians "shortly" because his pastor's heart yearned to know their "state" (2:19), or spiritual and natural condition, desiring and praying it was good. If Timothy visited them and reported this was so, it would "comfort" or "cheer" (NIV) Paul.[51] He was a good shepherd with a good heart. And he was wise!

---

51. This shows Paul's humanness. Like us, he was tempted to angst; but, spiritually mature, he cast all his worry-burdens on the Lord by prayers of faith with thanksgiving, as he taught us (Phil. 4:6–7). The same scenario played out in Thessalonica (1 Thess. 3:1–7).

Realizing evil spirits constantly wage war against every growing Christian and church (Eph. 6:10–18; Acts 20:28–31), good shepherds check up on the flocks under their care regularly. When all is well, they're comforted and cheered. When it isn't, after seeking God's mind in prayer, they send corrective counsel and motivating promises and warnings (as in all Paul's epistles, 1 Cor. chapters 3, 5, 6, 11; 2 Cor. 2:9–11). When their correction is received, they're again comforted, confident their Spirit-led counsel, when obeyed, will heal and restore the flock.

Are you an aspiring or practicing good shepherd? Keep an eye on your flock's condition and address every spiritual and natural need as it arises, personally or by proxy.

Are you a sheep with good shepherds? Pastors or elders who are godly, caring, unselfish, spiritually minded ministers? Comfort their hearts. Walk with God, examining yourself regularly and keeping your spiritual condition strong. If you stumble, quickly receive your shepherds' "rod" of correction (1 Cor. 4:21), realizing it's given to restore your soul-comfort and theirs—and the Good Shepherd's. And as His good sheep, say, "Thy rod and thy staff, they comfort me" (Ps. 23:4).

2:21 Everybody's out for himself! Of those Paul might have sent to minister to the Philippians he exclaimed disappointedly, "No man" was concerned for "your state," "for all seek their own!" (2:20–21). (So much for the fallacy that the entire early church was ideal!) Even if an exaggeration, Paul's statement stuns! He knew no ministers (elders) in Rome or nearby or perhaps anywhere he could fully trust to serve unselfishly and whose hearts were wholly set on Christ's interests. None! Only Timothy!

Some of these self-interested ministers may have been fullblown egotists, domineering Diotrepheses bent on usurping control of churches and ministries (3 John 9–11), building their own reputations, and disparaging anyone whose popularity rivaled theirs. Paul frankly warned the Ephesian elders of such hirelings (Acts 20:28–30). Most of the ineligible messengers, however, were probably sincere ministers who had simply not yet grown in grace to the point that they served Christ's interests "first" all the time (Matt. 6:33). If sent, they would have served with mingled motives and flawed faithfulness—and mixed results.

Self-serving shepherds commit three crimes: (1) they don't know Jesus' interests (preoccupation with their own agenda keeps them from prayerfully studying and discovering His, John 7:17); (2) they don't passionately love Christ's people (2:20; cf. 2 Cor. 12:15; 1 Pet. 5:1–4; John 21:15–17), and (3) consequently, they don't truly minister to them. For these hirelings, the ministry is a profession, not a passion, a means of gaining, not giving (John 10:12–13; cf. Matt. 20:28). So they don't expend the effort to consider, counsel, or intercede for Christ's struggling sheep. Consequently His sheep go unhelped, their sins unaddressed, problems unsolved, callings unrecognized, enemies unchecked, heresies uncontested, and schisms unhealed (Jer. 23:1–2). The worst hirelings actually prey on their sheep, fleecing them through hypocritical speech, twisted biblical interpretations, or fraudulent scams (2 Pet. 2:1–3; 1 Tim. 6:3–5).

Contrast Paul's selfless love for the Philippians:

> Another lesson to be learned from Paul's sending Timothy is the need for selflessness. Timothy was close to Paul and dear to his heart. If Paul ever needed Timothy, it was while he was there in Rome under house arrest. Yet

he was willing to sacrifice Timothy's companionship so that others could be helped.[52]

Paul also sacrificed the companionship of another valuable friend and aide, Epaphroditus, to help the Philippians (2:25–28). There's another possible reason why Paul couldn't send other ministers to the Philippians.

They may have been entangled in their own churches' internal chronic contentions or problems. (Ironically some of the Philippians' leaders themselves were snared in strife, eliciting Paul's passionate plea for peacemaking, Phil. 4:1–3.) One commentator notes, "This is one of the tragedies of church problems; they divert time, energy, and concern away from the things that matter most."[53] If Satan can keep us overburdened with our own personal or church contentions, we'll have no time or strength to minister to other Christians.

"All seek their own"—thus Paul acknowledged ecclesiastical demand was greater than ministerial supply; he had more missions than missionaries, more problems than peacemakers. Today many spiritually minded, Christ-centered overseers, bishops, superintendents, missionary boards, and senior pastors feel Paul's frustration. Willing to help?

Lay aside your interests to study Christ's. Learn to love Christ's people first, passionately and persistently. Like Paul, serve them sacrificially. Help solve, not stir, your church's internal squabbles, and rise above personal trials that previously hindered you. Then to your "Philippians" you shall go!

---

52. Walvoord and Zuck, *The Bible Knowledge Commentary: An Exposition of the Scriptures*, Phil. 2:19, note, quoting from Lightner, *Philippians*.
53. Wiersbe, *The Bible Exposition Commentary*, Phil. 2:19–21, note.

2:21 Jesus' interests. Paul lamented his fellow elders were ignoring "the things which are Jesus Christ's," or "what matters" to Him (NLT), "the work of Jesus" (NCV), "the cause of Jesus" (PHILLIPS)—or simply, Jesus' interests. These are all the things dear to Jesus' heart, His desires and goals and plans and methods to obtain them. He "travailed" (Isa. 53:11) in Gethsemane and bled on Calvary to obtain these interests.

Scripture confirms Jesus is interested in:

- Turning lost souls from atheism or false religions to Him (Luke 9:55–56; Acts 26:16–18)

- The spiritual condition of His people, or in Paul's words, "your state" (Phil. 2:20)

- Establishing churches in His (NT) order (1 Cor. 11:34; 14:40; Titus 1:5)

- Destroying sin and its (and its author's) deceptive, destructive influence (1 John 3:8)

- Saving us (Christians) from being controlled by our sins and sin nature (Matt. 1:21)

- Teaching us God's Word (2 Tim. 2:15), the core disciplines of His spiritual lifestyle (Ps. 81:13; 95:10; 1 Cor. 4:17), to walk closely with Him daily (Matt. 11:29; Luke 1:76; Gen. 5:22–24, 6:9), to walk in love (John 13:34–35; Phil. 2:1–4), and to offer acceptable worship (John 4:24; Ps. 29:1–2; Acts 13:1–2; 16:24–25)

- Sanctifying us entirely—in thought, word, and deed (John 17:17; 1 Thess. 4:3–8; 5:23–24)

- Transforming our characters to be like His (Rom. 8:28–29)

- Motivating us to fulfill our predestined life works—vocational, professional, or ministerial (Eph. 2:10; Acts 26:16–18)

- Uniting us in perfect harmony (John 17:23; Eph. 4:13–16) and revealing His glory—sensed presence and evident acts of compassionate power and grace—among us (John 17:22) to show the nations He is real (John 17:23) and draw many to Him (John 12:32)

- Continually strengthening our faith, hope, and love so we live and minister in these essential attitudes (Rom. 14:19; Eph. 4:11–12; 1 Cor. 14:26; 13:13)

- Thoroughly testing us to grow, establish, and prove our faith, obedience, loyalty, and patience—and demonstrate His unfailingly faithful care (1 Pet. 1:6–7; 4:12)

- The Holy Spirit actualizing (fulfilling) His high priestly prayer (John 17) and Paul's (the NT's) inspired visions of the mature church (Eph. 2, 4, 5)

- Reforming and reviving us and our churches whenever we revert to lukewarmness, sin, and corruption (Acts 3:19; Rev. 3:15–22)

- Preparing an eternal home for us (His bride) in heaven (John 14:2; 1 Thess. 4:17–18)

- Catching us (His tested people) away to be with Him before Israel's and the nations' final seven-year test, the Tribulation (John 14:3; 17:24; 1 Thess. 4:14–18; 5:9–10; Rev. 3:10)

- Reforming, reviving, and restoring Israel during the Tribulation (Matt. 10:6; 15:24; Rom. 11:25–29, esp. v. 26)

- Ushering in His thousand-year kingdom (Rev. 20)

- Ushering in the Father's eternal kingdom in the new earth and New Jerusalem (Rev. 21–22)

These are the things that interest, engage, drive, enthrall, and captivate Jesus. Beside these, other things—the worldly programs, passions, politics, prosperity, and other priorities that so often usurp our thoughts—mean little.

Specifically, here are some things in which He's *not* deeply interested:

- Our personal net worth (Luke 12:13–15; Acts 3:6)

- Our personal popularity in this world (Gal. 1:10; 1 Cor. 4:9–10)

- Religious externals (ornate church buildings, vestments, traditions, rites, rituals[54])

- The church's standing among world religions (Matt. 15:12–14; Matt. 22–23)

---

54. The two ordinances Christ specifically ordered, Baptism and Communion, are exceptions (Matt. 28:19; 1 Cor. 11:23–25).

- Worldly success, fame, and awards (1 John 2:15–17)

- Our exceptional physical appearance or strength (Prov. 31:30; Ps. 147:10)

- Our enjoying excessive leisure or pleasure (2 Tim. 3:4)

- The worlds of politics, sports, and entertainment[55]

- Which nation is presently considered the greatest

When these interests consume us instead of Jesus' interests, Paul laments—and Jesus grieves and groans! "He groaned in the spirit, and was troubled" (John 11:33). Why? He wants us to get interested in His interests. Are Christ's interests yours? They can be... today!

2:23 Lessons from God's waiting room. Paul planned to send Timothy to the Philippians "as soon as I shall see how it will go with me" (2:23; see 1:20). Thus he didn't yet know if his trial would result in his release or execution (though he hoped for the former, 2:24). Why? He was in God's waiting room.

God sometimes keeps us waiting to receive answers to prayers, discover the next step in His guidance or plan, or receive His deliverance in time of need. But God's waiting room isn't His jail. It's a well-disguised, oft-misunderstood blessing—and the company we'll find there is outstanding. Consider this list of waiters.

In Troas Paul waited hours, perhaps days, for God's guidance (Acts 16:6–10). Moses waited six days atop Sinai's summit

---
55. Though benign or beneficial in moderation, these things obsess many Christians to their spiritual loss, but not Christ.

Jesus' Kenosis—and Ours!

before God revealed His plan for the tabernacle and statutes for Israel (Exod. 24:15–16). Jeremiah waited ten tense days to receive God's guidance for Judah's discontent survivors (Jer. 42:7). Abraham waited twenty-four years to discover the name, time, and mother of his son of promise (Gen. 17:21). Ruth, Boaz, and Naomi waited one *very* long day before God confirmed Boaz was His choice to marry Ruth (Ruth 3:13, 18). Samson waited many weeks, perhaps months, for his hair to regrow so he would know if God had given him a chance to redeem his ruined ministry (Judg. 16:22). Paul waited a decade before knowing when, where, and how his apostleship and the Spirit's saving work would begin among the Gentiles (Acts 9:30; 11:25–26). He waited over two years in Caesarea to discover when and how he would travel to Rome (Acts 23:11; 24:27; 25:11–12). In exile on Patmos the Apostle John waited until "the Lord's day" dawned and Christ released His awesome Revelation (Rev. 1:9), and he continued waiting to learn if he would be released.[56] Why did God keep them waiting?

While they waited on Him, He worked in them—widely, deeply, thoroughly, and permanently![57] He wants to do the same in us.

In His waiting room God makes us more patient, dependent on Him, sensitive to His voice, discerning of His providential hand, responsive to His Spirit (Rom. 8:14; Rev. 14:4), Christlike in attitude, spiritually productive (farming well our valleys of delay), one with Him, and thus perfect or complete

---

56. According to early church sources John was exiled by the Roman emperor Domitian in AD 95 but released after Domitian's death and Nerva's accession in AD 96.

57. To wait "in" Christ is to patiently pursue our daily duties in close, sustained fellowship with Him; to wait out of fellowship is to grudgingly endure in pouty, murmuring discontent. The former builds Christlike character; the latter dismantles it.

in character. While awaiting our divinely appointed times of release, we learn and grow in these vital lessons of spiritual maturity:

- That God's Word, guidance, or intervention is so valuable it's worth waiting for
- That God richly rewards His patiently waiting servants (Job 42:10–17)
- To not rebel or rush to start "fires" of self-led works (Gen. 16:1–3; Isa. 50:10–11; John 21:3–5; 2 Sam. 18:19–32)
- To occupy well, using our time and pursuing our God-given work diligently
- To nourish our faith and closeness to Jesus daily, to sustain our hope
- That God never wastes time—while we wait, He works "all things" together for His good plan and our good blessing, and prepares us to manage well what He's about to give us (Rom. 8:28)
- That His time for everything is always best (Eccles. 3:11; 3:1–8; Gen. 8:13–16)
- That God never forgets where we are, however apathetic and inactive He seems (Gen. 8:1; Dan. 5:10–13; Acts 11:25; Exod. 3:4; 1 Kings 18:1; 2 Kings 11:4–5)
- That God faithfully fulfills everything He promises in His time and way (Acts 27:25)

- That it's better to suffer where God leads us (1 Kings 17:1–7) than suffer for leading ourselves (1 Sam. 27:1–7; 30:1–6)

- That our spiritual endurance (patient faith) grows as we wait on God submissively, patiently, hopefully (James 1:2–4; Rev. 3:10; Ps. 84:5–7; Rom. 4:16–21)

Is God delaying His guidance, deliverance, open doors, or other answers to prayer? Take courage; you're in His waiting room—and in excellent company! Learn well the vital lessons of spiritual maturity…until they mature you. Realizing "the testing of your faith leads to power of endurance" (James 1:3, WEY), endure patiently, or "move steadily on in the way, work, and will of the Lord, even when things are very different" from what you want or need.[58] How long? Until Christ opens the door of your waiting room to release you. Refuse to be an immature, unfinished Christian. "Let your endurance be a finished product" (James 1:4, MOFFATT).

2:25–30 Honoring Epaphroditus. Having lauded his more famous associate, Timothy (2:19–23), Paul now commends his lesser-known yet equally honorable aide, Epaphroditus.

Epaphroditus' name means "lovely, handsome, charming," implying his character was lovely and attractive to God and charming or winsome to men.[59] Whatever his physical appearance, Paul's inspired description of him confirms God saw the inner "beauty of the LORD" (Ps. 90:17), or Christlikeness, in

---

58. Mrs. C. Nuzum, *The Life of Faith* (Springfield, MO: Gospel Publishing House, 1956), 45.
59. Smith and Cornwall, *The Exhaustive Dictionary of Bible Names*, s.v. "Epaphroditus."

him—the "fruit of the Spirit" (Gal. 5:22–23) demonstrating daily that the Holy Spirit was having His way in Epaphroditus. Though we're not told when, where, and how, the evidence reveals he had gone through a personal kenosis (self-emptying), as Christ (2:5–8) and Paul had (3:4–10), and, steadily "working out" his own salvation (2:12–16), had become a thoroughly humble, Christlike servant of God. As his life thus steadily "lifted up" Christ's character for others to see, they were drawn to his Lord and Savior (John 12:32).[60] Therefore like Timothy, whom Paul previously lauded (2:19–23), Epaphroditus was a "vessel unto honor" (2 Tim. 2:21), and Paul instructs the Philippians to honor him and others like him: "Honor people like him" (2:29, NIV; see 2:30; Acts 15:25–26). Paul cites Epaphroditus' honorable qualities.

He was Paul's "true brother" (2:25, NLT), a born-again sibling and friend in God's family whose sweet fellowship Paul enjoyed. He was Paul's "companion in labor" (2:25), a helpful "co-worker" (NLT) in his apostolic ministry. He was Paul's "fellow soldier" (2:25), a spiritual warrior who by prayer, fasting, and suffering fought by Paul's side against demons, heretics, and false apostles (Eph. 6:10–18). To the Philippians Epaphroditus was "your messenger" (2:25), a trusted believer who carried the Philippians' gifts and messages to Paul and other ministers and churches. Paul further says he "ministered to my need" (2:25) by delivering the Philippians' monetary gift (4:10, 14–18) and apparently by afterward laboring manually to support Paul's ministry in Rome. "Ministered" is a translation of the Greek *leitourgos*, which means rendering priestly or ministerial

---

60. The same spiritual drawing occurred numerous times in Paul's life (Gal. 1:24; Acts 16:27–30).

service to a religious community.[61] This may imply Paul sent Epaphroditus to minister in his name in the local Roman churches or beyond.[62] (That he was entrusted to carry the Philippians' gift to Paul implies he was an elder, or trusted minister or deacon, in the Philippian assembly.) Epaphroditus also had great zeal—perhaps too much! Paul said he was "sick" (Gk. *astheneō*, "to be weak; or ill"[63]) and "near unto death" because of "the work of Christ...not regarding his life" (2:27, 30). This may mean Epaphroditus made himself sick by overworking while in Rome, or perhaps by pushing himself too hard on his long trek to visit and cheer Paul in Rome,[64] or by exposure to the elements during the journey, especially at sea,[65] or by a combination of these exceptional physical stresses. In any case, this showed he was willing to die, if necessary, to serve God's servant and people (2:30). Most importantly, he was love-driven, motivated by a strong (agape) love for his fellow Philippians. When sick, "he longed after you all [the Philippians], and was

---

61. C. Spicq and J. D. Ernest, *Theological Lexicon of the New Testament* (Peabody, MA: Hendrickson Publishers, 1994), s.v. "*leitourgos*."
62. If so, this would not have been novel. It is generally held that Paul trained disciples in Tyrannus' lecture hall in Ephesus and sent them throughout Asia Minor evangelizing and discipling (perhaps sometimes accompanying them), resulting in the founding of the seven churches of Asia (Rev. 1:11, plus that in Colossae) and the widespread growth of the faith throughout the province (Acts 19:9–10, 20, 26).
63. Swanson, *Dictionary of Biblical Languages With Semantic Domains: Greek (New Testament)*, s.v. "*astheneō*."
64. Wuest translates, "Having recklessly exposed his life" (2:30). Another source surmises, "It may have been that 'he fell ill on the road and nearly killed himself by completing the journey while he was unfit to travel.'" See Carson, France, Motyer, and Wenham, *New Bible Commentary: 21st Century Edition*, quoting from G. B. Caird, *Paul's Letters From Prison* (Oxford: Oxford University Press, 1976).
65. Craig S. Keener relates, "Travel conditions were dangerous and harsh, especially at sea [Mediterranean] in late fall and early spring, and these conditions decreased one's resistance to antiquity's many diseases." See Keener, *The IVP Bible Background Commentary: New Testament*, Phil. 2:25–30, note.

full of heaviness [distressed that they were distressed over his illness!]" (2:26). Thus he wished to return speedily to Philippi, if Paul agreed, to cheer them (2:28). These are the reasons why Paul ordered honors for Epaphroditus.

Two questions remain to be asked. First, are we honoring our Epaphrodituses (lesser-known assistants) or only our Timothys (better known ministers)? Ministers aren't effective nor do churches or ministries thrive without Epaphrodituses. Shouldn't we, like Paul, give our Epaphrodituses some well-deserved kudos—private words of praise, recognition in our meetings, assignments to higher service? Second, are Epaphroditus' honorable and winsome character traits growing in us? Why not? Today, in the stresses you face in your "Rome," let the charming "beauty of the Lord" grow in you by joyfully obeying God's Word and guidance and sacrificially serving His "Pauls" and people.

2:27 A love-driven servant. Sadly many Christians, even ministers, are too often driven by wrong motives. The Pharisees were driven by religious pride, envy, covetousness, sectarian rivalries, and other nefarious motivators. Paul noted in this epistle that some ministers in or near Rome were preaching Christ in envious competition against him, maliciously hoping to make his imprisonment harsher or even prompt Nero's condemnation (Phil. 1:15–18). But, like Timothy, Epaphroditus' motivation was pure.

He served for love of Christ and His people alone (Phil. 2:26). By placing his vaunted teaching on love (1 Cor. 13:1–13) in the middle of his lengthy discussion of spiritual gifts (12:1–31; 14:1–40), Paul implicitly taught us love should motivate all ministers and the use of all the Spirit's gifts. The Apostle John emphatically agreed that loving one another is our primary Christian and ministry duty (1 John 4:7–12). Why? They recognized Jesus commanded love (John 13:34–35; Matt. 22:39) and prayed the Father would make it real in us (John 17:21–23, 26).

Epaphroditus so identified with God's people that he was more distressed by their affliction than his. It didn't offend him that he was deathly ill (Phil. 2:27), but it stressed him greatly that news of his condition was grieving the Philippians! This, not the failure of any selfish plans or greedy ambitions, left him "longing" (homesick) and "full of heaviness" (2:26). In this he mirrored Paul's apostolic love for the Philippians (1:8).

Paul desired release from his incarceration only so he could continue helping the Philippians and other churches (1:21–25). Truly dead to selfishness, he lived to love Christians. He gave up the fellowship and assistance of Epaphroditus he so badly needed (while imprisoned!) to send him to relieve the Philippians' anxieties over his health—and Epaphroditus' angst over their angst (2:28)! This shows just how seriously Paul took Christ's prime command (John 13:34–35) and high priestly prayer that we abide in perfect loving unity (John 17:21–23, 26).

Like Paul's, Epaphroditus' love was strong, active, and urgent. He could not ignore or neglect his fellow believers' needs and still retain joy. Their needs drove him to intercession and their relief relieved him. Thus love dominated all his decisions. Whatever course of action best furthered the loving blessing of Christ's sheep, he chose it (John 21:15–17).

This love was typical of many early Christians. It was a key factor in Christianity's remarkable growth during the first three centuries despite persisting periodic persecution. Divided by their own proud rivalries and divisive attitudes, many pagan Romans exclaimed of Christians, "Behold how they love one another."[66] Consequently many from all walks of life came to Christ and His followers' humble, hidden house fellowships. Why? They wanted to experience the wondrous river of God's love flowing through them (John 7:37–39).

Is the same river flowing through us? Or are rushing streams of selfishness spoiling our witness? Let's emulate Epaphroditus' love-driven life until our neo-pagan peers come to receive our Lord and be revived and refreshed in the river of His love flowing through us.

2:27 Christ's compassions continue. Paul says when Epaphroditus was deathly sick, God "had mercy on him" by healing him (2:27). Thus this was a mercy healing.

Actually it was a triple mercy! God had mercy on Epaphroditus by extending his earthly life and service. He showed mercy on the Philippians, since Epaphroditus was one of their beloved leaders (elder, deacon) and they yearned for him to recover and return to them (2:26, 28). And He had mercy on Paul, who loved Epaphroditus and needed his services badly at this time, and who, already worn by many sorrows, didn't need another, "lest I should have sorrow upon sorrow" (2:27; cf. 1 Cor. 10:13). And that's not all.

Epaphroditus' mercy healing shows us Christ's compassion hasn't ceased. During His earthly ministry Jesus often healed, fed, taught, or delivered supplicants because of His compassion: "Jesus...saw a great multitude, and was moved with compassion toward them, and he healed their sick" (Matt.

---

66. This quote is attributed to Tertullian. Describing how many Romans spoke of Christians, he said: "Look," they say, "how they love one another" (for they themselves hate one another); "and how they are ready to die for each other" (for they themselves are readier to kill each other). See http://www.tertullian.org/quotes.htm (accessed March 31, 2015).

14:14).[67] It is likely that Paul and the others who interceded for Epaphroditus' recovery begged the same tender mercies of Jesus. Thus by raising him some thirty years after His ascension, Christ confirmed to them, and through Paul's letter, to us, that indeed He is "the same yesterday, today and forever" (Heb. 13:8). Like His unchanging character, Christ's compassions continue. As Jeremiah proclaimed before Christ's incarnation, so we hold after His ascension: "His compassions fail not. They are new every morning; great is thy faithfulness" (Lam. 3:22–23).

Remember this when praying for the sick, and ask our Father to heal them, even if "near unto death," for His great mercy's sake (James 5:14–18). Who knows how many valuable, honorable, overworked Epaphrodituses will recover and finish their work, how many Philippians will be cheered, and how many Pauls spared overwhelming sorrows?

2:28 Reaping the mercy we sow. Paul sent Epaphroditus on a mission of mercy—to relieve the Philippians' troubled hearts by the sight of him, their divinely restored, dearly beloved brother (2:26, 28). Earlier they had sent Epaphroditus on a mission of mercy—to relieve Paul in the heaviness of his Roman captivity (with the prospect of execution looming) with financial aid and Epaphroditus' sweet friendship and assistance (2:25; 4:18). Thus the Philippians received again the mercy they gave. So did Epaphroditus!

Epaphroditus had personally shown Paul mercy by undertaking the arduous trip from Philippi to Rome in his church's behalf to relieve the afflicted apostle, and by laboring to meet

---

67. During Jesus' earthly ministry He repeatedly practiced compassion (Matt. 15:32; 20:34; Mark 1:41; 5:19; 6:34; 9:22; Luke 7:13) and taught it (Matt. 18:33; Luke 10:33, 37). Shouldn't we pray expectantly for His mercies today?

his needs once in Rome. While there, and after recovering from his deadly illness, Epaphroditus had become "full of heaviness"—after hearing the Philippians were worried sick over his sickness![68] So Paul mercifully released him "the more eagerly" to return to Philippi to relieve this, his affliction (2:28). Thus Epaphroditus received again the mercy he gave.

These returning mercies underscore the universal biblical principle, "Whatever a man soweth, that shall he also reap" (Gal. 6:7).[69] More specifically they confirm we will reap the mercy (or cruelty) we sow in this life: "With the merciful thou wilt show thyself merciful" (Ps. 18:25). Are you sowing mercy today in your attitudes, words, deeds, reactions? Toward your family members? Fellow Christians? Friends? Coworkers? Neighbors? Strangers?

2:28 A holy love triangle. Among fallen human beings love triangles are troublesome, destructive, even deadly! But among spiritually mature, self-emptied Christians we find something refreshingly different: holy love triangles. Instead of each party being jealous and hostile about the other two sharing love, spiritually minded Christians enjoy and promote their friends freely loving one another. This epistle describes this.

In love the Philippians sent Epaphroditus to Paul to minister monetary assistance, sweet fellowship, and ministry assistance. Realizing their deep concern over Epaphroditus' illness, Paul relinquished his own fellowship with Epaphroditus to lovingly send him back to the Philippians to relieve and bless them. And he did so not reluctantly but "all the more eagerly" (2:28,

---

68. Apparently Epaphroditus' "heaviness" was intense. The same Greek word (*adēmoneō*) is used to describe Jesus' "very heavy" soul burden in Gethsemane (Matt. 26:37).
69. See Psalm 18:25; Proverbs 11:17; Matthew 5:7; Luke 6:36–38; 2 Corinthians 2:6–11; 2 Timothy 1:16–18.

NAS), or "at once" (MOFFATT), or "with increased haste and diligence" (WUEST). Thus instead of fighting over who would *hold* Epaphroditus' fellowship and service, Paul and the Philippians each joyfully *gave* this blessing to the other, and Epaphroditus was willing to go either way, ready to do whatever would foster the loving unity for which Jesus prayed and died (John 17:21–23, 26)! That's Christ's love. That's an envy- and jealousy-free threesome. That's a holy love triangle—and rare not only in the world but also in our churches.

Are we learning to be glad when our Christian friends and helpers enjoy fellowship with or ministry from other Christians instead of us? Or are we jealous when they love and are loved by other Christians, churches, or ministers and trying to spoil or steal their blessings? It's time we turn our unholy rivalries into holy love triangles. "Love is patient and kind. Love is not jealous.... It does not demand its own way" (1 Cor. 13:4–5, NLT).

Chapter Three

PRESSING TOWARD NEW GOALS!

Paul describes his abandonment of his old Jewish goals and glory—his personal kenosis—to pursue his new goals and glory. Forgetting his past, he's now zealously pursuing new goals: to know Christ, His power, His sufferings; to become spiritually perfect or mature; to fulfill the purpose of Christ's call on his life. He now has only one glory or chief delight: Christ! And only one hope: looking for "the Savior" to return…
Are these your goals, glory, hope?

3:1 The rarest rejoicing. In three references in this epistle Paul reminded the Philippians, and us, to "rejoice in the Lord," or delight in our Savior and His salvation (3:1; 3:3; 4:4). Repeating this command implies its importance and urges continuous practice: "Continue to rejoice that you are in Him" (3:1, AMP), or "be constantly rejoicing in the Lord" (WUEST), or "Whatever happens…rejoice in the Lord" (NLT). "In the Lord" means in the Lord's salvation, body (church-kingdom), and personal fellowship.

"In the Lord" we're saved from our sins and God's wrath (Matt. 1:21; John 5:24; Rom. 6:12–14) and granted a new, living way of sweet fellowship with Jesus daily (Ps. 17:15, AMP; Heb. 10:19–22). This alone is cause for rejoicing every hour of every day of every year.[1] We can draw near Jesus, talk to Him, and listen to His responses that come by the quickening of His Word in our reading and the work of His hand in our circumstances. But, strangely, as wondrous as this is, we rarely pause to consider or give thanks for our "so great salvation" (Heb. 2:3). Why?

We don't train ourselves to "give thanks" for "everything," beginning with our salvation (1 Thess. 5:18). Also, our adversary stirs up adversity constantly to keep us distracted with present problems in a deliberate strategy to eclipse the brilliance of our Sun of righteousness and His awesome salvation (1 Pet. 1:6). Saved from eternal torment, freed from sin's enslaving power, reunited forever with the source of life and joy, filled with His supernatural Spirit, taught by Him, convicted and comforted by Him, and bound for a perfect world without sin, suffering, or strife—*that's* what Jesus mercifully gave us through His cross. Heaven is very aware of these benefits we have in the Lord: "Forget not all his benefits" (Ps. 103:2). We should be also. Exactly what is ours in Christ?

We have His truth, fellowship, faithfulness, peace, favor, presence, protection, counsel, guidance, ministers, church, gifts, callings, answers to prayer, sustaining grace, strength, miraculous power, authoritative name, wisdom, end-time prophecies, and many other blessings! Whatever may come, these redemptive

---

1. The Scriptures certainly say as much. See Philippians 3:3; 4:4; Psalms 9:2; 33:1; 40:16; 63:11; 64:10; 97:12; 116:12–19; Habakkuk 3:17–18 (cf. 1 Sam. 1:8; Ps. 17:15, AMP); Luke 1:46–47; 10:20; John 5:24; Acts 2:26–27; 8:39; 16:32–34; Romans 5:2; 15:9–10; 1 Thessalonians 5:16; 1 Peter 1:6; 1 John 3:14.

benefits remain ours "in the Lord." No worldly problems (even poverty, James 1:9; or persecution, Rom. 8:35–39) are bitter enough to spoil them—if we don't become offended and disbelieving (Luke 7:23)!—and no worldly blessings are sweeter (Ps. 16:11). Whatever else may be wrong, troublesome, or incomplete in our lives, this remains right: Jesus has saved us from sin, judgment, and meaningless living, and as we abide, we are eternally safe "in Him"! Why not begin obeying now?

> *"Father, I rejoice in the Lord! Help me make this rarest rejoicing regular. Whatever You send my way, help me not be so troubled by my tests or uplifted by my triumphs that I forget to rejoice 'in the Lord' every day... until Jesus comes. Amen!"*

3:1 Impenitently repetitious. Paul said it was not "irksome" (3:1)—not bothersome or irritating—to him to periodically teach the Philippians "the same things," or the fundamental and practical but oft-forgotten truths of the faith (3:1). Why? For their spiritual protection from sin, error, and forgetfulness. Paul didn't originate this impenitent repetition of truth.

The entire Bible reveals that God Himself believes that in matters of eternal truth, redundancy is good! Scripture often repeats various themes, truths, and prophecies:

- The Psalms urge us no less than twenty-three times to "Praise ye the Lord" (e.g., Ps. 104:35).
- The New Testament bids us offer God thanks six times (1 Thess. 5:18; Eph. 5:20; Col. 3:15, 16, 17; Heb. 13:15) and repeatedly shows the Savior and saints doing so (Matt. 15:36; Luke 2:38; Acts 27:35).

- Five times God's Word declares "the just shall live by faith" (Hab. 2:4; Rom. 1:17; 2 Cor. 5:7; Gal. 3:11; Heb. 10:38).

- At least seven times the Bible states, using various wordings, God is "no respecter of persons" (James 2:1, 9; Deut. 1:17; Prov. 24:23; Rom. 2:11; Eph. 6:9; Col. 3:25; Acts 10:34).

- Three times the Bible asserts "whosoever" calls on the Lord shall be saved (Joel 2:32; Acts 2:21; Rom. 10:13).

- Twice God's Word anathematizes those who preach false gospels (Gal. 1:8–9).

- Deuteronomy contains many truths recorded in Leviticus (cf., Deut. 28; Lev. 26).

- Jesus spoke a memorable proverb about pride on three occasions (Matt. 23:12; Luke 14:11; 18:14).

- Jesus repeatedly warned His disciples to "watch and pray" (Matt. 26:41; Mark 13:33; Luke 21:36).

- Three of Paul's epistles charge us to "put off" the flesh and "put on" our new man (Rom. 13:12–14; Eph. 4:22–24; Col. 3:8–14).

Many more examples could be cited. Together they testify, as one commentator states, "It is good for us often to hear the same truths";[2] another adds, "Repetition is a vital part of learning."[3] But many Christians disagree.

---

2. Henry, *Commentary in One Volume*, 1865.
3. Walvoord, Zuck, and Dallas Theological Seminary, *The Bible Knowledge Commentary: An Exposition of the Scriptures*, Phil. 3:1, note.

We often tire of hearing variations of previously presented themes and complain. While some ministers repeat teachings due to poor organization, stagnant studies, apathy, or forgetfulness, Spirit-led ministers will repeat themes when the Holy Spirit prompts them to do so (when their people's spiritual condition calls for them). A. W. Tozer cited this as a mark of ministers with prophetic insight:

> What God says to His church at any given period depends altogether upon her moral and spiritual condition and upon the spiritual need of the hour. Religious leaders who continue mechanically to expound the Scriptures without regard to the current religious situation are no better than the scribes and lawyers of Jesus' day who faithfully parroted the Law without the remotest notion of what was going on around them spiritually.... They seemed wholly unaware that there was such a thing as meat in due season. The prophets never made that mistake nor wasted their efforts in that manner. They invariably spoke to the condition of the people.[4]

For instance, faith and patience may be taught not once but several times when a congregation is experiencing a lengthy test of faith and endurance. Humility may be taught after fresh victories to deter pride. Biblical morality, prejudice, or love may be reviewed when events call for decisions on these or other key subjects—even if they've been taught before. As pastors we must, therefore, be willing to repeat biblical themes whenever our congregations need them. Peter did so in his second epistle:

---

4. A. W. Tozer, *Of God and Men* (Harrisburg, PA: Christian Publications, 1960), 20.

"I will always remind you about these things—even though you already know them" (2 Pet. 1:12, NLT).

Personally, we may gain immensely by educational rumination—reviewing excellent books or documentaries (Phil. 4:8). Every time we revisit these familiar wells, we draw up something new, something more clearly understood, something more deeply grasped. Why? Our discernment of truth has increased. Our spiritual (and natural) insight grows the further we walk with God, seeking Him daily, studying His illuminating Word, and trusting and obeying Him in tests. With this enhanced insight we see new truths in old materials. So if the material is excellent, its review will be also; if it profited you originally, it will enrich you again.

A brief caveat. Of course we can run this principle into the ground. Excessive redundancy isn't productive. Typically after studying subjects adequately, we should move on to fresh material. It's intellectually stimulating to search "new things" (Acts 17:21; see 17:19–21), and we need intellectual stimulation as well as spiritual edification.[5]

Are we in the ministry ready to follow Paul's lead by not tiring of repeating themes—for motivation, not information—when our people need to hear them again, or more broadly, or in greater detail (2 Thess. 2:5)? If so, we'll find that if hearing

---

5. John Skidmore relates the following of Oswald Chambers: "I realized that I lacked the ability to give form in my mind and expression in words to what I knew in my heart. Mr. Chambers asked me what I read. When I told him, nothing but the Bible and books directly associated with it, he diagnosed the difficulty at once and said—'The trouble is you have allowed part of your brain to stagnate for want of use.' Then...he gave me a list of over fifty books...covering almost every phase of current thought. The outstanding result was a revolution which can only be described as a mental new birth...which by God's grace is still extending and expanding." See G. Chambers, *Oswald Chambers: His Life and Works* (London: Marshall, Morgan, & Scott, 1959), 94.

the truth once doesn't do the job, "hearing and hearing" will (Rom. 10:17)! And as Christ's students, are we willing to revisit and review familiar learning materials when the Spirit through our ministers or memories opportunely brings them to mind? If so, we'll agree with Paul that redundancy is good!

3:2 Watching for heretics and heresies. Using uncomplimentary symbolism ("dogs"), Paul warns the Philippians to be on guard against the appeals of the Judaizers, whose prime error was their insistence that Gentiles had to first become Jewish proselytes before they could be saved (Acts 15:1).[6] More broadly, the Holy Spirit through Paul here warns we should beware of all false teachers and destructive heresies.

Zealous but deluded professors of religion will eventually visit every church. Really, they must come! Why? God uses them to test our discernment and courage as we learn to differentiate their skewed teachings from the proper interpretation of Scripture and take firm stands against them. The New Testament repeatedly warns us of this challenge so we'll neither be surprised nor deceived when heretics try to infiltrate and convert us (1 John 4:1; 1 Tim. 4:1–6). It further instructs us to be patient with Christians of weaker faith, but never to the point they cause strife and divisions (Rom. 14:1, ESV). Instead we should "earnestly contend" with them, if able, refuting their errors by presenting clarifying biblical texts (Jude 3); if unable, we should defer this to our leaders who are usually better prepared to engage in doctrinal debates (Acts

---

[6]. The first Gentiles to be saved were in fact Jewish proselytes (Acts 2:10), but Christ demonstrated at Cornelius' home (10:34–48) and again at Antioch (11:19–21) His intention to save Gentiles *without* their first becoming Jews. The Judaizers insisted to the contrary, even after Peter related his vision (11:1–18) and later the first church council corroborated Peter's (and Paul's) position (15:23–24).

15:1–2). If after leaders correct them they persist in promoting their errors, we are to disassociate from them (Titus 3:10; Matt. 18:17). The Apostle John instructs us to not receive or support them or even wish them well since this helps them harm more unsuspecting souls with their false truths (2 John 10–11). These are uncomfortable but unavoidable scenarios, and we must deal with them to prevent church schisms and individuals' spiritual corruption and to demonstrate that we have the spiritual and moral courage to stand not only for but also against things, as Jesus did (1 Cor. 11:19; Matt. 22:29–32; John 4:22).[7]

Paul also calls heretics "evil workers" (3:2). To us this language may seem harsh. But have we considered, for instance, that those who preach false gods and religions, or false gospels, are misrepresenting God, serving Satan, and causing souls to be eternally lost. That's evil! Remember this the next time heretics knock on your door or visit your church and follow the simple biblical instructions above.

3:2 Apostolic irony. Like Martin Luther's pen centuries later, Paul's stylus sometimes released lethal irony. The apostle who wrote the Bible's definitive description of love (1 Cor. 13) could also, if he so chose, write with stinging sarcasm.

Knowing the Judaizers, like other Pharisaic Jews, called Gentiles "dogs," Paul called them the same: "Beware of dogs" (3:2)! (Even Jesus called the Syro-Phoenician woman a "dog" when severely testing her, Matt. 15:26–27.) Paul was probably

---

[7]. We do well also, however, to avoid overzealousness. It's not Christlike to be contentious, pugnacious, or rude (2 Tim. 2:24–26), or to refuse fellowship with other Christians over minor points of (non-salvific) biblical interpretation, manner of worship, or other issues that are clearly debatable. There we should remember the oft-quoted Christian motto, "In essentials, unity; in non-essentials, liberty; in all things, charity."

Pressing Toward New Goals!

further alluding to the fact that the Judaizers were, like wild dogs, always harassing him by following him wherever he ministered, persistently barking at his heels with their *ad hominem* criticisms and erroneous arguments, and biting him (and other godly teachers) by denying his apostolic authority, revelations, and biblical interpretations and thus forcing him to defend his ministry (2 Cor. 10:7–13; 11:22–12:19).[8] And his poison pen wasn't finished.

Since the Judaizers were so zealous to remove foreskins, he calls them "mutilators." One commentator notes, "Because circumcision had no spiritual value they were just *mutilators of the flesh*."[9] J. B. Phillips states:

> Be on your guard against these curs, these wicked workmen, these would-be mutilators of your bodies!
> —Philippians 3:2, Phillips

What's worse, Paul wrote the Galatians saying he wished the Judaizers would cut off their own foreskins instead of those of gullible Gentile Christians! Some translators feel he went even further: "As for those agitators, I wish they would go the whole way and emasculate themselves!" (Gal. 5:12, niv). Whew, that's graphic language!

And a fact not lost on Luther as he studied Paul's writings. When Luther spoke or wrote of enemies who opposed Christ or the Reformation, his language was sometimes equally piercing. "Great thieves go scot-free, as the Pope and his crew," was one of his milder comments.[10] Even fellow Reformers such

---

8. Henry, *Commentary in One Volume*, 1865.
9. Carson, France, Motyer, and Wenham, *New Bible Commentary: 21st Century Edition*, Phil. 3:1–2, note.
10. See http://www.goodreads.com/work/quotes/1167108-the-table-talk-of-martin-luther (accessed April 1, 2015).

as Zwingli were not safe from Luther's razor-sharp tongue. When the two differed on Communion, "Luther," exasperated, "said Zwingli was of the devil and that he was nothing but a wormy nut."[11] And Luther's quotes concerning Jews and Pope Leo were shockingly brutal and his language coarse. Did he draw inspiration from Paul's choice of words in Philippians 3:2? Or his anathema in Galatians 1:8–9?

Whatever Luther's inspiration—or excuse, it behooves us to remember we're neither Paul nor Luther and refrain from anathematizing folks or searing them with flaming sarcasm.

3:3 We are the circumcision. Paul's assertion, "We are the circumcision" (3:3), clearly implies, "we Christians are the true or spiritual Jews" (cf. Rom. 2:28–29).[12] Thus, it follows logically that the church (comprised of Christ- or Messiah-trusting, Spirit-filled, heart-circumcised Christians) is spiritual Israel (cf. Gal. 6:16, NIV, NLT, PHILLIPS, WEY), or its true spiritual seed

---

11. See http://www.christianitytoday.com/ch/131christians/moversandshakers/zwingli.html?start=2 (accessed April 1, 2015).
12. We conclude this because Paul asserted, "We are the true circumcision" (3:3, NAS). Also, because (a) circumcision is the most ancient and important sign of God's covenant with the Jewish people (Gen. 17:10–14; Rom. 4:11); (b) in this context, Paul is comparing the condition of the mostly Gentile Christians of Philippi with that of the Judaizers, who were Jewish Christians; and (c) in the larger context of the New Testament, throughout his writings Paul used "circumcised" or "circumcision" to refer to Jews as distinct from Gentiles, whom he usually referred to as "uncircumcised" (Rom. 3:29–30; Gal. 2:7, 9, 12; Eph. 2:11; Col. 3:11; 4:10–11). Further evidence lies in Jesus twice denying the authentic Jewishness of Christ-rejecting synagogues in Smyrna and Philadelphia, proving that *He* doesn't consider ethnic Hebrews true Jews if they reject Him (Rev. 2:9; 3:9) and thus implying He considers whoever receives Him a true Jew!

and substitute as God's current "princely" covenant people—though *not* its permanent replacement (Rom. 11:1–29).[13]

In this verse Paul gives three characteristics of spiritually circumcised Christians or spiritual Jews—Christians who, receiving Christ and His Spirit, put off their "flesh" life[14] to possess and grow in the essence of what it means to be a fulfilled Jew. Spiritually (or heart) circumcised Christians:

1. WORSHIP GOD IN SPIRIT AND IN THE HOLY SPIRIT (3:3). They worship spiritually, not merely ceremonially. Spiritual worship is inward, of and from our spirit (heart or spiritual core). Ceremonial or ritual worship is outward, performing religious rites and ordinances yet requiring no real inward change in the worshipper.[15] To worship "in the Spirit of God" (3:3, NAS) is to audibly, bodily, or silently express adoration for God in and with the Holy Spirit's personal inspiration and assistance.[16] Moreover the Holy Spirit:

---

13. While as Paul explained in Romans 11:1–29, the church currently holds the position of Israel as God's fruit-bearing branch in this age, it does not and will never hold its predestination. Every promise God made to ancient Israel will yet be fulfilled in the modern, spiritually reformed, Christ-worshipping Jewish people and homeland.
14. Many limit their understanding of the "flesh" to the grosser "works of the flesh" (Gal. 5:19–21), but more broadly "flesh" speaks of our old, fallen, independent nature in all its ways and works, including its more refined forms: religion, intellectualism, idealism, philosophy, philanthropy, and other humanistic causes divorced from Christ and His biblical revelation and redemptive purposes. Philippians 3:3–4 speak of this broader definition of the "flesh" (in which we often boast!), and the next verses (3:5–7) specifically describe Paul's religious "flesh."
15. This was true of virtually all first-century pagan religious cults.
16. The Judaizers whom Paul refers to in the preceding verse (3:2) did not worship "in the Spirit of God."

A. INDWELLS AND ENVELOPS US as He prompts, instructs, and guides us in worship—As we worship acceptably (in "spirit and truth," John 4:23–24), He visits us, is enthroned as God in our praise and worship (Ps. 22:3; Acts 16:24–25), and manifests in various ways how real His presence is (John 14:21, 23).

B. TEACHES US "expanded" or "charismatic worship"[17]—We "expand" our praise and worship by using unknown languages ("tongues") that exceed our natural means of expression (native language) and are given by the Holy Spirit's supernatural assistance (1 Cor. 14:2, 14; Acts 2:4, 11; Rev. 1:10). Paul personally worshipped this way (1 Cor. 14:14–15), apparently often (14:18), attested to its effectiveness (14:17), was thankful for it (14:18), and thus highly recommended it to us, though with the restraints of reasonable orderliness (14:27 33, 40).

C. SHOWS US other ways we worship God acceptably—by our obedience, ordinances, service, stewardship, charity, sacrifices, and anything we do "heartily, as to the Lord" (Col. 3:23), etc.

2. GLORY IN CHRIST ALONE (3:3). They "rejoice" (praise, boast) in Jesus their Messiah ("Christ Jesus") more than in any other person or thing and in the rich benefits they have as Christians.

---

17. I've borrowed the expression "expanded worship" from Jack W. Hayford's *The Spirit Filled Life Bible*, page 1804. I've taken the term "charismatic worship" from Craig Keener's *The IVP Bible Background Commentary: New Testament*, Phil. 3:3, note.

Even when suffering for Christ and deprived of worldly blessings and comforts they rejoice in their sweet, personal, untouchable fellowship with Him daily (Phil. 3:1; 4:4; Hab. 3:17–18; 2 Cor. 10:17; Ps. 16:11; 17:15; 27:4; Jer. 9:23–24; Acts 16:24–25).[18] See my entry, "The Rarest Rejoicing" (Phil. 3:1).

3. HAVE NO CONFIDENCE IN "FLESH" (3:3). They don't put complete trust or reliance in any "flesh" (unredeemed humanity), including:

   A. THE FLESHLY NATURE. They don't trust in the goodness, wisdom, strength, or ability of human nature unaided by divine grace, their own or anyone else's, unsaved or saved (John 2:23–25; 6:63; Rom. 7:18; Jer. 17:9).

   B. THE RELIGION(S) OF THE FLESH. In this context Paul describes his former confidence and glorying in Pharisaic Judaism (3:4–6) and how he abandoned trusting in rabbinic traditions and law-keeping to save him to trust in Christ alone and worship and serve Him in God's appointed way of righteousness "by faith" (3:7–14, esp. v. 9). Like Paul, spiritually circumcised Christians trust in God's biblically appointed way of righteousness and wor-

---

18. By contrast, the Judaizers boasted in circumcisions, rabbinic traditions, and other religious works (Luke 18:11–12).

ship (religion) alone, not man's unbiblical deities, doctrines, or traditions.[19]

Other New Testament references give additional characteristics of spiritually circumcised Christians. They:

1. Receive and walk in God's righteousness (Rom. 2:25–26; cf. Rom. 10:1–3)

2. Live by faith, relying on God's faithfulness and Word, as Abraham did (Rom. 4:9–11)

3. Obey God's commands (Word, guidance, checks) (1 Cor. 7:18–19; John 15:14; Rom. 8:14; Acts 16:6–8)

4. Put off (or voluntarily circumcise) their "sins of the flesh" (Col. 2:11; Gal. 5:13–24; 1 Cor. 6:9–11; Col. 3:8–14; Eph. 4:24–5:7)

Summing up, true circumcision (and Judaism) is spiritual, not physical, in nature. It occurs primarily in the heart, not the body (Deut. 30:6); in our manner of living, not in our ethnicity or dress (prayer shawls, yarmulkes); in the spiritual qualities of faith, humility, submission, and obedience, not compliance with outward religious rites and rituals ("ceremonies," Phil. 3:3, WEY). It consists of a Spirit-led, not carnally driven life; Christ-centered, not self-centered motives; a hunger to have more of the Spirit, not more bodily comfort or indulgence. It describes one who lives to please God,

---

[19]. Cain originated the religion of the flesh, or self-appointed, divinely unacceptable worship and righteousness when, in a spirit of pride, he worshipped God and sought righteousness *his* way (Gen. 4:2–5). By practicing Christ-rejecting, ceremonial (and obsolete) Judaism, unbelieving first-century Jews were unconsciously perpetuating the error and religion of Cain—righteousness and worship *their* way (Rom. 10:1–3).

Pressing Toward New Goals!

not himself or others; praise God, not merely men; delight in Christ's kingdom, not worldly leaders or nations; boast in God's works, not human achievements; hope in God's promises, not people's; seek God's help first, not man's; trust God's wisdom, not human knowledge; live and work in God's ways, not the world's. Such believers are cutting off "the things of the world" (1 John 2:15–17) daily to live more for the things of Christ (Col. 3:1–4).[20]

As you ponder this expanded description of spiritual circumcision, ask yourself where you may need spiritual circumcision. Then execute this rite of passage to the authentic, Spirit-filled, joyful Christian—and true Jewish—life. Have no more confidence in any flesh, rejoice in your Messiah Jesus daily, and worship God with your spirit and by His Spirit.

3:4–9 Paul's kenosis—and ours. After presenting the example of Christ's kenosis (self-emptying) and divine exaltation (2:5–11) and urging the Philippians to follow Christ's example of humility in thought and deed (2:12–16), Paul relates his own personal kenosis.

He first describes the religious "flesh" in which he formerly delighted and boasted—his perfectly pure Jewish pedigree with all its unimpeachable credentials (3:4–9). This religious résumé along with other New Testament passages reveals Paul was:

---

20. For more on spiritual or heart circumcision, see Deuteronomy 10:16; 30:6; cf. Leviticus 26:41; Jeremiah 4:4; 9:25–26.

- Duly "circumcised the eighth day" (3:5)[21] —circumcision was *the* distinctive sign linking one to the Abrahamic covenant (Gen. 17:9–14)

- Of undisputable Jewish ethnic origins, "of the stock of Israel" (3:5)—or a "pure-blooded" (NLT) Jew having not one but two Jewish parents (2 Cor. 11:22)

- From an honorable tribe, "of the tribe of Benjamin" (3:5)[22]

- Outstanding among his people, "an Hebrew of the Hebrews" (3:5)—or a Jew's Jew

- In an ultra-orthodox sect, "as touching the law, a Pharisee" (3:5)—Pharisees were "noted for being the most meticulous observers of the law"[23] (Mark 7:3–4; Acts 23:6)[24]

---

21. More evidence here that Paul didn't oppose Jews being circumcised, only Gentiles, if they did so imagining that such conformity to the law would save or spiritually mature them. Note he's careful to say all his former religious zeal, including circumcision, was but "dung" (3:8) (excrement or food scraps) when compared to being "in him [Christ]" (3:9) and having that righteousness that comes only "by faith" in Christ (3:9), not by fleshly circumcision or other Jewish legal observances.

22. The tribe of Benjamin famously produced Israel's first king, Saul, in honor of whom Paul may have been given his Hebrew name (Saul of Tarsus). Also, Benjamin was one of Jacob's two favorite sons, the other being Joseph. (Infamously, however, the tribe of Benjamin also caused Israel's tragic civil war, in and for which they were decimated; Judges 20:12–14.)

23. See Keener, *The IVP Bible Background Commentary: New Testament*, Phil. 3:5, note.

24. We hold a low opinion of the Pharisees today because Christ exposed their deep hypocrisies (Matt. 23:1–33), yet in first-century Israel, especially in Jerusalem, it was a badge of honor to be a Pharisee. They were widely respected for their dedication to the written and oral law.

- A strict Jewish separatist, "a Pharisee" (3:5)—"Pharisee" means *separated ones*, and this small but highly influential Jewish sect maintained strict separation from Gentiles, especially in dining, so as to not share their presumed idolatry (Acts 10:28)[25]

- Expertly trained in Mosaic law, "brought up in [Jerusalem] at the feet of Gamaliel" (Acts 22:3)—or taught the written and oral law by Gamaliel, the nation's most respected rabbi (Acts 5:34, 40a)

- Very zealous for his faith, "concerning zeal, persecuting the church" (Phil. 3:6)—so zealous for God and true Judaism that he violently persecuted followers of "The Way," whom he considered dangerous heretics following a messianic pretender (Acts 8:3; 26:9–12; Gal. 1:13)

- "Blameless" in right living, "touching the righteousness which is in the law, blameless" (3:6)—he obeyed all Jewish commands and ordinances, written and oral and, when he sinned, offered the sacrifices the Law requested (cf., Luke 1:6; 2:25).

- An up-and-coming religious leader in Israel—Israel's highest religious leaders entrusted Saul of Tarsus (Paul) with key commissions, particularly to lead their anti-Christian campaign (Acts 8:3; 9:1–2; Gal. 1:14)[26]

---

25. Ibid., Acts 10:27–29, note.
26. Thus by receiving Christ Paul abandoned his fast-rising religious career.

These boasts were Paul's treasured "gain" (3:7), his most cherished "assets" (ISV). Yet as Jesus stripped off His divine glory to become human and fulfill His Father's will, Paul also stripped away his religious glory (proud religious "flesh," 3:4) to have Christ and fulfill His call. Consider how Paul's kenosis tracked Christ's.

Like Jesus, Paul didn't consider his high religious status "robbery" (something to be clung to) but "made himself of no reputation" (Phil. 2:6–7) among Jews by receiving Christ. He immediately "took upon him the form of a servant" (Phil. 2:7) by calling Jesus "Lord" on the Damascus road (Acts 9:5–6), obeying His orders in Damascus (9:6–9), and serving Him as an evangelist and apologist (9:20–22). Thus humbled by conversion, he was, like his Master, "made in the likeness of [ordinary, religiously undistinguished] men" (Phil. 2:7) as he came and went "certain days" as just another congregant in the Damascus church (Acts 9:19).

As a Christian, Paul further humbled himself by beginning to be "obedient unto [the] death" of his self-will in Jerusalem (Phil. 2:8), as he accepted the Jerusalem church's initial rejection (Acts 9:26), deadly Jewish persecution (in Jerusalem and Damascus, 9:23–24, 29), and Christ's disappointing guidance (confirmed through the church's leaders) to return to Tarsus (Acts 9:26–30).[27] There in Tarsus, his hometown, he humbly "worked out his own salvation" (Phil. 2:12) for nearly a decade, as Christ had done for eighteen years in Nazareth, until recalled to ministry. Thus, again, now as a Christian, Paul thoroughly humbled himself.

---

27. To a zealous, new believer of Paul's caliber, burning with zeal to pursue his call, it was surely disappointing to be sent home to Tarsus to practice obedience rather than sent out to the nations to preach Christ!

And if that wasn't enough, he was prepared to go further. Besides what he had already lost for Christ, he vowed to abandon more, even "all things"—every pleasant blessing remaining in his life—if necessary, to finish his course: "I [am prepared to also] count *all things* but loss [for Christ]" (Phil. 3:8a); or, "Not only those things, but I think that *all things* are worth nothing compared with the greatness of knowing Christ" (NCV). So after his kenosis Paul wasn't regretful, withdrawn, and self-protecting. Rather he was ready for another, if God willed.[28]

Consequently God who had "highly exalted" Christ after His kenosis began honoring Paul also (cf. Phil. 2:9). Paul's rising began when Christ released him to teach in Antioch and the next year sent him on the first of three official (and one unofficial) highly fruitful apostolic missions.[29] In sovereign wisdom God intermingled these uplifting ministry experiences with sobering persecutions that, in Paul's words, kept him humble (2 Cor. 12:7; cf. Mark 10:28–30).[30] Enduring these deadly perils also qualified Paul as being, like his Lord, "obedient unto death, even the death of the [or his spiritual] cross" (Phil. 2:8).

---

28. Every day that Paul pressed forward in ministry, knowing more persecution could come at any time, proved this. Some twentieth-century Chinese ministers who, after suffering years of terrible imprisonment and torture for Christ's sake, vowed the same. If necessary, they were ready to return to prison rather than register their churches with the (Communist) government-controlled and monitored, theologically liberal, Three Self Patriotic Movement Church. Thousands of fully committed Christians do the same daily around the world.
29. Paul's three official apostolic missions are recorded in Acts 13:1–14:27; 15:40–18:22; and 18:23–21:3. His unofficial fourth mission was his trip to and ministry in Rome while in Roman custody (27:1–28:31).
30. For a sampling of Paul's sobering sufferings—rejections, hardships, abuses, imprisonments, stonings, death plots, and other cross-like humiliations for the ministry's sake—see Acts 13:50; 14:19; 16:16–24; 21:27–36; 23:1–2; 23:12–13; 24:27.

Therefore God also gave Paul "a name...above" (Phil. 2:9) many others in biblical literature and church history. To this day Christians everywhere honor the name "Paul," studying his letters, teaching his theology, marveling at his ministry, wondering at his sufferings, and praying for his grace. In Paul's time even Peter acknowledged Paul's writings were inspired and lauded their profound wisdom (2 Pet. 3:15–16), though Jews continued demonizing him, Athenians dismissing him, and Romans ignoring him (2 Pet. 3:15–16). Millions since have symbolically "bowed the knee" to Paul's Christ-given apostolic authority by obeying his teachings and have "confessed" his revelations and prophecies are inspired (Phil. 2:10), giving "glory to God" (2:11) for Paul's ministry (Gal. 1:24). Finally, as an overcomer, Paul will rule with Christ, receiving a position of authority in the Millennium (Rev. 2:26–27; 3:21). Many then will figuratively "bow" their knees to Christ's delegated authority vested in Paul in whatever office he holds just as the Egyptians bowed to Pharaoh's authority delegated to Joseph.[31]

Thus, ultimately, the servant will be as his Lord—emptied, humbled, and raised to honor and power in God! Here's food for thought.

Compared to Christ's divine glory, and even Paul's religious "flesh-glory," the things that are gain to us may seem infinitesimally small. But the same principles apply to us that applied to them. Let us too, then, walk faithfully with Christ as He leads us through our own kenosis. A wonderful, new Spirit-filled life awaits...and exciting, new, eternal goals.

---

31. Note how Pharaoh's authority was comingled with Joseph's decrees in his name (Gen. 41:40–44, 53–57).

3:7–15 Paul's new goals. After tearing up his formerly impressive Jewish résumé, Paul authored a list of his new goals as a Christian. These spiritual life objectives were to:

1. BE FOUND "IN HIM" (3:9). When Christ returns (3:20), Paul wants to be found not living in sin or self but entirely "in him" (3:9)—in Christ's body, as a living, abiding, growing believer-cell; in Christ's fellowship, walking ever more closely with Him daily; in Christ's ministry, serving Him with increasing effectiveness in His calling and gifting.

2. REST IN GOD'S RIGHTEOUSNESS (3:9). Finished with seeking right relationship with God by works of the law, Paul trusted Christ alone and rested in "the righteousness…of God" (3:9), which he received by grace and "by faith" in Christ crucified (Eph. 2:8).

3. KNOW CHRIST PERSONALLY (3:10). Paul desires to "know him in an experiential way" (v. 10, WUEST), not superficially, but "deeply and intimately" (AMP); not merely in public worship, academic study, or by others' testimonies but in his daily personal experience. By steadily and prayerfully seeking, studying, obeying, and worshipping Christ, Paul aims to increasingly know every aspect of His character and ways

(Ps. 27:4; John 8:31; Matt. 7:23; 11:28–30).[32] This persistent, passionate pursuit of *more of Christ* is the essence of eternal life (John 17:3), our heavenly vocation, and the source of the zeal that propels us toward the "mark" of fulfilling our destiny in Christ.

4. EXPERIENCE CHRIST'S RESURRECTION "POWER" (3:10). Paul desires to know "the power shown by his resurrection" (3:10, PHILLIPS), again, not academically but "experientially" (WUEST). This divine power (Greek, *dunamis*) is the same that energized "his resurrection" (3:10). Paul hopes not merely to study but also to witness, receive, and minister this power (Acts 1:8; Mark 16:17–20; Eph. 1:17–18; 3:20; Luke 18:27).[33] This same power that works physical miracles also brings spiritual rebirths and revivals (Acts 3:19) and strengthens us to suffer long adversities with a joyful spirit (Col. 1:11–12).

5. EXPERIENCE CHRIST'S "SUFFERINGS" (3:10). Knowing the deepest bonds are formed when people suffer together, and that Christ left some

---

32. Specifically, he aimed to know Jesus' acts, words, and ministry as revealed in the Gospels; and His heart (John 17:1–26), humility (Phil. 2:5–6), servantship (2:7; John 8:29), obedience (Phil. 2:8), sufferings (3:10), joy (Matt. 25:21, 23; John 15:11), truth (17:17), voice (our recalling His Word opportunely, Acts 11:16), love, correction (Rev. 3:19), glory (1:10–17), eternal power and authority (5:11–14), guidance (Rom. 8:14; John 10:4), peace (14:27; Col. 3:14), presence (John 14:21), appearing (14:1–3; 1 Thess. 4:16–18); judgeship (John 5:22, 27; Acts 10:42; 2 Tim. 4:1), and generalship (Rev. 19:11–16, 19, 21; Ps. 24:7–10).
33. This "power of the Spirit" (Luke 4:14; Acts 10:38) was first seen in Paul's ministry in Acts 13:9–12. Other manifestations of the Spirit's miraculous power followed (Acts 14:3; 14:8–10; 14:19–20; 16:16–18; 19:11–12; 20:6–12; 28:1–6; 28:7–10).

of His (non-redemptive) sufferings for Christians to bear (Col. 1:24), Paul desired to experience "his [Christ's] sufferings" (3:10). These adversities come for Jesus' name, righteousness, and truth's sake (Matt. 5:10–12), not due to sin or selfishness (1 Pet. 4:15). This "joint-participation" (WUEST) in suffering is our Christian duty (1:29).[34] Though naturally bitter, suffering brings us the sweetest fellowship with Jesus (Dan. 3:25; Acts 27:20, 23–24) and other sufferers (2 Tim. 1:16–18; Phil. 1:7; 4:14, 18) and brings God the sweetest worship (Acts 16:24–25).[35]

6. BE CONFORMED TO CHRIST'S "DEATH" (3:10). To "conform" is to shape something to a mold or model. Paul saw Christ's utterly obedient spirit as a model. He sought to be "obedient unto death" (2:8) in his sufferings for Christ's sake—injustice, betrayal, cruel treatment, public humiliation, all for doing God's will—and so experience Christlike death in: mortification, or the death of the control of his sin and self-will (Col. 3:5, 3–10; 1 Cor. 15:31); meekness, or the death of his pride (excessive self-esteem) (1 Pet. 5:5–6; Luke 14:10; Rom. 12:3); and ultimately

---

34. For Paul, this meant being hated, denounced, and persecuted by the very Jewish relatives, people, and leaders who formerly respected him (Acts 9:20–24, 29).

35. Suffering also marks the true minister. When pressed to defend his apostolic call and ministry, Paul pointed to not his many converts, church plants, miracles, travels, or writings but to his sufferings as proof that his apostleship was authentic (2 Cor. 11:22–12:11). In the same spirit, many leaders in some of China's most prolific house church networks consider their sufferings a primary qualification for leadership. See Luke Wesley, *Stories From China: Fried Rice for the Soul* (Waynesboro, GA: Authentic Media, 2005), 118.

martyrdom, the death of his body as a consummate sacrifice and witness for Christ's sake (Acts 7:59–60; 14:19).

7. EXPERIENCE CHRIST'S RESURRECTION (3:11). Since Jesus' death led to His resurrection, and resurrection is the portal to eternal life, Paul yearned that his sufferings too would lead to his resurrection with divine favor: "that one way or another I will experience the resurrection" (3:11, NLT). We too may be raised in Christ's favor:

  A. From spiritual death to spiritual life, when we're born again (John 3:3–8; 5:24) or revived after backsliding (Luke 15:24, 32)
  B. From carnal (unspiritual, unbiblical) thinking and living to spiritual attitudes and habits (Rom. 6:1–2, 4; 8:1; 8:6; Gal. 5:16)
  C. From spiritual "death" experiences—seasons of discouraging defeats, delays, and apparent failures of God's promises, prophecies, or ministries (John 12:24; Rom. 4:19–21)—to new seasons of joyful fulfillment
  D. From physical death or near-death experiences to fully restored vitality, when raised from deathly illness or injury

or resuscitated after expiration (John 11:43–44; 12:9; Acts 9:39–41; 14:20)[36]

E. From bodily decay to a glorified body, when by His supernatural re-creative power Christ raises our bodies from graves, tombs, dust, and waters and renders them immortal (Job 19:26; 1 Cor. 15:50–55; 1 Thess. 4:13–16; John 5:28–29; 1 John 3:2–3; Rev. 20:12–13)

8. BECOME SPIRITUALLY MATURE (3:14). The "mark" (lit. *goal, target*) Paul was pressing toward in his personal life was twofold. The first part was Christian perfection, or spiritual maturity, which manifests in consistently spiritual (Christlike) thinking and living. Acts reveals that by God's grace he reached this goal in life. It was also his central goal in ministry "to present every man perfect in Christ Jesus" (Col. 1:28; 1:22). Scripture, including Jesus' sayings, urges us also to be "thus minded" (Phil. 3:15).[37]

---

36. God occasionally, though rarely, grants supernatural resuscitations so (a) people can finish their life works and (b) Christ's unchanging and compassionate works of power may be known (Heb. 13:8). Christ raised three people from death, Peter raised one, Paul another (and apparently was raised himself once, Acts 14:19–20), Luther's prayers raised Melanchthon, and many others since have been brought back after unexpectedly expiring. Medical science (by CPR, AEDs) is reviving people every day that only a half century earlier would have passed away. I personally know two such individuals who've experienced this in the last few months, one who was without pulse for eleven minutes (my eighty-six-year-old father, Rudy Hinnant) and another for twenty-eight minutes (my friend David Earl). Can't God, then, also supernaturally revive expired ones for His sovereign purposes, if He sovereignly wills? On Luther's prayer, see: http://home.comcast.net/~gracelife/rim/luthheal.htm (accessed March 31, 2015).
37. For other scriptures calling us to seek spiritual maturity, see: Matthew 5:48; 13:20–21; 19:21; Luke 8:13–14, 15; Romans 12:1–2; 2 Corinthians 7:1; 13:9, 11; Ephesians 4:12; 1 Thessalonians 3:10; Hebrews 6:1–2; James 1:4; 3:3; 1 Peter 5:10; 1 John 2:5; 4:12.

9. **Fulfill Christ's calling** (3:12). The second half of Paul's "mark" was to complete the ministry works for which Christ apprehended him in Damascus (3:12–13; Acts 26:15–18; 9:15–16; Eph. 2:10). To "apprehend" this he forgot the past, focused on the present, and steadily pursued the goal: "I follow after...[by] forgetting...[and] reaching forth...[and] I press [on]" (3:12–14).

10. **Receive Christ's rewards** (3:14). Paul had a clear hope Christ would reward his service and sacrifices (Heb. 6:10; 11:6). Using athletic language, he described himself running a race to receive a "prize" for his faithfulness and sufferings (Phil. 3:14).[38] Winners of ancient Olympic events won olive branch wreaths, red woolen ribbons, and palm branches.[39] Paul's anticipated "prize" consisted of Christ's commendation, nearness to Him in the kingdom, promotion to higher service there, a "hundredfold" restoration of his losses,[40] and other joys (Matt. 25:21, 23; Luke 19:17; Rev. 2:26–27; 3:12, 20–21; 2 Cor. 5:9–10).

---

38. Paul was racing against Satan's rulers of darkness, not other Christian light-bearers. His fellow Christians, including ministers, were his friends, not his competitors, those who by their love and prayers helped him run around or through satanic hindrances, entanglements, and barriers to finish the race Jesus planned for him ("my course," 2 Tim. 4:7). To Paul, "winning" meant faithfully finishing that course, not accomplishing more than other ministers.
39. See http://www.olympic.org/Documents/Reports/EN/en_report_658.pdf (accessed March 31, 2015).
40. For the crosses we bear and natural blessings we relinquish to follow His call, Christ promised a "hundredfold" (something much greater than our loss) recompense in this life (Mark 10:28–31; Matt. 10:39b).

Pressing Toward New Goals!

Paul's lofty new goals show us he practiced what he preached. He exhorted the Colossians to "set your affection on things above, not on things on the earth" (Col. 3:2), and his life goals prove his own heart also was set on heavenly, not worldly, ends. Is yours?

Are Paul's new goals yours? Or does your heart passion burn for other ends that, frankly, will pass when this present Christless social order passes? If so, reset your heart and the direction of your "race" by making Paul's spiritual objectives yours: "Let those of us who are mature think this way" (Phil. 3:15, ESV).

3:4 Playing the fool to make others wise. By briefly boasting to the Philippians of his former religious "flesh"—how great a Pharisee he had been (3:5–6)!—Paul lowered himself to speak as a chattering, boastful fool (Prov. 10:8, 10). "Whoever thinks he can rely on that [his flesh], I can outdo him" (Phil. 3:4, MOFFATT).[41] Why did he speak as a fool?

To make us wise. Paul hoped the Philippians, and every Christian who learned of this epistle,[42] would pause to consider the outstanding religious "flesh" he gave up to pursue the humble but spiritually rich path Christ set before him, and then choose to follow Paul's footsteps in their own lives. Have we made that choice?

---

41. Paul also "spoke as a fool" to the Corinthians when to disprove the boastings of false apostles he was forced to assert the authenticity of his apostolic call (which they were denying) by among other things listing his many sufferings for Christ's sake (2 Cor. 11:16–33; 12:11–12).
42. Since it was the early Christians' practice to copy apostolic letters and share them with other churches, Paul would have understood that he was instructing not only the Philippians but also many other Christians to whom his letter would be read aloud (Col. 4:16; Acts 15:30–31; 16:4).

Are we following Paul's footsteps in humility? Or are we still glorying in our religious past or any other aspect of our old life and its false paths to fulfillment? Also, do we like Paul love Christ enough to look foolish (weak, defeated, humiliated, insignificant; 1 Cor. 4:9–10) for a season, if necessary, to finish our obedience and receive spiritual power, discernment, and wisdom to make others wise?

3:4–14 The chief of zeal. During his years as a rising Pharisee Paul had been very zealous (3:6; Gal. 1:13–14). When he abandoned his former religious ambition to become a Christian (Phil. 3:7) his core enthusiasm remained unchanged. The new Paul was just as zealous as the old—but for new spiritual goals.

These verses (3:4–14) describe a man all-out for Judaism becoming all-out for Christ. Instead of longing for Pharisaic religious success, Paul became insatiably hungry for more of Jesus: "Now I long to know Christ" (3:10, PHILLIPS). Acts and the epistles show repeatedly Paul was just as enthusiastic, driven, fearless, and indomitable as a Christian as he had been while a Pharisee (Acts 14:19, 20–21; 21:13). Nothing about him was lukewarm; he was all in or all out but never in between.[43] Yet Paul seemed oblivious to his great zeal, as if he thought it was normal for a Christian. It was in another area that he felt himself the greatest.

To Timothy he described himself self-deprecatingly as "chief" of sinners since before his conversion he had severely persecuted the church (1 Tim. 1:13–15). But he was in fact the undisputed chief of zeal. His lavishly passionate language—"I long," "I follow after," "[I'm] reaching forth," "[I] press toward the mark

---

43. Paul was the *opposite* of the Laodiceans whom Jesus rebuked for lukewarmness (Rev. 3:14–16). We may conclude Jesus loved Paul's enthusiasm as much as He loathed the Laodiceans' indifference.

Pressing Toward New Goals!

for the prize," (Phil. 3:10, Phillips; 3:12, 13, 14)—betrays a flaming heart and dynamic spiritual lifestyle constantly moving forward in God's truth and work. It also suggests one reason Paul overcame his zealous antagonists: he out-zealed them! Paul's experience wasn't the first time a zealous sinner became a zealous saint.

It happens more often than we think. Many unbelievers who are very enthusiastic about their vocation, profession, art, trade, sport, or religion become equally enthusiastic for Christ upon conversion. And God loves it! Why?

God is zealous—burning, ardent, glowing, focused, intense about everything He loves and does, especially the key fulfillments of His redemptive plan! Prophesying of Christ's future millennial reign, Isaiah declared, "The zeal of the Lord of hosts will perform this" (Isa. 9:7); or, "the passionate commitment of the Lord...will make this happen" (NLT). Because He is "passionately committed" in everything He does, He wants us to be the same: "I would thou wert...hot" (Rev. 3:15). His Word commands us to be zealous for *Him*—His truth, presence, people, calling, return, purposes, and ways of living and working—as Paul was (Phil. 3:10). He asks us to do "whatever" we do zealously, or "heartily, as to the Lord" (Col. 3:23) and "with thy might" (Eccles. 9:10). He honors zeal and inspired Paul to laud Epaphras for praying constantly and "fervently" with "great zeal" (Col. 4:12–13). He laments when our zeal declines: "Thou hast left thy first love" (Rev. 2:4). And He challenges us to receive all necessary correction (including that for lack of zeal!) zealously: "Be zealous...and repent" (Rev. 3:19). Vital as it is, raw zeal is not enough.

To please God and benefit us and His people, our zeal must be correctly informed. We must be zealous for truth, not error (Rom.

10:1–3). Our zeal must also be controlled. Furnaces are constructive, but wildfires are destructive (Gen. 34:1–31; 2 Sam. 21:1–2).[44] Our zeal must be limited, not excessive, to avoid burnout. We want our zeal to "consume" us spiritually, but not physically (Ps. 69:9, NAS)! Paul heard God's call for zeal and responded, pleasing Him and becoming an exemplary leader in Christian zeal. Will I do the same? Will you?

Are you apathetic or ardent, less or more committed to Christ than you were in your former worldly pursuits? For the kingdom and King's sake, imitate the chief of zeal!

3:12–14 Paul's plan for pursuing perfection. Paul shares his plan for pursuing spiritual perfection. Spiritual perfection is not sinless perfection (or the supposed "eradication" of our sin nature in this life) but rather *spiritual maturity* marked by the full growth and complete development that produces spiritual adulthood[45] or consistent Christlikeness.[46]

The steps Paul took toward this goal of spiritual perfection are:

1. NEVER ASSUME PERFECTION (3:12, 13). "I count not myself to have apprehended [perfection]" (3:13). Paul realized the pride of presumption stagnates growth. All seeking ends when we

---

44. Three striking examples of excessive, misdirected, and destructive zeal for God during the Medieval Age are the Crusades, the Inquisition, and "Christian" persecutions and expulsions of European Jews.
45. J. B. Phillips translates "perfect" as "spiritually adult" (Phil. 3:15). See J. B. Phillips, *The New Testament in Modern English*, revised edition (New York: MacMillan Publishing Co., 1972), 415.
46. Every born-again Christian is positionally perfect before God by virtue of being clothed with Christ's righteousness and having His nature within—who alone is intrinsically, sinlessly perfect. Our spiritual perfection is a process, not an experience, in which Christ's perfections (graces, fruit, Gal. 5:22–23) increasingly manifest in our lives by the work of the Holy Spirit as we continue trusting and obeying Him.

attain our goals, so if we assume attainment prematurely, our seeking ceases...short of perfection. So Paul "cast down" self-flattering thoughts (2 Cor. 10:5) and any line of reasoning that concluded he was already "brought to that place of absolute spiritual maturity beyond which there is no progress" (Phil. 3:12, Wuest) and clung to the humble facts. This sober attitude kept him humble, hungry, and growing.[47]

2. Have a clear spiritual goal (3:12). "I follow after [my goal]...this one thing I do" (3:12–13). With singular focus Paul pursued a two-part goal: (a) to be spiritually "perfect" (3:14–15), and (b) to "apprehend" (fully grasp and discharge) Christ's call to ministry on his life (3:12; Eph. 2:10; Acts 26:15–18). This goal was clear, not obscure; heavenly, not worldly; centered on pleasing Jesus, not Paul or others; Paul's only life goal, not one of many dividing his affections and energies (Gal. 1:10; James 1:8).

3. Forget past achievements and failures (3:13). "Forgetting those things which are behind" (3:13). Good or bad, our past is gone; we can't change it. But our present and future are before us, ready to be made. Never glory in past accomplishments or mourn past failures, as one mood leaves you too high, the other too low, and both

---

[47]. This is true for churches and ministries as well as individual believers. None of us dare assume we have arrived. "Those who think they have grace enough give proof that they have little enough, or rather that they have none at all; because, wherever there is true grace, there is a desire of more grace." See Henry, *Commentary in One Volume*, 1866.

stunt current progress. Ponder past triumphs and defeats long enough to learn from them, and then release them into Jesus' all-powerful redeeming hands. We can't grasp the future while still clinging to the past.

4. REACH OUT FOR NEW THINGS IN CHRIST (3:13). Paul bravely and steadily reached out to "those things which are before" or things he'd never experienced before (3:13). He refused to fear change or new experiences or challenges, choosing instead to trust the Holy Spirit's sovereign guidance unquestioningly (Prov. 3:5–6; Acts 16:10). He was ever content but never rutted in his present experience, or as the hymnist wrote, "Ready to go, ready to stay...ready to do His will!"[48] Never fear God-led changes, only self-led stagnation. Reach out and embrace new studies, works, missions, ministries, tasks, tests, and other challenges in God's will. Forward movement keeps your soul fresh, strong, and refilled with the Spirit.[49]

5. PRESS ON FOR THE "PRIZE" (3:14). Paul had only one gear: forward! "I press forward...to press on to the goal" (3:12, 14, MOFFATT). This "pressing" speaks of his persistence. Whatever his days—exciting, mundane, painful, or happy—Paul persisted in his spiritual duties. Why? He

---

48. "Ready" by A. C. Palmer. Public domain.
49. In the words of Robert Browning, "Ah, but a man's reach should exceed his grasp, or what's a heaven for." See Robert Browning, *Men and Women* (Boston, MA: Ticknor & Fields, 1864), "Andrea del Sarto." See also http://www.poetryfoundation.org/poem/173001 (accessed March 31, 2015).

knew rewards awaited if he faithfully persisted in walking and working in Jesus' ways. Are you persisting in His ways of prayer, Bible study, intercession, service, giving, enduring with difficult people, and other spiritual duties? Need more inspiration? Remember:

> A. YOUR CALLING IS "HIGH" (3:14). Indeed it's uncommon, otherworldly, heavenly, from Jesus Himself. Just as surely as He called the ancient apostles (Mark 3:13–19) and prophets (Jer. 1:4–10), the sovereign Lord has tapped you for His service. Let this honor lift and ennoble your spirit to bear persisting opposition, challenges, and dishonors with grace, even joy.
>
> B. A "PRIZE" AWAITS (3:14). Spiritually awake, Paul kept his eyes on the prize. He was sure Christ would reward him, in His time and way, for all his "works" of devotion, service, and suffering (2 Cor. 5:10; 2 John 8; Heb. 11:6; 6:10; Gal. 6:7–8; 2 Chron. 15:7; 1 Cor. 15:58). This confidence he would reap all the good he sowed kept him sowing, awake, inspired.

We know this plan worked for Paul, because in his last epistle (AD 67–68) he announced he was ready to go home, he had finished his course (completed his ministry), he had kept his faith (thus it, and he, was purified, proven, and mature), and a "crown" (reward) awaited him in heaven (2 Tim. 4:6–8). So Paul's plan for pursuing perfection was, well, perfect!

It still is, if you and I desire to be spiritually perfect and are willing to follow Paul's plan. As stated earlier, the Spirit through Paul urges our hearty agreement and compliance: "Let all who are spiritually mature agree on these things" (Phil. 3:15, NLT).

3:14 Our high calling. Paul declares our calling as Christians is "high" (3:14). And it is, so high it's the highest calling!

This world has many elevated vocations and professions (education, medicine, social service, government, etc.) that inspire their practitioners with the knowledge that they're helping lift others to a higher plane of life. And they are. But the humblest Christian has a loftier calling.

We're called to live and work in God's higher ways: spiritual thinking (Rom. 8:6; Phil. 2:5; Col. 3:1), spiritual life disciplines, Christ's values (Matt. 6:33; Ps. 71:19, NLT), closeness to Jesus, divine love, Christlike ministry to others all around us (Matt. 20:28), sweet unity with other Christians, and the hope of heavenly bliss.[50] As we study and live in these heavenly things daily, Christ steadily elevates our lives in spirit, thought, habit, and influence until we reach the ultimate elevation—His presence!

But Satan has other, lower plans. He intends to use his demons and servants to pull us down from our high calling: "They plan to topple me from my high position" (Ps. 62:4, NLT); or, "They plan to push me from my place" (MOFFATT). Typically he does so through or by:

- DISTANCE—encouraging us to live independently, at a distance from Christ, instead of in daily dependence on Him through devotional reading,

---

50. Specifically we eagerly anticipate: (1) a coming translation and heavenly rendezvous with Jesus (the Rapture, Phil. 3:20–21); (2) life in a utopian, thousand-year, Christ-ruled kingdom on this present earth (the Millennium, Rev. 20:1–6); and (3) eternal life in God's presence in a pristine new heaven and earth and a New Jerusalem populated only by the redeemed (Rev. 21–22).

prayer, worship in the "secret place" (Ps. 91:1; Matt. 6:3–4, 6, 17–18), and fellowship with spiritually minded believers

- DIVERSION—trying to confuse us as to our gifting and calling so we'll work at cross-purposes with Christ instead of sweet union with Him in His yoke (Matt. 11:28–30)

- DISTRACTION—trying to entangle and preoccupy us with worldly interests and activities until we have no time left to seek God, intercede, or serve in ministry (2 Tim. 2:4)

- DISOBEDIENCE—tempting us to not comply with God's Word, call, or guidance

- DIVISION—trying to separate us from other Christians, whose fellowship and assistance we need, by provoking us to hold unloving or unforgiving attitudes toward them

- DISBELIEF—trying to convince us we're so carnal, weak, or foolish we'll never be able to think and live spiritually and there's no use in praying for ourselves or others

- DEGENERATION—luring us to abandon our spiritual quest and return to unspiritual living, fleshly sins, or wasteful indulgences (2 Tim. 4:10; Luke 21:34)

- DISLOYALTY—encouraging us to abandon good Christians and ministers merely because they're experiencing defeat, distress, reproach, or loss (Acts 13:13; 15:37–38)

- DISCOURAGEMENT—trying to get us to condemn or pity ourselves over sin habits, failures, rejections, or unrelieved adversities

- DEFIANCE—trying to use our adversaries' relentlessly defiant opposition of our walk or work to crush our hopes and initiatives (Matt. 13:21)

- DECEPTION—spreading false teachings that confuse us, block our fellowship with Christ and other Christians, hinder our spiritual growth, and spoil our fruitfulness

- DESIRE—surprisingly, urging us to excessive zeal, knowing fanaticism, asceticism, or rushing into ministry unprepared all hinder spiritual growth and divine usefulness (2 Sam. 18:19–32)

These and other devilish devices halt spiritual elevation—our rising steadily higher in heavenly thinking, living, and ministry. We won't escape them automatically; steady effort will be required. Why?

It's easy to come down from "seeking those things which are above" (Col. 3:1) to unspiritual thinking and living. The daily pressure of critics, demons, monotonous duties, and "all kinds of trials" (1 Pet. 1:6, NIV) often leave our hearts low and heavy. In these uninspired valleys many stop "pressing toward" the "mark" of our high calling (Phil. 3:14) and accept spiritual defeat as inevitable. But it's not. Our calling remains high but, by God's grace, well within our reach. However low and long our oppressive situations, we must refuse to stay down in spirit and, remembering our high calling, rise to it.

In your present valley, are you resigning to lowness or rising higher? Remember Paul's inspiring example to the Philippians, and keep pressing onward and upward in Christ: "I keep going on, trying to grasp that purpose for which Christ Jesus grasped me" (Phil. 3:12, PHILLIPS).

3:15 He still corrects wrong thinking. Paul assured the Philippians that if they were "otherwise minded," not thinking spiritually or from God's viewpoint (in this context not seriously pursuing the "mark" of spiritual maturity, 3:12–14), the Lord would faithfully "reveal even this unto you" (3:15). More broadly, this shows Paul believed the Lord monitors and corrects our thinking. Are you "otherwise minded"?

Are your typical daily attitudes immature, still self-serving and self-centered rather than Christ-centered and love-driven? Is your thinking carnal more often than spiritual? Are your life goals only of this world and not anchored in Christ's coming kingdom? Do you address challenges and adversities with your human reason alone and forget to apply your faith in God? Are your beliefs heretical instead of biblically sound? Are you apathetic and dismissive about spiritual maturity instead of being eager to study and seek it as Paul was? If in these or other areas of thought, intent, or desire your thinking isn't Christlike, Christ wants to correct you.

Many imagine that once we're saved, He's content to leave us as we are. Oh, how wrong they are! Christ is a patient, persistent, passionate perfectionist. From the moment we receive the Savior on earth to the moment He receives us in heaven, He continues transforming us in every area of our soul and life.

This spiritual maturity progresses as we renew our minds to think consistently like Christ.[51] Thus He constantly corrects us when our thinking is anything less than His (scriptural).

We see Christ frequently doing this in His interactions with His twelve disciples (Luke 9:48, 50, 55–56).[52] He even tried to lovingly correct His enemies' wrong thinking whenever He could (Mark 3:1–5; Matt. 22:21, 29–33). After His ascension He continued doing so with the seven churches of Asia Minor (Rev. 2–3; esp. 3:17). The writer to the Hebrews assures us Christ's corrective work continues and is a sure sign of His love (Heb. 12:5–6) and, if we receive it, our sonship (12:7–8). How faithful and loving of Him!

Isaiah assures us our Father will send us a word of correction if we "turn" from His guidance (Isa. 30:21). Paul here adds the comforting promise that Christ will alert us when our thinking is off.[53] How He does so isn't specified. He may correct us by His Spirit working quietly in our conscience, by His Word as we read or study it, or in many other ways. Often He sends correction through spiritually mature ministers and elders He places in our lives to help us grow (1 Thess. 5:12–13; Heb. 13:17). Are you ready and willing to receive His correction?

Whenever Christ alerts you that you're "otherwise minded," receive His correction—and thank the perfect One for patiently perfecting your thinking!

---

51. We renew our minds to think like Christ only by steadily studying God's Word and trustfully and submissively obeying it in our daily tests (Rom. 12:2; 2 Tim. 2:15).
52. For more examples, see: Matthew 18:1–4; 18:21–22; 19:13–15; Mark 3:31–35; Luke 7:39, 40–47; 19:11; John 20:24–29; 21:20–22; Acts 1:6–8.
53. This means only that He will alert us to our wrong thinking, not force us to change it. He leaves full leeway for the exercise of our free will (Gen. 4:6–7).

3:16 Walking by the same rule. Paul urged the Philippians to continue pursuing spiritual maturity by living by the same "rule" (3:16), or standard of righteous conduct, they had already been taught (John 8:31; Phil. 4:9).[54] At base Christianity is not merely a creed, theology, liturgy, or set of rites but a walk, a lifestyle, a relationship, and Christ's teaching gives us the "rule" for that life. So Paul redirects his readers to right living as Christ defined it, or "his righteousness" (Matt. 6:33).[55] Paraphrasing, he urged, "Keep living up to what you've learned and believed, to Christ's pure teaching, and don't lower or change your standards of faith and right living for any reason." Thus they would progress toward spiritual maturity (3:12–15).

This is a call to Christian integrity, or wholeness of character in pursuing faithfulness to God: "Only let us hold true to what we have already attained and walk and order our lives by that" (3:16, AMP). It's easy to step back from what "we have already attained," because it is very demanding—requiring constant self-examination and confession of sin, purity in thought as well as deed, a life of studying and obeying Scripture, faithfulness in duty or ministry, the willingness to suffer for so living, and the humility to love, not loathe, our enemies (Matt. 5:38–48). Will we hold tightly to this, "his righteousness" (Matt. 6:33), without conforming to any other standards—the teachings of other religions, or the values of our generation, family, or friends, or those of our neighbors, coworkers, fellow students,

---

54. "Rule" is translated from the Greek word *kanōn*, meaning a "cane" or straight reed or rod. Figuratively this refers to the Word of God, the spiritually straight rule or measuring stick we use to determine the true standard of Christian faith, practice, and teaching. Hence we call those books we hold to be inspired "the canon (*kanōn*) of Scripture." See J. Strong, *A Concise Dictionary of the Words in the Greek Testament and The Hebrew Bible* (Bellingham, WA: Logos Bible Software, 2009), s. v. "*kanōn*."
55. As Jesus did His disciples (Luke 6:46–49) and James his readers (James 1:22–25).

or associates? Christian integrity in motive, thought, and life demands a constant supply of God's grace, and Paul assures us God will give it and we'll find it sufficient for us to "do all things" through Him (Phil. 4:13; 2 Cor. 12:9). Though difficult, this life is also very rewarding.

Living faithfully by Christ's "rule" will bring us rich benefits. It will win Christ's favor, increased closeness to Him, more of His Spirit, steadier peace, increased joy, biblical insight, approval for service (2 Tim. 2:15), new commissions (Acts 13:1–2), and the deep assurance we'll be rewarded at the finish line or "mark" (Phil. 3:14) of our Christian service (2 Tim. 2:5; 4:6–8). Are you walking by "the same rule" today?

3:16 Think like me—maturely! After saying the spiritual mature will be "thus minded" (3:15), Paul exhorted the Philippians to "mind the same thing" (4:16), or, "Let us be of the same mind" (NKJV) or "the same thing think" (YLT). By "same thing" he was referring most immediately to his foregoing theme of pursuing spiritual maturity (3:12–15). Thus he urged them "think like me, maturely!"[56] This was no surprise.

Knowing Christians are thought-driven creatures, Paul often addressed our thought life. He ordered the Romans to transform their lives and souls "by the renewing of your mind" (Rom. 12:2). He warned them of the consequences of remaining "carnally minded" and the benefits of becoming "spiritually minded" (8:6). He further advised them against proud thoughts and in favor of humble ones: "not to think more highly" of themselves but "to think soberly" (12:3). To the Galatians he

---

56. Numerous excellent translations (NIV, NAS, NLT, ESV, NCV, ISV) omit this charge to "mind the same thing" (Phil. 3:16), yet on reflection how can we "walk by the same rule" (3:16) of Christ's righteousness if we don't "mind the same thing" as Paul and other spiritually mature ones?

revealed proud thinking leads to self-deception (Gal. 6:3). He challenged the Corinthians to not think too highly of one minister in comparison with others (1 Cor. 4:6). He charged his ministerial protégé Timothy to shun thoughtless talk and study Scripture diligently: "Study to show thyself approved unto God" (2 Tim. 2:15). Later in the Philippian epistle he charged his readers to "think on" things that were worthy, virtuous, or exemplary (Phil. 4:8). Why the exhortations to think right?

Paul knew this was the key to living right. To change the life one must change the mind. Spiritually mature Christians think maturely, whereas chronically immature ones do not. I'm sure he also remembered Jesus stating we should love God with "all thy mind" (Luke 10:27). The evidence suggests the Philippians responded to Paul, "minding the same things" he did, and maturing.

Are you responding? Stirring your mind to read, think, meditate on, and discuss Scripture, teachings, counsels, and testimonies that inspire spiritual maturity? Why not? As you "mind the same thing," you'll find fresh inspiration to "walk by the same rule" (3:16).

3:17–19 Live like me—and Jesus! Paul unashamedly presented his lifestyle as an example for the Philippians to follow, not once but twice in this epistle (3:17; 4:9). Why? He knew he was following Christ's example. So he was really saying, "Follow me as I follow Jesus."

How confident he was to be able to say without misgivings, "Take me as your example for Christian living," or, "Copy me" (3:17, MOFFATT). This is the language of a man utterly convinced of the truth and accuracy of what he's believing, teaching, and practicing. Paul recommended his life and ministry example often, "everywhere in every church" (1 Cor. 4:17). He clarified this by adding he wanted his Christian students to follow not all his attitudes, mannerisms, and habits but his Christlike ones, "my ways which are in Christ" (1 Cor. 4:17). No yearning for hero worship or mindless conformity here. To the contrary Paul wanted believers to follow his example with their eyes wide open, so if he should depart from Christ's ways (as on occasion even Moses, David, and more recently Peter had, Gal. 2:11–14), discerning it they would follow his wisdom but not his errors.

To show his "follow me" wasn't laced with any delusion of personal superiority, Paul added, "And observe those who walk according to the pattern you have in us" (Phil. 3:17, NAS). Or, "Follow others living like me as we follow Christ." Paul further ordered his ministerial protégés, Timothy and Titus, to be examples to the churches (1 Tim. 4:12; Titus 2:7) and, as already noted, without hesitation recommended Timothy's example (Phil. 2:19–24), as well as Epaphroditus' (2:25–30). So clearly Paul understood his spiritually exemplary life was but one of many, Christlike but not singular. Thus his thinking was humble, holy, and healthy and his counsel safe.

In the next two verses he added a bold, vital warning:

> But *don't* follow the beliefs and practices of the "enemies of the cross" (false teachers and self-serving ministers). Weep for them, with me, because their "end" (goal), "God" (ruler), "glory" (delight, boast), and "mind" (thinking) are all tragically wrong. They take pride in things other than Christ, His glory, and His kingdom. They think carnally, not according to the Spirit's viewpoint expressed in God's Word. They teach the Scriptures but don't make scriptural decisions

in their private lives and ministries. Their goals are all temporal, of this world, not of God's eternal purposes and kingdom.

—Philippians 3:18–19, author's paraphrase

Such warnings weren't peculiar to Paul. The Apostles Peter and John also warned the saints of misleaders and heretics and redirected them to follow godly leaders (2 Pet. 2:1–22; 1 John 4:1; 3 John 9–12). Jesus did the same (Matt. 23:1–33, esp. v. 3).

Are you confident enough of God's truths, grace, and ways, and your daily practice of them, that you can say, "Copy my example"? Are you bold enough to warn others to avoid indisputably false teachers and self-serving ministers, yet humble enough to realize that many others model Christ as much as you? If so, you're living like Paul—and Jesus.

3:18–19 The "enemies of the cross." Weeping, Paul warns of "enemies of the cross." Their opposition was apparently not so much against Christ's general claims, sayings, or ways as it was "the cross." They seem to fall into three categories.

First, they rejected salvation by Christ's cross alone. Then as now these "enemies" include but are not limited to the advocates of other religions, who obviously deny Christ is the only "way" to heaven (John 14:6). But they're not alone. Professing Christian ministers are also enemies of the cross if they insist we must add good works to Christ's sacrifice on the cross to be saved. Many today teach cross-plus-works (or grace-plus-works) salvation.[57] In Paul's day the Judaizers taught obedience to the Jewish law, particularly circumcision, was necessary for salvation, for which insistence Paul vigorously opposed them (Acts

---

57. Jehovah's Witnesses, Mormons, and orthodox Roman Catholicism, with its insistence on keeping the seven sacraments, are among these.

15:1–2; Gal. 2:21–3:1) and they him. But he states here they were not only his but also Christ's enemies! While claiming to be Christ's advocates, they were in fact His adversaries, working in His name against His very plan of salvation…by His cross alone.

Second, they were Christian ministers who rejected bearing crosses for Christ's sake. The Judaizers devised their compromised doctrine to retain the Jews' favor and thus avoid their persecution (Gal. 6:12). Other ministers simply desired to please people more than Jesus, again to not make waves (John 12:42–43). These accepted Christ's cross but rejected their own sufferings for His sake—a core part of true Christian discipleship Christ, Paul, Peter, and the writer to the Hebrews explicitly called us to accept (Luke 14:25–27; Matt. 16:24; Phil. 1:29–30; 1 Pet. 4:12–19; Heb. 12:1–4). Their refusal to suffer rejection or persecution for Christ betrays them as being self-serving and self-protecting if not self-indulgent Christians (1 Tim. 6:3–5).

Third, they were false Christian teachers who were apparently indulging their lower fleshly appetites. One commentator notes, "In contrast to the Judaizers," who were rigidly righteous, "other false teachers perverted Christian liberty and took freedom from the Law as license to sin."[58] Many were influenced by the early Gnostics who taught bodily acts didn't affect one's soul or salvation, thus leading some Christians to live licentiously (Rom. 16:17–18).[59] Others were apparently gluttonous and/or slothful. Paul said their carnal desires had become their true, controlling "god" and had set them on course for spiritual ruin, the loss of rewards, and the wasting of their poten-

---

58. *The Spirit-Filled Life Bible*, Phil. 3:17–21, note, 1806.
59. Other Gnostic groups asserted that because (as they taught) the body was a hindrance to spirituality, it should be rigorously disciplined, which often encouraged futile and sometimes fanatical asceticism.

Pressing Toward New Goals!

tial fruitfulness for Christ (Phil. 3:19). Peter describes them as having walked briefly with Christ and then defecting to live again for money, pleasure, and pride, misleading or offending many in the process (2 Pet. 2:1–22). They ignored the values, truths, and ways of God's eternal kingdom: "This world is the limit of their horizon" (3:19, Phillips).

Significantly Paul said there were "many" such enemies of the cross (3:18). This is more evidence that degeneration, heresy, and encroaching apostasy troubled even the first-century church (c. 60–63).[60] Enemies and their errors still trouble us.

Today "enemies of the cross" are not limited to proponents of false religions and false forms of Christianity (teaching grace-plus-works salvation). Many are ministers professing the core doctrines of evangelical Christianity who reject the believer's responsibility to carry crosses of rejection and persecution for Christ's sake. Personally, they compromise (denying Christ's exclusive claims, John 3:3–7; 14:6) or take other evasive action rather than endure suffering. Their teaching reflects their living, as they encourage others to live worldly, compromised, self-centered, pleasure-seeking lives that bring no Judases, thorns, or crosses.

As in Paul's day, all the errors mentioned in Philippians 3:19 are to some degree present in these false ministers and their followers. Their "mind" (or outlook on life) is unspiritual and fixed exclusively on "earthly things." They "glory" (delight, boast) in the wrong things, things praised by this world, and not in the things of Christ and His kingdom. Thus they boast about things of which they should be ashamed: "That which they esteem to be their glory is their shame" (3:19, Wuest). While professing "Christ is Lord," they actually serve the false "gods"

---

60. See this commentary's note on Phil. 2:21, "Everybody's Out for Himself!"

of their "bellies," their bodily appetites or other strong desires of their fleshly nature (refined or gross). Jesus said some have "ravening," or wildly insatiable, appetites for worldly things and sins (Matt. 7:15; cf. 1 John 2:15–17). In a word, their "end" will be "destruction"[61] —the loss of their salvation, if unregenerated (Matt. 7:21–23), or their rewards (partial or complete), if saved (1 Cor. 3:15; 2 John 8).

With "many...enemies of the cross" still roaming, Christ needs you to be a friend, not a foe, of His cross. If you trust His work on the cross alone to save you, patiently endure your crosses for His sake, and refuse to indulge the selfish or sinful desires of your fleshly nature, you're a friend of the cross. May many friends of the cross arise in these last days.

3:18 A faithful shepherd. Paul reminded the Philippians that he had "often" warned them of false teachers: "of whom I have told you often" (3:18; cp. 3:2).

Ever the faithful shepherd, Paul did the same in Ephesus, warning the believers there "night and day" for three years (Acts 20:31) and taking time from his crowded travel itinerary to give one final warning to their elders when he knew he wouldn't see them again (Acts 20:17–38). In other epistles he issued many similar warnings to other churches and leaders all round the Mediterranean world (2 Cor. 11:3–15; Gal. 1:6–9; 2:1–5; 3:1; 5:1, 7–12; Col. 2:8–10; 2 Thess. 2:1–5; 1 Tim. 4:1–5; 6:3–5; 2 Tim. 2:16–18; 4:1–4; Titus 3:9–11). This diligence in warning God's people and their leaders of spiritual dangers is a mark of a faithful, loving shepherd ever mindful of Christ's words to His first undershepherd, Peter (John 21:15–17), and

---

61. "Destruction" is taken from the Greek *apoleia*, meaning "ruin, loss, waste." See Swanson, *Dictionary of Biblical Languages With Semantic Domains: Greek (New Testament)*, s.v. "*apoleia*."

thus ever watchful, alert, and ready to warn Christ's sheep whenever the need arises (Ezek. 3:17).[62]

If pastors, elders, and mentors are to be faithful watchmen over God's people, they must warn their people not occasionally but "often" of the spiritual dangers lurking on every side. Why? Satan's attacks on our faith, devotion to Christ, and service to His people are relentless, his wiles crafty, and his workers ubiquitous (Eph. 6:10–13). Our loving care for other believers begins when we begin taking Hebrews 3:13 seriously: "Exhort one another daily, while it is called Today, lest any of you be hardened through the deceitfulness of sin."

Will you "exhort" your fellow believers—stirring their faith with biblical conversations, urging them to righteous action, dissuading them from unrighteousness—not weekly but "daily"? If so, you're on your way to becoming a faithful shepherd, whether a pastor, elder, or mentor.

3:18–19 He wept for his enemies too. Paul wept while describing the enemies of the cross: "Of whom I…now tell you even weeping" (3:18). Some may find this surprising.

We know Paul wept over the Christians and churches he oversaw (Acts 20:18–19, 31; 2 Cor. 2:4), but we wouldn't expect him to shed tears over ministers who were working against Christ's truth and cause—and were maligning Paul! Though Paul knew their sin, he also discerned their captivity. By returning to self-centered or sinful living and receiving false teaching after they knew the truth, these enemies (Judaizers, Gnostics, other heretics) had come under Satan's control. Barring repentance, they were headed not for a joyous, bright,

---

62. For more on Paul's superb spiritual shepherding, see this commentary's notes on Phil. 1:3–7, "Marks of Great Christian Leaders," and Phil. 1:27, "What Good Shepherds Desire."

God-lit city but a tragic, dark, teeth-gnashing eternity. A man of extraordinary sensitivity, Paul was deeply grieved and prayed, as Christ instructed (Matt. 5:44), they might come to repentance (2 Tim. 2:24–26; 2 Pet. 3:9). Meanwhile hot tears ran down his cheeks.

This wasn't Paul's natural kindness at work. It was the love of God, the very compassion of Christ, who Himself wept over His own Jewish people as they, having rejected the love of the truth He so richly gave them, went about to crucify Him and get on with their lives (Luke 19:41–44). As Paul consistently obeyed God in mercy trials (not prejudging or misjudging, not condemning, ever giving, always forgiving, Luke 6:36–38) and prayed for his enemies, the love the Spirit "shed abroad" in his heart (Rom. 5:5) grew ever wider, deeper, stronger. As he informed the Philippians of the tragic end of his enemies, he was spontaneously moved by it all—as Jesus is every day when sinners continue rejecting Him and Christians stop loving Him and turn to worldly loves. Why? He knows barring repentance they're headed for tragedy (Ps. 73:17–20).

A similar transformation occurred in David. He began his long, painful wilderness trial imprecating that God would summarily judge King Saul for persecuting him (Ps. 35:5), yet later, responding to God's correction, twice spared Saul's life and pleaded with Saul to repent (1 Sam. 24:1–8; 26:5–20).[63] Why? He no longer wanted Saul to be judged, though he knew he would be if he didn't change. Upon hearing of Saul's tragic,

---

63. David's episode with Nabal was another mercy trial. Through Abigail, God taught His developing king again not to "return evil for evil" to his enemies, even a Nabal (1 Sam. 25:32–35; Rom. 12:17–21)! That David continued this in his mercy trial with Shimei many years later shows the lesson was deeply and permanently learned (2 Sam. 16:5–14).

violent death, David grieved, eulogizing Saul for his good works yet sorrowing over what might have been (2 Sam. 1:17–24).

Is this divine love stagnant or growing in you? Are you imprecating or interceding for your enemies? If you've received Christ's nature and Spirit, He can make you like Paul and David. Obey God in your mercy trials, pray for your enemies' repentance, do them good whenever possible, and never retaliate against them, and Christ's love will grow deeper, wider, and stronger until one day you too will weep over your enemies.[64]

3:20–21 Kingdom colonists—eager to go home! Philippi was a Roman colony populated by retired Roman soldiers and other Roman citizens proud of their empire and citizenship. Paul reminded the Philippian Christians, many of whom were registered Roman citizens,[65] that they were first, and eternally, citizens of heaven and should be eagerly anticipating going there when Jesus reappears (3:20–21).

Roman colonies were "little Romes" in which transplanted Roman citizens modeled the Roman lifestyle to subjugated non-Roman nations.[66] Colonists were expected to obey Roman law, respect Roman religion, preserve Roman language (Latin), and promote Roman customs, all to "Romanize" their host nations and increase the glory of Rome and Caesar. For this

---

64. Though there will be a "great gulf fixed" (Luke 16:26) in eternity between the saved and the lost, Jesus' words—"they which would pass from hence [paradise] to you [in hell] cannot"—imply the redeemed would reach over to bring them in, if they could; yet, knowing God's utterly loving and unerringly just nature, they will fully accept and praise His perfectly fair judgments (Rev. 16:5–7).
65. When children were born in a Roman colony such as Philippi, their names were registered as citizens. Similarly when we're born again, our names are written in heaven's register of citizens, the Lamb's book of life (Luke 10:20; Rev. 20:12, 15). Whatever your trials or difficulties, remember to praise God that you're a registered citizen of heaven!
66. Wiersbe, *The Bible Exposition Commentary*, Phil. 3:17–21, note.

service Roman colonists received all the rights, privileges, and benefits of citizenship, including a parcel of land, tax exemption, the right to elect local magistrates, the right to a hearing, the right of appeal, and protection against scourging. Paul saw parallels between Roman colonists and Christians.

He informed the Philippian Christians that they were kingdom colonists: "We are [really] a colony of heaven" (3:20, MOFFATT). (He had previously charged them to live honorably as heaven's citizens to honor Christ and His gospel, 1:27.)[67] Their local fellowship was planted to model God's kingdom in the midst of men's empires, to "kingdomize" Macedonians who didn't yet know heaven's King. They were to remain loyal to their King, His laws, and His ways, and speak His language: truth spoken in love (Eph. 4:15). By doing so they would glorify Him and His kingdom—their true, eternal home (Rev. 21:1–22:5). For this service they would receive enviable rights and privileges: fellowship with the King daily, His unerring guidance, His loving correction, a gift and calling with which to serve Him, insight into His Word and plan, His Spirit's comforting help, material provision, a home reserved in heaven (John 14:1–3), the honor of representing the King in this world (as His ambassadors), and the right to appeal to Him concerning all earthly problems (Phil. 4:6–7).Why tell them they were kingdom colonists?

Perhaps they'd forgotten this and were unconsciously putting their Roman citizenship first. They, and we, must remember that we "have a higher citizenship and really are only aliens on this Earth."[68] To help them look heavenward, Paul briefly describes the wondrous event by which they will for the first time visit their eternal homeland. We call it the Rapture.

---

67. See Philippians 1:27, note, "As Citizens of Heaven."
68. *The Spirit-Filled Life Bible*, 1806.

Pressing Toward New Goals!

Jesus, whom they should be eagerly "looking for," will appear and "change" their "lowly [mortal] body" to be "like his glorious [immortal] body" (3:20–21). Thus he emphasizes the radical bodily transformation necessary for us to inherit heaven (1 Cor. 15:49–51; 1 John 3:2). Paul says this "looking" is not a vague, apathetic wish but a focused, active anticipation. "Look for" (Phil. 3:20) is taken from the Greek *apekdechomai*, meaning "to look forward [to] eagerly."[69]

Thus these translations:

> We eagerly await a Savior from there...
> —NIV

> We are waiting with longing expectation for the coming from Heaven of a Saviour...
> —WEY

> We, with our attention withdrawn from all else, are eagerly waiting to welcome the Saviour...
> —WUEST

Why did Paul remind them, and us, that we're citizens of heaven yet to receive immortal bodies and should be eagerly "look[ing]" forward to Jesus' appearing? Four reasons are sure.

First, so we won't believe and seek the life-goals of the worldly minded "enemies of the cross" he's just described, or any other religious, political, social, or political advocates who ignore Christianity's heavenly aim (Matt. 6:19–21; Col. 3:1–4) and only "mind earthly [worldly] things" (3:19). To highlight the contrasting viewpoints presented in verses 19 and 20 (between

---

[69]. J. P. Louw and E. A. Nida, *Greek-English Lexicon of the New Testament: Based on Semantic Domains*, electronic ed. of the 2nd edition, (New York: United Bible Societies, 1996), s. v. "*apekdechomai*." *Apekdechomai* is also used in Romans 8:19, 23, 25; 1 Corinthians 1:7; Galatians 5:5; Hebrews 9:28.

the "enemies of the cross" and Christians earnestly "looking" for Christ), several excellent translations begin verse 20 with the conjunction, "But..." J. B. Phillips states:

> This world is the limit of their horizon. But we are citizens of heaven...
> —Philippians 3:19–20, Phillips

Second, Paul realized Jesus' pre-tribulation appearing is a purifying hope. So did John: "Every man that hath this hope in him purifieth himself even as he is pure" (1 John 3:3). Thus it's a "blessed hope" inspiring holiness, closeness to Christ, and loving unity among believers (Titus 2:11–13). Believing we need to walk closely with Jesus to be sure we'll be taken when He appears (and kept "from" the hour of tribulation, Rev. 3:10; 1 Thess. 5:9–10) keeps us on our toes spiritually. It spurs us to turn from all besetting sins to faithfully seek, worship, obey, and serve the King now in our present trials (Rev. 1:9).

Warren Wiersbe notes:

> There is tremendous energy in the present power of a future hope. Because Abraham looked for a city, he was content to live in a tent (Heb. 11:13–16). Because Moses looked for the rewards of heaven, he was willing to forsake the treasures of earth (Heb. 11:24–26). Because of the "joy that was set before Him" (Heb. 12:2), Jesus was willing to endure the cross. The fact that Jesus Christ is returning is a powerful motive for dedicated living and devoted service *today*.[70]

Third, Paul didn't want the Philippians living in dread of the coming Antichrist and tribulation (2 Thess. 2:7–10).

---

70. See Wiersbe, *The Bible Exposition Commentary*, Phil. 3:17–21, note.

Many Christians today who've been taught Jesus won't appear before the tribulation are "eagerly awaiting" Antichrist more than Christ![71]

Fourth, Paul didn't want the Philippians obsessing over or distracted by present political problems. Eagerly looking for Christ's return helps us not be unduly entangled in the endless contentions and futility of our present nation (and citizenship) and its increasingly secular, deeply troubled culture. If our country fails, another awaits us in heaven whose righteousness and glory will never fade (Heb. 11:13–16). If our leaders err, we have another—an all-wise Head of state—to trust and excitedly anticipate daily. When He appears, finally, we'll fully experience Him, our new nation, and our new bodies, all by the awesome work of the Holy Spirit's power (3:21). That's good news!

It's better than any the Philippians were receiving from Rome or we're receiving from Washington. My fellow colonist, are you delighting in your heavenly citizenship or boasting in (or fretting over) your present citizenship? If you'll begin "eagerly awaiting" Jesus' appearing, you'll abandon worldly goals, purify yourself, stop trying to identify the Antichrist, and not be discouraged when your nation or its leaders err. Be Christ's faithful kingdom colonist—eager to go home!

3:21 Our amazing new body. When Jesus appears (3:20), abiding Christians will not only be suddenly caught up to be with Him but also experience a radical bodily change (3:21).[72]

---

71. There are at least six major views of the last things: pre-tribulational premillenialism, mid-tribulational premillennialism, prewrath premillennialism, post-tribulational premillennialism, postmillennialism, and amillennialism. This commentary advocates the pre-tribulational premillennialist view.
72. For Paul's description of the catching away of the church and the glorification of our bodies, see 1 Thessalonians 4:15–18; 1 Corinthians 15:49–53; 2 Corinthians 5:1–3.

Our mortal bodies will be "glorified" or made immortal, "like his glorious body" (3:20). Our new bodies will no longer be limited or affected by the consequences of sin.

Paul's description, "our lowly body" (3:20), is not a criticism of the awesome human machine but rather an acknowledgement that sin has had a degrading effect on the human body. In our present state, we're subject to:

- WEAKNESS, thus after exertion we need restoration through sleep
- SICKNESS, thus we need medical cures and prayers of faith
- INJURY, thus we need healing and therapy
- PAIN, thus we need anesthetics
- AGING, thus our strength and vigor are gradually decreasing
- DEATH, which all except Christ's translated ones must face
- LIMITATION, thus the manner and speed by which we move about is restricted

Redemption removes all these sin-induced problems and brings us back to the physical condition Adam and Eve were in before the Fall (Gen. 1–2)—with some amazing improvements!

Since "we shall be like him [Jesus]" (1 John 3:2), our glorified bodies will have some special features seen in Jesus' glorified body. Though material, Jesus' body could appear and disappear (John 20:19, 26), experience transport from one location to another, and even change appearance (Mark 16:12; Luke

24:15–16). Strangely, though bloodless, Jesus' body could also eat (Luke 24:39–43). Jesus' glorified body also released great light, a physical manifestation of the spiritual light with which He was filled (Acts 26:13; Rev. 1:16; 21:23; 22:5). Since these elements are present now in "his glorious body" (Phil. 3:21), we'll experience them in our glorified state.

Loosed from our mortal limitations and infirmities, we'll be wondrously free, always strong, healthy, pain-free, awake, and youthful. We'll be able to enjoy eating and drinking (Matt. 26:29; Rev. 19:9), transport ourselves at will (cf. Acts 8:39–40), transform our appearances,[73] all while ever shining (releasing, reflecting Christ's glory within, Dan. 12:3) and never aging, weakening, or expiring…forever! That's our amazing new body—and another reason we should "eagerly look" for Jesus (3:20)!

3:21 The "working" that subdues all things. Paul mentions the "working" by which God will ultimately subdue everything and everyone to His sovereign will. It is the awesome power of the Holy Spirit: "That power of his which makes him in command of everything" (3:21, PHILLIPS). Paul prayed we might fully understand and believe in this power (Eph. 1:19).

In this context Paul states "the working" will power the Rapture of the church—the sudden catching up of all prepared believers worldwide to rendezvous with Christ in heaven

---

73. This ability to change our appearance will apparently be like that of the angelic guardians to God's throne, the seraphim and cherubim, who are described with slight variations in form by Isaiah, Ezekiel, and John (Isa. 6:2; Ezek. 1:5–14; Rev. 4:6–8). Angels also have the ability to change their bodily appearance and have sometimes appeared in human form (Gen. 19:1, 5; Heb. 13:2). Also, in glory we will be "like him [Jesus]" (1 John 3:2), and He changed His appearance after His resurrection, appearing in "another form" to two on the Emmaus Road (Mark 16:12) and to Mary Magdalene, who initially mistook Him for a gardener (John 20:14–15).

(1 Thess. 4:15–18; Matt. 25:10)—and the simultaneous transformation of believers' bodies from a mortal to an immortal state (Phil. 3:20–21; 1 Cor. 15:49–53). The same divine "working" created the universe, started and stopped the worldwide flood, parted the Red Sea, opened and closed the Jordan River, powered Jesus' miracles, raised Him from the dead, and will one day destroy the entire creation and create another. Thus by this power Christ will "subdue all things unto himself" (Phil. 3:21). Let's examine His "working" more closely.

Christ has power over all people. "Behold, I am ... the God of all flesh; is there anything too hard for me?" (Jer. 32:27). While He has ordained free will, He sovereignly breaks any will, when necessary to build His kingdom or relieve the oppressed. If we're selfish, foolish, or wicked enough to defy Him, sooner or later He'll bring us low (Dan. 4:37; Matt. 23:12). Conversely, when we're serving His will, no matter how powerful or proud our opponents, Jesus can put them on their face in one flash of divine power (Acts 9:1–6; John 18:4–8). He subdued Pharaoh, Nebuchadnezzar, Haman, Herod, Hitler, and will yet subdue Antichrist, so whom should we fear (Ps. 27:1–3)? Ultimately all God's enemies will bow to the Spirit's convicting or crushing power, acknowledging Christ's lordship.[74]

Christ has power over all material things. He demonstrated this when walking on water, halting the wind, re-creating maimed limbs, raising dead bodies, transporting His disciples' boat suddenly to the shore, causing fish to retrieve coins, multiplying bread and fish to feed thousands, and performing other stunning physical miracles recorded in the

---

74. See Genesis 26:26–28; 44:14; Exodus 12:31–32; Ezra 6:1–14; Esther 6:10–11; Psalms 47:2–3; 60:12; 66:3; 72:9; 110:1; Proverbs 16:7; Isaiah 2:11; 45:22–23; Daniel 3:26–30; Romans 14:11–12; Philippians 2:10–11; Revelation 3:9.

New Testament and the Old (since before the Incarnation Christ worked miraculously as the "Angel of the Lord," Exod. 3:2; 14:19–25; Judg. 6:11; 2 Kings 19:35). For His compassion, name, gospel, and plan's sake, He still works physical miracles today (Heb. 13:8).

Christ has power over the spiritual realm and all spirits, including Satan and his demonic hosts. Though the devil and company are supernatural, Christ's power is omnipotent—game over! Jesus demonstrated this superiority in His ministry of exorcism and delegated it to the church in His absence (Mark 5:1–13; 16:17; Luke 10:19–20; Acts 16:16–18; 19:11–12; Ps. 91:13). If we abide safely submissive and obedient to Christ, demons cannot have at us, thanks to Christ's covering blood and angels (Ps. 91:9–12; Job 1:10; Eph. 6:10–18).

Finally, Christ directs our times and circumstances. Daily He controls ordinary people and events that are beyond our control, all to serve His work in our souls and purpose in our lives. "He changeth the times and the seasons" to facilitate His plan (Dan. 2:21) and "causes all things to work together for good" for those who obey Him and His calling (Rom. 8:28, NAS). If we keep step with His guidance, we'll find Christ makes "everything beautiful in its time" (Eccles. 3:11, NKJV).[75]

If we believe Christ thus "subdues all things," we won't fear willful enemies however powerful, physical impossibilities however daunting, demonic resistance however stubborn, or seasons of adversity however long. Abiding and praying in faith, we'll endure our tests of faith confidently and patiently until we see

---

75. There's nothing more beautiful than God's providential control of events, times, and seasons in the Book of Esther. There we see Him working all things—even a king's insomnia—together to deliver His people from imminent catastrophe, bless them with exceptional leaders (Mordecai and Esther), and preserve them for the coming of Messiah.

enemies surrender, demons yield, and miracles as needed—all in God's time. Are you doubting this all-powerful "working" and living in fear? Or are you comforted by it, knowing as you walk with Christ, Christ works for you?

Chapter Four

STANDING FAST!

Paul begins his final words with the charge, "Stand fast!" But he does more than exhort. Ever the teacher, he shows us precisely how to stand fast against everything and everyone that would move us from Christ and His will. We must be peacemakers, work as a team, always rejoice, be gentle, turn our anxieties into prayers, cultivate God's peace, develop our intellect, do what we're taught, always be content, believe we can meet every challenge with Christ's help, give generously, receive all Christians, and much more. Sound too hard? Not at all! Paul assures us if we're willing, to our delight, we'll find we can "do all things through Christ" who strengthens us... to stand fast!

4:1 Oh, how he loved them! Paul's language—"dearly beloved and longed for, my joy"—reveals an extraordinary love. He was passionate, not passive, about those he pastored. The Philippians weren't just loved; they were, Paul asserted twice, "dearly beloved" (4:1). He didn't just enjoy seeing them; he "longed for" them. That's passionate pastoring.

Such affection is nothing less than the Messiah's love implanted in His ministers. Due to its inspiration the entire New Testament is in a sense Christ speaking to His church—the Head of the church addressing the members of His body through the pen of appointed writers (2 Tim. 3:16; 2 Pet. 1:20–21). Thus Paul's love here is not merely his but also Christ's expressed through him. Everyone in leadership should pray for this grace. Why?

Excellent leadership is always driven by love.[1] That Paul was one of the highest authorities in the church—an apostle—suggests that the proper way to seek higher levels of leadership is not to shamelessly self-promote but rather to passionately and practically love those to whom we're ministering! If we'll have Christ's love for them, we'll have it for anyone, anywhere, anytime (Luke 16:10).

Pastor, teacher, elder, counselor, mentor, Sunday school instructor, are you passive or passionate about those you're helping? Are they "dearly beloved" or barely loved? "Longed for" or left alone? It's time to get passionate about pastoring (John 21:15–17; 1 Cor. 8:1; 1 Pet. 5:1–4).

4:1–23 How to stand fast. In closing, Paul urges the Philippians, "Stand fast" (4:1), or "stay true to the Lord" (NLT), as he had the Ephesians when closing their epistle (Eph. 6:10–18). This was his second charge to "stand fast" in this letter (Phil. 1:27). Why these repeated exhortations?

A wise watchman, Paul realized Christians are under constant attack from Satan, demons, and workers of iniquity, all intent on moving them from their faith, hope, love, devotion, fellowship,

---

[1]. The same is true of any effective, productive leader. I remember hearing the legendary football coach of Grambling University, Eddie Robinson, say, "You've got to love them to lead them."

and service. Thus he reminded the Philippians to "be standing firm in the Lord" (Phil. 4:1, WUEST)—never routed, moved, or shaken, and only rarely forced to retreat—against the forces and people trying to stop, stumble, or turn them.

By using the conjunction "Therefore" (4:1), or "So then" (YLT), he refers to his preceding statements reminding the Philippians of their "high calling" (3:14) and hope (3:20–21). As citizens of heaven eagerly awaiting Jesus' return, they should follow Paul's spiritually mature example by pressing toward the goal of fulfilling the purpose of Christ's calling in their lives (3:13–16). In this heavenly calling and hope they should, they must, "stand fast" on earth.[2] But there's more.

He tells them how to do so. Moffatt suggests the entire fourth chapter is an expansion of its first verse, Paul's detailed instructions on how to "stand fast."

> This is how you are to stand firm in the Lord, O my beloved.
> —PHILIPPIANS 4:1, MOFFATT

Thus after charging them to "stand fast in the Lord," he laid down a series of commands that construct a practical means, or roadway, by which they could reach that spiritual end.

They are:

- Remember your first citizenship is in not Rome but heaven—and you're going there soon ("Therefore" [4:1] links the previous thought, 3:20–21).

- Remember you are your pastor's "joy and crown" (4:1)—by standing strong in Christ you will bring

---

2. Or, in Christ's words, they must "hold fast" to the truths they've received (Rev. 3:11).

him (or her) great satisfaction and rewards now and at the judgment.

- Eliminate the divisions among you, especially among your leaders (4:2).

- Have "the same mind" (4:2)—New Testament attitudes, goals, and purposes.

- Be peacemakers: "help" others with their disagreements and duties (4:3), or "lend a hand to these women" (MOFFATT) (Matt. 5:9).

- Foster a team spirit—as "true yokefellows" (4:3) always united, "in perfect cooperation with me *as a team of athletes* would" (WUEST), no longer stubbornly independent but working together, synchronizing, synergizing.

- "Rejoice in the Lord always" (4:4)—remembering you are saved (written in the "book of life," 4:3; Luke 10:20; Rev. 21:27), give thanks and rejoice daily.

- Practice "moderation," or patience and gentleness with others (4:5)—since you're already saved (4:3), Christ is "at hand" (4:5),[3] and He will return soon (4:5).

---

3. As Paul states, Christ is "at hand" (4:5), or so near He's *within reach*, to help you with your needs and problems (4:6–7; Heb. 13:5), reassuringly touch you with the hand of His Spirit as you pray and worship (John 14:21, 23), speak to your heart in guidance (Rom. 8:14), examine and, as needed, correct you (Heb. 12:5–6; Rev. 2:1), humble and halt your enemies (James 5:8–9), release you from your trials (1 Cor. 10:13), and, ultimately, this world (Phil. 3:20–21; 1 Thess. 4:16–18).

Standing Fast!

- Refuse, remember, and replace (4:6–7)—refuse to worry[4] (even in persecution, 1:28–30), remember to pray about "every" problem large or small (4:6), and thus replace your worrying habit with a prayer and faith habit.[5]

- Let God's supernatural "peace" guard and judge you (4:7–9b)—protecting your mind from troubling thoughts and assessing whether you're trusting God in your tests (4:6–7), thinking right (4:8), and "do[ing]" what you've learned (4:9; Col. 3:15).

- "Think on these things" (4:8)—develop your mind, broaden your knowledge, and hone your analytical skills by reading, pondering, and discussing excellent biblical and nonbiblical materials (Mark 12:30; 2 Tim. 2:7).

- Diligently practice ("do") what your ministers have taught you (Phil. 4:9; James 1:22–25).

- Financially support godly ministers and ministries (Phil. 4:10, 14–16), knowing your giving:

    1. Is being registered on "your account" in heaven (4:17)

    2. Is blessing those who've blessed you (4:18)

---

4. One of Oswald Chambers' favorite sayings was, "I *refuse* to worry," with emphasis as indicated! See D. W. Lambert, *Oswald Chambers: An Unbribed Soul* (Fort Washington, PA; Christian Literature Campaign, 1968), 21.
5. Habitually pray with "supplication" (4:6), or strong pleading; "thanksgiving" and faith, your thanksgiving showing your confidence God has answered "when you pray" (Mark 11:24; cf. 1 John 5:14–15); God's surpassing "peace," His reward for your choice to trust Him.

3. Is a sweet sacrifice that pleases God and marks you as a true New Testament believer-priest (4:18)

4. Ensures God will always support you with His inexhaustible supplies (4:19)

- Be "content" in every circumstance of life (4:11–12; Heb. 13:5).

    1. Never complain or "speak in respect of want" (4:11a; 1 Cor. 10:10).

    2. When adversity is prolonged, persevere ("stand fast") in contentment (Phil. 4:1, 11; James 5:7–8); the longer our trials, the sweeter our fruit of the Spirit (Gal. 5:22–23).

    3. Remember God changes our seasons; after we learn to be "abased," He'll let us "abound" (Phil. 4:12; Dan. 2:21; 1 Pet. 5:10).

- Be positive, cultivating a can-do-in-Christ attitude (Phil. 4:13; 2 Cor. 12:9; ct. John 15:5b).

- Practice godly correction—as Paul kindly but directly corrected Euodia and Syntyche (Phil. 4:2; Eph. 4:15) and Christ corrected the churches of Asia Minor (Rev. 2:4; 3:18–19).

- Practice Christian commendation—praising all who do well, as Paul did the Philippians (Phil. 4:15) and Christ the churches of Asia (Rev. 2:2–3; 3:8).

- Remember, by "standing fast" you're glorifying God (Phil. 4:1, 20).

- Lovingly "greet," or receive into fellowship, all believers—whether from prisons ("with me," 4:21) or palaces ("of Caesar's household," 4:22)—not just those of your own group.

- Pray for "grace" for yourselves and others daily, especially in difficult times (4:23).

If practiced faithfully, these simple instructions will enable any Christian to stand strong, perfectly immovable in faith, hope, devotion, fellowship, and duty whatever his (or her) adversities (Matt. 7:24–25; Luke 6:46–48). Are you standing fast? Or have the winds of adversity blown you away from Philippians 4?

4:2 A personal appeal. After his general appeal to "stand fast," Paul now makes a very personal, powerful appeal ("I beseech," or beg!) for two leaders, Euodia and Syntyche, to mend their differences and maintain the harmony of loving cooperation.[6] What were their differences?

We can only guess. Some suggest they each hosted church assemblies in their homes, one of Jewish believers and the other Gentiles.[7] Others surmise they were two strong-willed women, each unwilling to yield to the wishes of the other, even when it

---

6. While all church disunity is harmful, divided leadership is especially so. If leaders are united, the Spirit flows freely through them and God "commands the blessing" on the congregation (Ps. 133:1–3); if not, His working is hindered. This is why God came down so quickly when Miriam and Aaron misjudged Moses (Num. 12:4). As the primary leaders of Israel's women, priesthood, and congregation respectively, their disunity was threatening the welfare of the entire nation (12:1–16).
7. Robertson, *Word Pictures in the New Testament*, Phil. 4:2, note.

concerned the welfare of their entire local church body. What a shame!

You see, these women weren't recent converts or inactive church members; they were leaders! Paul honored them by choosing them as his coworkers, "who labored with me in the gospel" (4:3). So he apparently found them faithful, gifted, and committed, genuinely outstanding Christians—but with a hole in their armor! So here he's doing damage control, seeking to repair their breach by taking space in this inspiring church letter to address their uninspiring carnal attitudes. Personally. Pointedly. Passionately! Why?

A wise master builder, he knew his building must be sound, without cracks. As a passionate perfectionist, he was striving for spiritual perfection, or consistent spiritual maturity, not only in his life (3:12–14) but also in those he shepherded (3:15–17). Seasoned and experienced, he knew this couldn't exist where there was ongoing, stubborn, senseless disunity.

Does Paul's personal appeal personally appeal to you? Are there any chinks in your spiritual armor? Even one? Never let unpleasant or contentious Christians keep you from forgiving, forgetting, and fostering unity—the sweet spiritual harmony for which Christ bled and prayed. Through Paul He's "beseeching" your full, unhindered, as-to-Christ cooperation. Who knows what might happen "suddenly…from heaven" when your church, ministry, Bible study, or prayer group is "all with one accord in one place" (Acts 2:1)?

4:3 Helping or hindering the healing? After appealing to Euodia and Syntyche, Paul continued appealing—this time to an anonymous "yokefellow" (perhaps Synygus) to help the two ladies stop contending and start cooperating. Whoever he was, this yokefellow was a peacemaker of Paul's molding and mind. The lesson?

When believers in our churches, ministries, families, or other organizations aren't getting along, we should do what we can to reconcile them. We can urge them to forgive, because Jesus commanded it (Mark 11:25–26). We can challenge them to examine themselves to see if their own bad attitudes are causing their animosity (Ps. 139:23–24; Prov. 4:23). We can remind them that to receive mercy they must give it (Ps. 18:25; Luke 6:36–37). We can recall Jesus' prayer for unity and urge them to seek unity to please Him (John 17:21–23). And if reason fails, fear may prevail.

A little reminder of sin's consequences never hurt anyone. We can remind contentious Christians that failure to comply with Christ's command to "love one another" (John 13:34–35) will give Satan a "place" (Eph. 4:26–27) in our hearts to trouble us and an "advantage" (2 Cor. 2:9–11) to hinder our work and prayers—and what's worse, may stir the "wrath of the Lamb" against us (Eph. 4:30–5:2, 6)! Sometimes even dire warnings fail to inspire change. So we must pursue plan B.

If one contender is so hardened that we can't soften his spirit, we may by counseling the other at least stop the open contention. It takes two to tango—and argue (Prov. 15:1; Rom. 12:17–18). Or we may ask their pastor or elders to counsel them. Or we may ask others close to them—spouses, children, friends—to talk to them. Sometimes friends are more effective than ministers in healing troubled relationships. Whatever plan we pursue, we must pray—fervently, persistently, and in the Spirit—until their hardness is melted and love restored. Any of the above appeals may succeed with prayer, but none will without it. We never know the precise innermost thoughts troubling our divided sisters or brothers, but the Holy Spirit does and can address them with perfect wisdom if we'll continue addressing Christ in prayer (Eph. 6:18; Rom. 8:26–27). But peace won't come if we ignore divisions. Nor will we be peacemakers. Or blessed!

"Blessed are the peacemakers," Jesus declared, for they know Christ is pleased with them (Matt. 5:9). Paul was blessed, as was his anonymous "yokefellow." Will you be? If we ignore broken relationships, we hinder their healing and the unity of our local body of believers. Let's help, not hinder, the healing of the body.

4:3 Women in ministry. Here's proof women helped Paul in ministry—and he let them! What's more, he spoke glowingly of them as faithful spiritual warriors: "These women...they have fought at my side in the active service of the gospel" (4:3, MOFFATT).

Thus, while unsure of the nature and extent of Euodia's and Syntyche's ministries, we're sure Paul didn't prohibit them, or other women, from ministering.[8] Some believe Euodia and Syntyche were deaconesses. Others hold they were teachers, exhorters, or counselors in the Philippian church. Like Lydia, they may have been among the Jewish women who resorted to

---

8. Christianity was liberating to formerly marginalized women and slaves, who now enjoyed new spiritual equality in Christ and His churches (Gal. 3:28). Apparently some women took their freedom too far. Some chattered or (typically uneducated) blurted out uninformed questions during Bible teachings. Others apparently did so over their husband's objections or challenged their husband's authority at home. Responding to this, Paul permitted women to pray and "prophesy" in meetings (1 Cor. 11:5), but asked them not to overrule their husbands or speak disruptively but rather to listen and learn quietly, asking questions of their (better educated) husbands at home. It was a "shame" upon the men for women to teach only because this meant the men, who typically should be leading and teaching (1 Tim. 3:1–7), were either unable or unwilling to do so (1 Cor. 14:34–35).

the place of prayer outside of the city where Paul first preached the gospel to the Philippians (Acts 16:13). If so, since they were converted first, it's possible, even in their patriarchal Greco-Roman world, that they had some leadership role and later helped Paul in evangelizing their city and teaching God's Word to the women in their congregation.[9]

Since there is neither male nor female in Christ (Gal. 3:28), and the New Testament gives examples of women in ministry, we should follow Paul's example and not forbid women to minister or, if God wills, serve as pastors or teachers. While male leadership is the indisputable biblical norm (1 Tim. 3:1–7, 8–13), female leadership is a biblically valid exception when necessary, as we see in the cases of Deborah and Esther. In such cases godly women would of course remain respectful of male overseers, their fathers, and, if married, their husbands.[10] So if God's exceptional call is on women to minister, rather than censure them we should help them. Thus Paul charged the Philippians, "Help those women" (Phil. 4:3). Surely Christ was leading him.

Christ Himself was assisted by females, whom He also permitted to be His disciples—a very exceptional thing in His male-dominated culture in which rabbis had only male

---

9. R. Jamieson, A. R. Fausset, and D. Brown, *Commentary Critical and Explanatory on the Whole Bible* (Oak Harbor, WA: Logos Research Systems, Inc., 1997), Phil. 4:3, note.

10. Deborah's first mention describes her as "a prophetess, the wife of Lapidoth," who "judged Israel at that time" (Judg. 4:4). That her husband is mentioned is, I believe, more than a rhetorical formality. It subtly hints that while she was in authority over the nation (4:5), she was still under authority to her husband in their home. The first mention of the prophetess Huldah also names her husband Shallum with similar implications (2 Chron. 34:22). In both examples the usual rule (male headship) and rare exception (female leadership) are both validated. We should embrace both in their proper time and place in God's sovereign will so we won't foolishly suffer Jezebels or suppress Deborahs.

disciples (Luke 8:1–3). Though rare, female leadership is validated by Jewish and Christian history.

Miriam prophesied and led worship in Moses' day. As stated above, Deborah and Esther were divinely approved judicial, military, and political leaders (Judg. 4:4–15; Esther 9:23–32). Huldah was a prophetess and royal counselor during Josiah's reign (2 Chron. 34:22–28). Priscilla helped her husband, Aquila, privately instruct the distinguished Alexandrian teacher Apollos (Acts 18:26) and may have helped him pastor their house church (Rom. 16:3–5). It seems clear Philip's unmarried daughters prophesied regularly in his house church (Acts 21:8–9). The Apostle John addressed his second epistle to an "elect lady" who may have been an eldress, prophetess, or deaconess (2 John 1).[11]

Much more recently Phoebe Palmer was a key leader and preacher during the nineteenth-century Holiness movement, whose ministry was received by many Methodist ministers in homes, churches, and camp meetings in America and abroad. Palmer inspired Catherine Booth, whose inspired preaching and leadership skills helped her husband, William, establish the Salvation Army. Countless women played key roles in temperance and other reform movements in America and other nations. Hudson Taylor was prominently assisted by women in his missionary work in China. Many foreign missionaries have been women. Aimee S. MacPherson was a gifted evangelist, pastor, and denominational founder whose preaching made "Sister Aimee" arguably the most notable preacher in America during the 1920s and 1930s. Besides her miraculous healing ministry, Kathryn Kuhlman was an able Bible teacher

---

11. While some scholars hold John was referring to the local church as the "elect lady," I believe he was in fact addressing a female.

whose meetings were attended by ministers and seminary students. Numerous female pastors, evangelists, and teachers are presently being used by God in an obvious way. God has used female ministers (evangelists, pastors, overseers, missionaries) very prominently in the amazing work He has done in China over the last half century. What do these facts imply?

When defending his ministry at Cornelius' house, Peter's rationale was simple: If God gave the Spirit to the Gentiles, who was he to object (Acts 11:17)? Similarly, if as we see above, God is pleased to use women in ministry, who are we to object?[12] Granted, their use as pastors is exceptional, but if they're divinely called, it's valid—or Deborah's and Esther's judicial and political authority (over women and men) was a divine mistake! Let there be no mistake, God's sovereign call is key: If His calling, gifting, and anointing are evident in a woman's ministry, if Christians are being blessed and churches edified, if the Holy Spirit is using her, who are we to object? In such cases we should help, not hinder female ministers.

When Paul charged the Philippians to "help those women," I'm sure they did. Will we? Are we helping or hindering our women in ministry? Receiving them in the ministries to which God has called and gifted them or blindly rejecting them due to their gender?

4:3 The book of life. Paul refers to the Lamb's "book of life," in which every Christian's name is entered when he or she is born again as a citizen of heaven, just as newborns' names were logged as Roman citizens in ancient Philippi.[13]

---

12. Lest, as Gamaliel warned, we fight against the Lord (Acts 5:38–39).
13. "Anciently, free cities had a roll book containing the names of all those having the right of citizenship." See Jamieson, Fausset, and Brown, *Commentary Critical and Explanatory on the Whole Bible*, Phil. 4:3, note.

"The book of life," therefore, is the official registry of heaven's citizens, Jewish and Gentile (Dan. 12:1). Among books, none is more important. Among people, none are as secure as those written in it. But even they shouldn't be presumptuous.

While asserting the eternal security of the believer (John 5:24; 6:37), the Bible also, in some puzzling apparently contradictory texts, reveals the possibility of names being "blotted out" (Ps. 69:28; Exod. 32:32–33; Rev. 3:5). It is self-evident that one's name can't be "blotted" (erased, wiped out) unless it is first written, so this clearly suggests the disturbing but undeniable possibility of loss of salvation—someone's name being first written as one saved and subsequently blotted out as lost, as was the case with Judas (John 17:12). If so, what for?

While we can't be dogmatic, here's one possibility. This extraordinarily rare retraction of salvation may be reserved only for those following the example of Judas—whom the Father first "gave" to Christ yet was subsequently "lost" (John 17:12). Judas not only abandoned Christ and His disciples but also returned to attack them in a willful, rebellious persecution. If Christians follow his dark example by falling away and subsequently attacking Christ's existence,[14] deity, gospel, ministers, or people, like Judas, they too may be lost.[15] There is clear biblical precedent for the retraction of divine promises for heinous

---

14. I speak here of professing Christians who fall from faith so fully they renounce Christ, deny His sole Saviorship, and fully adopt and promote atheism or other false religions (Islam, Buddhism, Hinduism, Universalism, Christ-rejecting Judaism, etc.).
15. To Judas' rebellion we add blaspheming the Holy Spirit—attributing the works of the Holy Spirit to the devil. The Pharisees committed this, the unpardonable sin, by publicly declaring that Jesus' miracles were the work of not the Holy Spirit but demons (Mark 3:28–30). Additionally, anyone who worships the Antichrist and takes his mark in the tribulation period will be irretrievably lost (Rev. 14:9–11). These are heavy truths, but who better to face and share them than truth-loving, truth-freed Christians (John 8:31–32, 36).

sins against God's people (1 Sam. 2:12–17, 22–25, 29–30; Ps. 82:6–7). This explanation, if correct, helps reconcile the Bible's assertion of eternal security with its warning of loss of salvation. Every born-again believer is securely registered in the eternal kingdom of God—unless they turn and rebel, actively fighting against the King and kingdom.[16]

Those who (bolstered by a superficial, dogmatic assurance of eternal salvation) boast so confidently that because they're saved they can "do anything they want" without fear of losing salvation are also clearly ignorant of the dire consequences of sin. Surrendering to any sin brings one under bondage—again—to sin's master, Satan (Rom. 6:16). He begins controlling the life, not Christ. Our spiritual life is cut off from nourishment unless and until we repent. If we continue stubbornly practicing sin, we're walking in the dark, used by Satan whenever he wills against other people to cause them to stumble and God's plan to hinder it (2 Tim. 2:25–26). Our discernment becomes confused, our bodies are weakened, and we risk divine chastisement, even death (1 Cor. 11:29–32). We waste our lifetime, ruin our destiny, harm those we love, dishonor Christ, disillusion unbelievers with Christianity, give demons free rein in our minds and use of our bodies, and become our own worst enemy. We pierce ourselves with many sorrows—and never know the sweet peace of God, the flowing joy of the Lord, the warm sunshine of Christ's approval, and, most importantly, the

---

16. For the truly born-again Christian, unconfessed sins, wrong attitudes, unworthy ministry works, apathy (Rev. 3:15–16), or lukewarmness will cause varying degrees of loss of eternal rewards and privileges in the kingdom of God, but not of salvation (1 Cor. 3:12–15; 2 Cor. 5:10–11; 2 John 8; Rev. 3:11). Those who persist in doing so against God's warnings will lose Christ's approval for service and incur a measure of His fearful wrath and judgments, perhaps including early departure from this life (Heb. 6:4–8; 10:26–31; 1 Cor. 11:30–32; 1 John 5:16b).

deeper things of intimacy with Christ, the Spirit's ways, and full insight into the riches of God's Word. Even if by grace we remain saved, we will forfeit honor, usefulness, the memory of a fulfilled life, nearness to Christ, and authority in His kingdom! Forever! With no chance to change our situation! Still eager to "do whatever you want"? It's time we abandon all flippancy about salvation doctrine and start seriously walking with God in righteousness and holiness in this life!

In the larger biblical context, some "blotting" references refer only to one's family name being blotted out of the unofficial social registry, or collective memory, of one's people or nation, and thus deprived of honor (Ps. 109:13). Christ assured the overcomers in Sardis, many of whose names had been blotted from the local Jewish synagogue's registry,[17] that their name wouldn't be "blotted out" of His book (Rev. 3:5), yet withheld this reassurance from their spiritually dead brethren (Rev. 3:1–3). He prompted John to warn anyone removing or increasing the words of the Revelation (or the Bible itself, say, by claiming inspiration for extra-biblical works[18]) risked dire consequences (Rev. 22:18–19), including having his "part" in the book of life (or some translations say, the "tree of life" and "holy city") taken away. This alludes to the loss of rewards or possibly salvation, if being denied fruit from the tree of life means one

---

17. In the first century, due to its ancientness (predating Roman religions) Judaism enjoyed legal exemption. Thus Jews were not required to worship Roman emperors or gods. Christianity, though widely misunderstood, enjoyed protection under the covering of Judaism, since Romans initially considered it a Jewish sect. When Christians were expelled from synagogues and their names removed from their rolls, they were then viewed as practicing an illegal religion and exposed to persecution. This was the argument the Jews hoped to prove against the Corinthian Christians...until Gallio refused to hear their case (Acts 18:12–13).

18. This has occurred in modern times with the Mormon's claims concerning the fantastical writings of Joseph Smith in the Book of Mormon and his other so-called inspired works.

cannot live eternally (22:19; Gen. 3:22–24). Those who take the Antichrist's mark are eternally doomed, and thus not written in (or blotted out of) the book of life (Rev. 13:8; 17:8; 14:9–11). Interestingly, the book of life will be used at the Great White Throne judgment of the wicked dead, but only to confirm that those judged are in fact not saved (Rev. 20:12–15). Only those who remain written in the Lamb's book will enter New Jerusalem (Rev. 21:27; Heb. 12:22–23). That's what's written of the "book of life" (Phil. 4:3).

Is your name written in it? If so, are you thankful, rejoicing daily that, whatever your troubles, you're headed for New Jerusalem *forever* (Phil. 4:4; Luke 10:20)—yet not arrogantly presumptuous about this salvation and foolishly ignorant of the dire consequences of sin?

4:4 Rejoicing "in the Lord." Twice in this verse and four times in this epistle Paul instructs us to "rejoice in the Lord" (4:4; 3:1, 3). Why this counsel?

There are two spheres of rejoicing in our lives: in the world and in the Lord. We rejoice in the world when worldly blessings come our way, joys or advantages or successes in this temporal realm. But Paul isn't referring to these things.

Rather, he's calling us to rejoice in what we have "in the Lord," or by virtue of our being a born-again believer: "Find your joy in him" (4:4, PHILLIPS). These are all the benefits of Christ's redemption, the joys and advantages and victories He gives us in this life and the next. "Forget not all his benefits," the psalmist reminds us (Ps. 103:2), yet even the most spiritually minded Christians sometimes lose sight of them due to the distractions and pressures of our ongoing testing process. (See my note, "The Rarest Rejoicing," Phil. 3:1.) Therefore Paul reminds us four times in this letter to remember the blessings we have "in the Lord" and rejoice in them regularly: "Delight, gladden yourselves in Him" (4:4, AMP). Paul didn't originate this idea.

Throughout Scripture the Spirit prompted sacred writers to in various ways enjoin us to "rejoice" in God. They are:

- "Rejoice in the Lord" (Ps. 33:1; 97:12; Isa. 41:16; 61:10; Zech. 10:7)

- "Be glad in the Lord" (Ps. 32:11; 64:10; 104:34)

- "Delight...in the Lord" (Ps. 37:4; Isa. 58:14)

- "Glory in the Lord" (1 Cor. 1:31; 2 Cor. 10:17)

Why this repetitive prod to rejoice in the Lord rather than in the world? Only the joys we have in Christ are untouchable. Satan may "touch" all our worldly blessings if God permits (Job 1:11; 2:5), but he can't touch any of our spiritual blessings in Christ—our time with Jesus, the nourishing truth of God's Word, the comfort of the Holy Spirit, the privilege of prayer and its answers, the peace of God, the hope of Jesus' return, fellowship with like-minded Christians, our duties or ministries in the body of Christ, and so forth. These delights remain ours daily, no matter how many waves of adversity overwhelm us or arrows of affliction strike us.

The Bible showcases numerous believers who remembered that whatever their adversities in the world, they still had their advantages in the Lord. Their faith-driven, sacrificial rejoicing in Him enabled them to endure the unendurable and overcome against all odds. Habakkuk faced down national desolation in joyful confidence in God (Hab. 3:17–19). Paul endured shocking injustice and intense physical abuse (Acts 16:24–25). Hannah got the victory over long, bitter barrenness (1 Sam. 2:1). David rose above cruel, relentless persecution climaxing in personal catastrophe (1 Sam. 30:6). Are you learning from their displays of overcoming faith and relentless rejoicing?

Have your worldly blessings diminished—or departed? Continue rejoicing "in the Lord," and He'll meet you. The Spirit of God will faithfully revive and strengthen you and fully restore your fellowship with Jesus and effectiveness in His service. And that's not all. Unable to sour your soul, Satan will be frustrated! So "Rejoice in the Lord, always!" Recall your benefits, offer thanks, worship the Lord, bless His name, sing praises to Him, all to please Him! (And frustrate Satan.)

4:5 On being gentle—and why we should be. Paul ordered the Philippians to display "moderation," and to motivate them added, "The Lord is at hand" (4:5). Let's look deeper.

"Moderation" (Greek *epieikēs*) means variously "gentle (mild tempered), reasonable, fair, kind, yielding (to others' needs or wishes), forbearing, forgiving." This describes someone who is gentle, considerate and patient with others, and therefore not excessive, hasty, pushy, or unreasonable. It portrays someone who is loving and therefore reacts to difficulties, rejection, or mistreatment with humble kindness. Or, to simplify, it describes someone who is Christlike! Most versions translate *epieikēs* as "gentleness" (NKJV, NIV) or "gentle" (NAS, NCV). Elsewhere Paul uses a different form of this word (*epieikeia*) to describe the "gentleness of Christ" (2 Cor. 10:1).

The KJV translators' choice, "moderation" (2:5), gives us an alternate interpretation. One who is gentle and forbearing is likely to not only be moderate (mild mannered) in handling irritating people and problems but also prone to use "moderation" in all things—that is, to control himself, enjoying but not overindulging in the acceptable pleasures and comforts of life (1 Cor. 7:31). Why? Perhaps he remembers Christ's warning that overindulgence in these things may "choke" the fruitfulness of God's Word in our lives (Luke 8:14) and render us unprepared for Jesus' return (Luke 21:34).

Leaving no doubt, Paul specified why we should be gentle with people and exercise moderation in all things: "The Lord is at hand" (4:5). Something "at hand" is present, so near one can reach out and touch it. Paul is telling us (1) Jesus is present with us by His Spirit (Matt. 28:20b; Heb. 13:5), and (2) His bodily return is near (Rev. 22:7, 12, 20). Paul's declaration of Jesus' nearness is strikingly similar to James' declaration of Christ's soon coming as Judge: "The judge standeth before the door [ready to come to you with justice]" (James 5:9). Like Paul, James suggests awareness of the nearness of Judge Jesus should encourage us, in his words, to "be…patient" and "murmur not one against another" because "the coming of the Lord draweth near" (James 5:8–9). So both inspired writers agree: we should be gentle, reasonable, and forbearing with others because the Lord is near.

More specifically, "at hand" implies:

1. He's present to judge (examine) us, ready to commend, correct, or chasten us (Rev. 2–3).

2. He's present to judge our adversaries, returning their treatment of us (Gen. 12:3).

3. His coming is imminent, or "may occur at any moment" (WUEST).

> 4. He's present to help us, so close we can quickly touch Him through prayer—and as quickly receive His reassuring strength, guidance, and assistance to meet all our needs (Phil. 4:6–7; Acts 23:11; 27:23–24).

Truly, remembering Christ is present—and thus observing us—encourages us to act and react with gentle Christlikeness. Who wants to fail or deny the Lord in His full view as Peter did? Understanding He's present to deal with unreasonable or hateful adversaries helps us rest when we're mistreated (Rom. 12:17–21; Prov. 16:7); we don't have to strive to deliver ourselves from reproach or injustices when Christ is fighting for us. Believing He could appear to take us away at any moment stirs us to be ready, watching, worthy, and wise—and therefore to be very careful to treat people not curtly, but kindly; not unfairly, but fairly; not hastily, but patiently; not vengefully, but forgivingly. Knowing He's "at hand" to help with every problem enables us to transfer all our anxieties to Him through prayer; when we're confident Jesus is helping us, it's much easier to be gentle and forbearing with everyone, even those who constantly trouble us.

What have you let "be known unto all men" lately (Phil. 4:5)? Gentleness or irritability? Forbearance or fury? Moderation or excess? Believe Jesus is at hand—and act like it.

4:6–7 Practicing God's peace. By inspiration Paul ordered the Philippians to do four things in these verses that are absolutely vital to living a victorious life:

> 1. Refuse to be anxious about *anything*. However important or urgent your needs or problems, start

by firmly refusing to worry about it. And, yes, "nothing" (4:6) means nothing! We're without excuse for succumbing to worry.[19]

2. Ask God's help with *every* problem, large or small.[20] Don't pray vague generalities but "definite requests" (AMP). Or, "Tell God every detail of your needs," (PHILLIPS); or, "Let your requests be unreservedly made known in the presence of God," (WEY). And, yes, "everything" (4:6) means everything! No problem must be faced without prayer.[21]

3. Trust God to faithfully hear and answer. As Christ expressly taught us, when you pray, believe He has answered you immediately, without any evidence other than His promise (Mark 11:24; 1 John 5:14–15; Dan. 10:12–14; John 14:14; 15:7–8).

4. Express your faith in Him "with thanksgiving" (4:6). Thanking God for answers that He's promised but we've not yet seen expresses and strengthens faith of the highest order (Matt. 8:5–10; Luke 1:45; John 20:29; Rom. 4:16–21).

---

19. The order of the commands in this context suggests that "rejoicing in the Lord always," practicing "moderation" (gentleness), and remembering Christ is "at hand" will free us from chronic anxiety and precondition us to meet problems in a more positive frame of mind (Phi. 4:4, 5, 6).
20. No problem is too small to pray about since, if left to fester, even the smallest anxiety will grow to spoil our disposition, day, and witness. Wise Solomon warns, "The little foxes...spoil the vines" (Song of Sol. 2:15).
21. Paul repeatedly teaches us throughout his epistles to pray continuously (Eph. 6:18; 1 Thess. 5:17), and his experience models his teaching (Acts 16:25; 1 Thess. 3:10; 2 Tim. 1:3).

Standing Fast!

This is a very challenging discipline, since we're usually tempted to fret about something daily. If practiced diligently, this *anxious for nothing, praying about everything* exercise will produce a Christian who consistently rests in God's surpassing peace (or walks in "the way of peace," Rom. 3:17) whether circumstances are wonderful, monotonous, or terrible. One commentator notes, "Prayer and peace are closely connected. One who entrusts cares to Christ instead of fretting over them will experience the peace of God to guard him from nagging anxiety."[22] When habitual, this exercise forms a strong, secure "sound mind" (2 Tim. 1:7) well guarded against the corrosive effects of Satan's relentless psychological warfare (2 Cor. 10:3–5; Eph. 6:16; ex., 1 Sam 27:1).

Through Paul Christ is ordering us to form a new habit, a new way of handling adversity. The old habit consists of worrying, reasoning, complaining, and depending solely on human means and wisdom. Thus though we profess Christ, in the practical problems of life we forget Him! Of this "worry-your-way-through-the-mess" methodology, one commentator notes:

> What is worry? The Greek word translated "anxious" (careful) in Philippians 4:6 means "to be pulled in different directions." Our hopes pull us in one direction; our fears pull us the opposite direction; and we are pulled apart! The Old English root from which we get our word "worry" means "to strangle." If you have ever really worried, you know how it does strangle a person! In fact, worry has definite physical consequences: headaches, neck pains, ulcers, even back pains. Worry affects our thinking, our digestion, and even our coordination.[23]

---

22. *The Spirit-Filled Life Bible*, Phil. 4:6–7 note, 1806.
23. Wiersbe, *The Bible Exposition Commentary*, Phil. 4:1–9, note.

This old way of being pulled in different directions emotionally and strangled spiritually every time troubles arise dishonors and grieves God because it implies He can't, or worse, won't, meet our needs and solve our problems. It also ignores Christ's key teaching commanding us to "take no [anxious] thought" for our worldly necessities (Matt. 6:25–34). Therefore we must abandon our old way and replace it with a new habit of utter God-reliance through prayers of faith and thanksgiving. One source states simply, "Do you want to worry less? Then pray more! Whenever you start to worry, stop and pray."[24] Hence Paul's teaching.

The new way Paul taught, lived, and inscribed in this epistle brings several wonderful benefits:

1. We release our anxieties to God. Talking to God about our frets and fears and asking Him to help shifts the burden of the situation to Him. "Cast thy burden upon the LORD, and he shall sustain thee," the psalmist says, promising if we do so, "he shall never suffer the righteous to be moved" (Ps. 55:22). Peter echoes him, "Casting all your care upon him; for he careth for you" (1 Pet. 5:7). This anxiety transfer spares us the emotional, nervous, psychological, and physical damage caused by the stresses of life.

2. God releases His peace into our hearts. As we "pour out" our heart to God in believing prayer, He pours peace into our heart (Ps. 62:8). And not just any peace, but "The peace of God which surpasses all power of comprehension" (Phil. 4:7,

---

24. *The Life Application Study Bible*, Phil. 4:6–7, note, 2022.

Wuest). Its supernatural, sustaining strength is the best medicine available—a miracle drug sure to relieve our troubled hearts, clear our confused minds, and restore our shaken confidence that God will meet "all our needs" (Phil. 4:19). Filled with this peace, we can live truly carefree lives, ready to give ourselves wholly to Christ, His will, and others' needs.

3. God's hand is released to help us. Our prayer and thanksgiving exhibit the faith—the utter, childlike God-confidence—that pleases God (Heb. 11:6). This releases His hand to help us providentially or when necessary supernaturally (Acts 12:7, 11).

4. God is honored. By thus depending on God in our difficulties, we show others Christ is real and as ready to help us today as in the days of His flesh. Thus He is honored and "lifted up" in our lives, and others are drawn to Him (John 12:32).[25]

We'll never know these sweet benefits if we never take Philippians 4:6–7 seriously. Instead, we'll continue facing problems the same old way. Every day we'll displease and dishonor God because we're practicing the opposite of His will: we're complaining, fretting, or fearing about "everything" and

---

25. The most God-honoring, extraordinary life of faith I know of was that of George Mueller. To learn more about his lifelong practice of Philippians 4:6–7 in meeting the needs of his family, a very large orphanage, many schools, more than one hundred missionaries, and numerous other ministries, all by prayer alone, I recommend George Mueller, *Answers to Prayer* (Chicago: Moody Press, 1984).

praying in faith about "nothing." While many things in our lives are uncertain, two are certain: first, anxieties will arise daily; second, we'll handle them or they'll handle us.

Tired of the corrosive effects of recurring worry? Yearning to live daily in God's amazing peace? Enough to change your ways? If so, please and honor God by following Paul's instructions, not occasionally but habitually. Make your new motto *anxious for nothing, praying about everything*. Practice God's peace daily. Every time you meet a new problem large or small, instead of letting Satan use it to take you from walking in peace to going to pieces, take your problem to the Lord and let Him take you from anxiety to prayer to peace.

4:7 About the peace of God. This text promises not human but divine peace, not natural but supernatural tranquility, the mighty, flowing, unique "peace of God"!

This God serenity is the very marvelous, indescribable tranquility and blissful absence of agitation that fills God's own heart and heaven—the very atmosphere of New Jerusalem![26] This is the peace promised us and nothing less. It "is so great we cannot understand it" (NCV), "exceeds anything we can understand" (NLT), and "goes far beyond anything we can imagine" (ISV). This explains why some of the truly saintliest saints had at times such a preternatural quality about them. They were so miraculously kept and held steady, clear, and fruitfully active

---

26. Perhaps this is why God chose Jerusalem, His city of peace (Heb. 7:2), as the capital of His ancient Jewish people and a type of the capital of the new world in which all the redeemed will live forever. Jerusalem means "founded in peace; teaching peace...double peace"—or *founded in and teaching the double or twofold peace of God*. This "double peace" follows when we (Jerusalem's elect citizens) are redeemed and, receiving God's own tranquility by grace, live thereafter pursuing twofold peace: with God and with men (Ps. 34:14; Heb. 12:14–15). For the definition quoted, see Smith and Cornwall, *The Exhaustive Dictionary of Bible Names*, s.v. "Jerusalem."

in the most turbulent, cruel, or terrifying moments (Dan. 3:25; 6:16–22; Acts 16:28; 21:40). Why? Not because they had exceptionally strong wills, physical constitutions, emotional control, or superior schooling. No, they were immersed in, filled with, and held by God's powerful peace!

The same overcoming tranquility is our rich legacy from Jesus: "Peace I leave with you, my peace I give unto you" (John 14:27). It is a sweet fruit produced in us easily and naturally when the Spirit is present and having His way in our lives (Gal. 5:22). We are called to live in this divine serenity (1 Cor. 7:15), and it marks us as authentic citizens of Christ's kingdom—which will be filled with peace (Rom. 14:17)! It comes to us through God's Word (John 16:33) and manifests when we choose to interpret the events of our lives, especially those adverse, from the spiritual viewpoint of God's Word (Rom. 8:6). God releases it to us afresh every time we do "good"—obeying His good will or doing good deeds to others (Phil. 4:9; Rom. 2:10). Every decision to trust God enables Him to refill us with His peace (Rom. 15:13, NIV). Every fresh visit of God's presence in our lives brings a revival of peace (John 20:19, 26); therefore He often graciously visits us in fearful times (20:19). He imparts this peace when commissioning us for His service (John 20:21) and releasing His Spirit upon us (20:22). We should pray often for more of God's peace (1 Cor. 1:3; 2 Thess. 3:16) and for our churches to be filled with it (1 Cor. 14:33). We should let God's peace be our judge, helping us decide whether we're walking in or out of the light and what is and isn't God's will (Col. 3:15). We should diligently maintain God's peace so we'll be found living "in peace" when Jesus appears (2 Pet. 3:14).

But the choice is ours. Paul didn't try to force the Philippians to walk in God's peace, nor will our Father attempt to coerce us. We're free to continue living in our anxieties or form the habit of living in God's peace. But it's not much of a choice.

Why be agitated when you can be calm, cool, and collected? Why live under damaging psychological pressure when you can live internally stress free? Why be anxious at heart when your soul can mount up and soar through your day with heavenly serenity? Why let troubling thoughts hold your mind hostage when your thoughts can be unrushed, orderly, and productive? Ponder, possess, and practice Philippians 4:6–7—and the amazing peace of God!

4:8 Ordered to think! After listing several worthwhile subjects, Paul ordered the Philippians, "Think on these things" (4:8), or "fix your thoughts on" them (NLT), or "cherish the thought of these things" (WEY). The apostle had spoken: they were to start thinking! Seriously! Deeply! Often! Why this command?

Paul knew our actions almost always flow from our reservoir of thoughts. To act righteously we must think righteously. So he recommended right thinking first (Phil. 4:8), before urging right action (4:9). "Think excellent things, then you'll do excellent things."

Our first response should be to immerse ourselves in prayerful, devotional Bible study (2 Tim. 2:15). God's Words are God's thoughts. These Spirit-filled, powerfully active, holy intellectual agents move us to righteous living. If we "meditate day and night" in them, we'll "do all that is written therein" with increasing frequency and ease (Josh. 1:8). We must also seek excellent Bible teaching, so our beliefs will be sound. Biblical rumination, recalling and thoughtfully pondering meaningful Bible verses we already know, helps nurture our biblical thinking. Diligent self-examination, screening our minds to reject unbiblical thoughts, helps guard our right thinking. Conscientiously obeying these biblical truths in the situations of life establishes them—and sound biblical thinking (or a "renewed" mind, Rom. 12:2)—in our lives (Phil. 4:9; 2:12–16; James 1:22–25). This thinking, cultivating, protecting, and doing of biblical truth is the born-again believer's foundation for a lasting, close walk with Christ.

It has been said:

> Sow a thought, reap an action;
> Sow an action, reap a habit;
> Sow a habit, reap a character;
> Sow a character, reap a destiny.[27]

But additional right thinking must be built atop this scriptural foundation if we want to be fully developed Christians. Paul didn't limit the Philippians' intellectual life to Bible study. To the contrary, he urged them to study "whatever" (4:8) was worthwhile. Specifically, any subject matter that is:

- TRUE—established as factual and real; not rumor, hearsay, conjecture, premature judgments, scientific theories, or imaginations (excellent fiction or inspired allegories excepted); whatever agrees with biblical revelation; whatever models or promotes faithfulness

- HONEST (OR HONORABLE)—inspiring honest, honorable speech or conduct; discouraging

---

27. Wiersbe, *The Bible Exposition Commentary*, Phil. 4:8, note.

falsehood; anything demonstrating the principle of 1 Samuel 2:30[28]

- JUST (OR RIGHTEOUS)—showing fairness, justice, equality; promoting unbiased, impartial treatment of everyone; court decisions stopping villains and relieving victims (Esther 7:10; Acts 18:12–17); examples of people reaping what they sow (Gal. 6:7)

- PURE—clean, moral, upright; not corrupting, defiling, or degrading; not tabloidish or sensational with shameful content

- LOVELY—beautiful, admirable, wonderful; mirroring the characteristics of Christ, the consummate lovely One (Ps. 90:17; Gal. 5:22–23)

- OF GOOD REPORT—worthy of consideration, conversation, and communication to others; changes for the better in people (repentance), nations (reforms), conflicts (resolutions), churches (revivals), ministries (how Christ is using them, Acts 11:21)

- EXCELLENT (OR VIRTUOUS)—reflecting or promoting high morals, ethics, or ideals; outstanding or exemplary conduct or achievement;

---

28. Repeatedly the Bible, history, and life attest to God's promise, "Them that honor me I will honor" (1 Sam. 2:30). Thus Paul, whose faith, testimony, and ministry under duress had honored God during a long, harrowing, hurricane-ravaged voyage, subsequently received honor from Him through the governor and people of Malta (Acts 27:21–25; 28:10).

praising and prompting the beliefs, habits, and traits of virtuous character and living[29]

- PRAISEFUL—bringing due appreciation or commendation to good men and women; or inspiring heartfelt thanks, testimonies, or songs of praise or worship that honor God

So Paul sets the margins very wide. There's a lot we're authorized to think about—and by implication, avoid.

You see, Paul's command is equally an order *not* to think on "whatever" is the opposite of the things he sanctions: things false, dishonest, unjust, impure, ugly, unhelpful, immoral, or without anything praiseworthy.[30] Remember that the next time you visit your TV, DVD store, magazine stand, or the Internet.

We can, however, learn from not only Christian but also non-Christian sources. Some feel secularists have nothing to teach us, and that's right concerning the core teachings of our faith and worldview. But God often gives thoughtful unbelievers worthy insights concerning many worldly and some spiritual and moral issues. Henry writes, "We should not be ashamed to learn any good truth of bad men."[31] As disciples and lovers of truth, we should agree with truth whoever speaks it. Indeed, secular scholars, scientists, writers, editorialists, historians, journalists, and even humorists frequently offer opin-

---

29. "Virtue" (Phil. 4:8, KJV) is translated "excellent" or "excellence" in numerous modern translations (NIV, ESV, NAS, NLT, ISV). Excellence speaks of one who excels, rises above, goes beyond, or stands out from the norm, and is thus superior. Do we pause to ponder individuals, organizations, and leaders that excel and why they do so?
30. How much of our intellectual energies are wasted on the meaningless, often mean-spirited, lie-riddled, and sometimes juvenile political contentions that pour out of media outlets daily, especially during campaign seasons?
31. Henry, *Commentary in One Volume*, Phil. 4:8, note, 1867.

ions, witticisms, philosophical observations, and practical life lessons of immense value to us in this complex and often confusing world.

Thinking and study have two general effects on us. They may "puff" us with the illusion that we're becoming more knowledgeable than others (1 Cor. 8:1), or humble us by causing us as we continually research new topics to realize just how many fields of knowledge there are about which we know little or nothing (8:2).[32] So we should study hungrily yet humbly, asking always, "Lord, how may I obey this knowledge in my life and help others with it?" (Phil. 2:3–5, 6–8; Rom. 12:3; Col. 3:12).

Moreover, because they're inspired, Paul's thoughts are really Christ's. Not just our apostle but our Head speaking through him wants us to be a thinking people: curious, well informed, reflective, growing daily in biblical and relevant human knowledge. Jesus is on record as saying we should love God with not only all our heart, soul, and strength but also with "all thy mind" (Matt. 22:37; Mark 12:30; Luke 10:27). Thus while studying "unspiritual" topics like biography, geography, history, science, or current issues, we should ask the Lord to bless our thinking: "Lord, show me Your hand, plan, intervention, and biblical principles and patterns in this subject matter." Our Teacher, the Holy Spirit, will answer. Why?

He knows thinking sharpens our mind, enabling us to grasp and analyze subjects more quickly and accurately. So does thought-provoking, spiritually and intellectually stimulating conversation (Prov. 27:17). Cultivating our intellectual

---

32. Searching for truth is a blessed frustration. We're blessed when we discover what we've been searching for, yet frustrated because alongside it we find new subjects, events, terms, and people we want to explore! There seems no end to it all! "Be careful...much study wears you out" (Eccles. 12:12, NLT). So take rests—but never stop studying!

powers makes us less susceptible to Satan's subtle strategies; a thoughtful Christian will catch the misinformation, doubletalk, and biblically unsupported teaching the thoughtless Christian misses.[33]

The Old and New Testaments alike urge godly meditation since it cultivates awareness of and closeness to God. Isaac apparently formed a habit of going out into the field in the evening to "meditate" (Gen. 24:63, reflect and "rehearse or go over a matter in one's mind"[34]) on his father's God and His plan for his life. Meditation also develops memory—and lack of meditation forgetfulness (Ps. 78:11; 106:13). Meditating believingly on God and His Word creates deep, peaceful trust and stability in our lives (Ps. 26:3, NLT) and, combined with an active intellectual life, helps develop the "sound [strong] mind" (2 Tim. 1:7) we need to withstand the barrage of false doctrines, academic skepticism, political spin, and sharp reproach we must correctly analyze in these last days.[35]

God rebukes us, His people, for thoughtlessness, or lack of due reflection on His faithful, loving care over our lives (Isa. 1:3; Mark 6:52). The Scriptures, therefore, urge us to meditate (to "consider," be "mindful," "muse," "remember," or "think") on many subjects: God's Word (Ps. 1:2; 119:15, 23, 48, 78, 97, 99,

---

33. Even with the Holy Spirit's warnings, we may fail to distinguish between deceivers, heresies, and other satanic diversions and the genuine servants, messages, and works of God if we don't take the time to ponder the key clarifying scriptures the Spirit brings to mind (Acts 11:16). The simple wisdom of the man born blind proves we don't have to have a PhD to be thoughtful and insightful (John 9:30–33)—and visited, enlightened, and comforted by Jesus (9:35–38)!
34. R. L. Harris, G. L. Archer Jr., and B. K. Waltke, editors, *Theological Wordbook of the Old Testament*, electronic edition (Chicago: Moody Press, 1999), s.v. "meditate."
35. We'll never overcome our strong-minded "adversary, the devil" (1 Pet. 5:8) if we remain weak minded, fearfully minded, double minded, carnally minded, high minded, or incuriously dull minded. So study! Think! Meditate!

148), His goodness (104:34), His work (77:12; 143:5; Eccles. 7:13), creation (Ps. 8:1, 3–4; 19:1); miracles (1 Chron. 16:12; Mark 6:52), providence (Eccles. 9:1), human life (Eccles. 4:1, 4, 15), wisdom (Ps. 49:3), adversity (Eccles 7:14), dreams (Dan. 7:8; 8:5; 9:23), fulfillments (Luke 3:15), our pre-conversion bondage (Deut. 15:15), our past stubbornness (Deut. 9:7; Hosea 7:2), our neglect of God's will (Hag. 1:5, 7), His past training in our lives (Deut. 8:2), and others' needs (Heb. 10:24). As we meditate on these things, the Spirit gives us insight into their meaning and how we should respond: "Think about what I am saying, because the Lord will give you the ability to understand everything" (2 Tim. 2:7, NCV).

By thus accentuating the positive, we avoid the negative (Gal. 5:16). Cultivating study of excellent things helps us avoid unworthy thoughts, strengthen our intellect, love and honor God with "all our minds," and so win the crucial battle for our minds, "bringing into captivity every thought to the obedience of Christ" (2 Cor. 10:5). Are you winning or losing this battle?

Today take your thought life seriously. Discipline your mind and make it Christ's servant. Don't say you can't develop intellectually because you didn't excel in school, don't have a university degree, or never liked to read. That's no excuse; you're in Christ now, a new creature with limitless potential![36] Many of

---

36. A. W. Tozer's formal education was surprisingly limited. He never had the benefit of university or seminary training—and only attended high school *one* day! But after his conversion he obeyed Paul's command—studying his Bible diligently and prayerfully, reading voraciously and widely, reflecting deeply and often, and writing thoughtfully and cogently—and became one of the twentieth century's most cerebral, articulate, and deeply spiritual evangelical thinkers and authors. His insightful, incisive, power-packed words stimulate the faith and holy desires of thousands today through his books. What might God do in you if you too "think on these things"? See James L. Snyder, *In Pursuit of God: The Life of A. W. Tozer* (Camp Hill, PA: Christian Publications, 1991), 35.

the Philippians had little or no education, but they obeyed Paul's order. Follow their lead. "Think on these things"—not trivia or trash but "whatever" is excellent, praiseworthy, spiritually edifying, or intellectually stimulating. You'll never be the same.

4:9 Ordered to obey! After ordering the Philippians to think, Paul immediately challenges them to convert their fine thinking into finer living. Specifically, they must "do" (4:9) what they have:

- "LEARNED" (4:9)—Christ's spiritual truths and life lessons they've grasped intellectually from the oral and written instruction of Paul and other ministers

- "RECEIVED" (4:9)—the truths and lessons they've already accepted and begun to practice in their daily lifestyle

- "HEARD" (4:9)—the truths, lessons, and examples they've acquired by the reports and testimonies of other Christians and leaders, including Paul; while some ancients told tall tales, Christians told "Paul tales"—reports of the amazing things God did in and through Paul in the various cities and nations around the Mediterranean[37]

---

37. Thanks to Dr. Luke penning them in Acts, we marvel at and speak often of these "Paul tales"—Paul's midnight prayers while suffering causing an earth-quaking divine intervention, Paul's Ephesian ministry turning all Asia Minor on its head, Paul prophesying deliverance on board a foundering ship in a hurricane, Paul healing everyone on Malta in Jesus' name, Paul being the target of numerous death plots (Acts 23:12–13), and so forth. My, how rapidly these *true* tales of God's amazing power and grace through Paul must have circulated through the first-century assemblies!

- "Seen in me" (4:9)—the truths, lessons, and examples they've witnessed firsthand in Paul's self-emptied, Christ-centered, truth-loving, love-driven lifestyle—his humility, devotion, prayer, sacrificial obedience, suffering, mercy, and charity—during his time with them in Philippi; Acts 16 tells this amazing story of Paul's Christlike living.

If they comply, obeying these truths and lessons in their daily lives, Paul promises:

> The God of peace [and the peace He gives] shall be with you.
> —Philippians 4:9

Why this urgent charge to "do" what they've learned? Paul realized if we only study and think yet fail to act on our excellent thinking, all our study is worthless. God gives truth to transform, not inform us. If we remain unchanged, we become unapproved. We're as foolish as the "silly" women Paul castigated for being zealous about biblical studies but unconcerned with biblical living—and dangerously self-deceived (2 Tim. 3:6–7; James 1:22–25; Matt. 7:21–23; Rev. 3:17).

Paul's exhortation is also a stark contrast to the pagan religions of his day. The Greek and Roman gods didn't demand high standards of moral or ethical conduct from their adherents, only that they comply with ceremonial rites, feasts, and offerings. Paul put the Philippians on notice that Christ was no Greco-Roman deity. He demands His worshippers change! They weren't just to study this new "way"; they were to walk in

Standing Fast!

it, living their learning every day, every hour, every minute.[38] The word "do" (4:9) refers not to a single act but rather to a continuous practice. Paul was saying, "These things habitually practice" (Wuest), or "Hold fast to them" (Wey). Why is persistent obedience important?

It is the only way to perfect godly or spiritual living. We perfect every activity, sport, art, craft, or profession by practicing it, often daily. We would never think of considering our abilities or gifts perfect after one act. We accept that continuous practice is necessary to fully develop our singing, painting, tennis, golf, knitting, woodworking, oratory, writing, and so forth. Similarly Jesus exhorts us to "continue in my word" (John 8:31) by not only persistently studying but also persistently practicing the spiritual truths we're learning. This alone will enable us to grow in grace until we become spiritually mature or "perfect" (Matt. 5:48; Heb. 13:20–21). There's more.

Consistent obedience also increases our inner peace. By promising the obedient, "The God of peace shall be with you" (4:9), Paul also promised the peace He gives—the "peace of God that passeth all understanding" (4:7). More of God's supernatural, undisturbable, inner tranquility, isn't that reason enough to live what we're learning?

Steady implementation of our instruction also takes us farther down the road of the deeper life in Christ. It enables us to learn more from God's Word, discerning new insights and applications in familiar Bible passages. It raises our viewpoint so we begin to see ourselves, others, our tests, our

---

38. If we reject this central duty to change our thoughts and ways to obey our Lord, ironically, like the pagans of Paul's day, we also gravitate toward impotent religion that emphasizes symbols and rituals but neither produces nor requires substantive life changes (2 Tim. 3:5)—and delivers no inner peace (Phil. 4:9b).

adversaries, and even current events with a spiritual mind. Best of all, it causes Jesus to draw closer to us—when we seek Him, during our workday, in the heat of trial, as we travel, when we least expect and most need Him (Luke 24:13–32). Why? He gives Himself fully to those who obey Him fully. Oswald Chambers said:

> An elevated mood can only come out of an elevated habit of personal character. If in the externals of your life you live up to the highest you know, God will continually say "Friend, go up higher" [to a higher standpoint...in the insight of your character]...
>
> Never let God give you one point of truth which you do not instantly live up to. Always work it out, keep in the light of it.[39]

For all these reasons God often tests us repeatedly in the same area of obedience. Though we've obeyed in these issues before, He requires us to obey again, and again, and again. To become spiritually mature, deeply peaceful, more discerning in God's Word, raised to God's viewpoint, and closer to Jesus, we must practice our trust and obedience not once or twice but many times in many circumstances over many years. That's why God kept Moses in Midian, Paul in Tarsus, David in the wilderness, Joseph in prison, and even Jesus so long in Nazareth. They were practicing the truths and ways—daily spiritual life disciplines—of God, which, once perfected, they passed on to thousands.

The reverse is equally true: If not practicing obedience, we're practicing disobedience. And perfecting it! There are already enough Christians who are perfectly disobedient. Do we want

---

39. Oswald Chambers, *My Utmost for His Highest* (New York: Dodd, Mead, & Company, 1935), 87.

to join them? And grieve Christ? And forfeit the peace, viewpoint, fellowship, and loving favor of "the God of peace"? There's no middle ground here. We're either practicing obedience or disobedience.[40] Jesus confirmed there are basically two kinds of Christians, implementers and ignorers of His Word (Luke 6:47–49). Implementers become instrumental in God's hands; ignorers become irrelevant. So Paul got in the Philippians' faces about this matter of obedience.

Like his previous command to "think," Paul's "do" was not a suggestion but an order. The Philippians responded well, becoming persistent practitioners of the Word and instrumental in God's hands. It's time we respond.

Let's consistently and repetitively "do" the biblical truths and life lessons we've "learned" from our ministers; "received" already and begun to obey; "seen" in our Paul's (pastors, elders, mentors, spiritual fathers and mothers); and "heard" from our "Paul tales"—the exemplary, inspiring God-stories in Acts, Christian history, Christian biographies, and present-day overcomers' testimonies. Soon our living will be as fine as our thinking. We'll be mature, peaceful instruments in God's hands.

Are you implementing or ignoring? "Doing" or deferring?

4:10 God's sweet providence and Paul's sweet humanness. Paul's heart was overjoyed when Epaphroditus arrived with the Philippians' loving letter and keenly needed contribution: "I rejoiced...greatly that now at the last your care of me hath flourished again" (4:10). Why was he so blessed?

They lifted his burden. Paul was a prisoner in Rome, chained to soldiers around the clock, abandoned by many Christian

---

40. If in doubt of this vital truth, a prayerful reading of 1 Samuel 15 will clarify the matter.

friends, and facing the very real prospect of being executed at the whim of the emperor. (Would you feel good if *Nero* were your judge?) But while he stayed close to the Lord, continued his ministry from his "hired house" (Acts 28:30–31), and I'm sure found God's grace sufficient and sustaining, always the thought of his upcoming hearing was there overhanging. Just then, while carrying this crushing burden, out of the blue a messenger arrived with a letter and financial gift from one of his favorite congregations, the Philippians! How sweet! Paul knew the timing of their gift was not accidental but providential.

Providence is God's omniscient foresight working through ordinary people, circumstances, and events to prepare blessings or aid for His people to help them do His will. It is seen prominently in the stories of Joseph, Ruth, and Esther. One commentator states:

> The Word of God clearly teaches the providential workings of God in nature and in the lives of His people. The word "providence" comes from two Latin words: *pro*, meaning "before," and *video*, meaning "to see." God's providence simply means that God sees to it beforehand.... It is the working of God in advance to arrange circumstances and situations for the fulfilling of His purposes....
>
> Life is not a series of accidents; it is a series of appointments. "I will guide thee with Mine eye" (Ps. 32:8)... "And when He putteth forth His own sheep, He goeth before them" (John 10:4). This is the providence of God, a wonderful source of contentment.[41]

Paul also rejoiced "greatly" because their timely, generous gift was "an evidence of their affection," and of "the success

---

41. Wiersbe, *The Bible Exposition Commentary*, Phil. 4:10, note.

of his ministry among them."[42] Truly, what he had labored to produce in them—mature Christlike living and love—was evident in their gift. Seeing Christ's hand using them, He realized afresh His work in Philippi, though viciously opposed, was not in vain; it was victorious! This gave him a minister's greatest joy (2:2; 4:1; 1 Thess. 2:19; 3 John 4).

He was furthermore being rewarded. Paul was reaping in joy the love he had sown in tears (Ps. 126:5–6). He had ministered sacrificially to the Philippians in their spiritual need (Acts 16:16–24); now they were supporting him sacrificially in his material need. It's the beautiful symmetry of God's promised reciprocation (Gal. 6:7) and Jesus' principle of giving (Luke 6:38). Realizing this, Paul could have boasted of how effective his ministry labors had been. Instead he reacted with characteristic thankfulness and humility.

Observe his unselfishness. One source notes, "Paul was always thankful for help but never made any demands upon his converts to support him. Here he does not speak of it to get help from them, but to praise them for their help."[43] And rather than ask the Philippians to reassure him by pledging future gifts, he reassured them God had noted their sacrificial giving on their heavenly "account" and would without fail "supply all your need" in the future (4:19).

Also observe his sweet understanding. He assumed the best, not the worst, about the Philippians, crediting them for wanting to give to him earlier but not being able to do so: "I know you have always been concerned for me, but you didn't have the chance to help me" (4:10, NLT). Apparently Epaphroditus related this to Paul when he arrived (4:18). Their inability to

---

42. Henry, *Commentary in One Volume*, Phil. 4:10, note, 1867.
43. *Dake's Annotated Reference Bible*, Phil. 4:10, note, 218.

support Paul earlier was probably due to their not knowing his whereabouts or if he had even survived his voyage or hearing.

Paul's sweet response confirms this: Inside the marvelous ministry machine we know as the Apostle Paul was a tender, sensitive, needy, vulnerable human heart just like ours. He was in the fullest sense a man of God—full of God and yet fully a man (Gal. 1:24; 2:20)—like Elijah and capable of both soaring and sinking. While standing in awe of Paul's exploits in Christ, we need to remember this super shepherd's human feelings and needs—and those of our local shepherds.

However efficient, gifted, and seemingly unflappable our ministers may seem, they have the same intimate heart and life needs we have, *plus* more or less of Paul's burdens of ministerial studies, teachings, writings, intercessions, troubleshooting, travels…and various thorns, nails, and crosses! What kind "gift" may you send them today? A thank-you note? A visit to their home for conversation and coffee? Financial, material, or other assistance? An invitation for a meal at your home or an evening out? Such sweet gifts will lift their burdens, boost their spirits, and increase their labors for the kingdom (and the fruit on your account! 4:17).

And if they're extraordinarily burdened, your thoughtfulness may be God's providence sweetening their bitter times and blessing them as much as the Philippians cheered Paul: "I was made very happy in the Lord that now you have revived your interest in my welfare." (AMP).

4:11–12 Taught of God. Paul's words, "I have learned…I am instructed" (4:11–12, KJV), reveal he received the Holy Spirit's personal instruction. Thus he was taught of God.

We believe Paul's extraordinary heavenly instruction began in the Arabian Desert and continued during the numerous visions Christ gave him (Gal. 1:11–12, 15–17; 2 Cor. 12:1–5). Christ's grand plan for the church, His uniting of Jews and Gentiles in one body, the Rapture of the church, the Antichrist, Israel's present and future place in God's plan, and especially the gospel of salvation by God's grace alone—these and other revelations, Paul asserts, were taught him by the Spirit, not by any man:

> The gospel which was preached by me is not after man. For I neither received it of man, neither was I taught it [of man], but by the revelation of Jesus Christ [by the Spirit].
> —GALATIANS 1:11–12

But in Philippians 4 the Spirit's instruction was of a much more personal nature. He was Paul's personal Teacher, and Paul's providentially arranged circumstances were His classroom. The Spirit "opened" Paul's inner ears (Isa. 50:4–5) and "spoke" (brought to mind or conscience) biblical truths to Paul to correct his thoughts, attitudes, desires, motives, speech, and behavior, thus changing his life habits from the innermost to the outermost! Daily He instructed Paul more precisely to help him eliminate his unchristlike ways and conform more perfectly to Christ's will and image (Rom. 8:29). This instruction wasn't in a church or school but in Paul's Spirit-filled soul. This very personal education shouldn't surprise us. Jesus called the Holy Spirit the *Paraklētos*, or one called alongside to help, and added He would "teach you all things" and "bring all things to your remembrance, whatever I have said unto you" (John 14:26).

Paul testifies this marvelous private coaching was ongoing in his life. So he felt himself above human instruction?

Certainly not! "I am instructed" also implies human instruction. Paul humbly and hungrily received instruction from Jewish rabbis in Tarsus; the great rabbi, Gamaliel (Acts 22:3); Ananias of Damascus (Acts 9:17–19a); the Damascus Christians (Acts 9:19b); Peter, the apostles, elders, and Barnabas[44] (Acts 9:27–28); and probably the other excellent, more experienced ministers in Antioch (Acts 13:1).[45] All these teachers contributed to the intellectual or spiritual learning of this man who testified, "I have learned."

Yet his Instructor in Philippians 4:11–12 is neither sage nor saint but the Spirit. The blessed Teacher worked secretly in Paul's heart, applying biblical verses to the situations of his life, convicting him, guiding him, checking him, inspiring devotion to Christ, leading him in prayer, prompting and instructing his worship, and urging improvements in his lifestyle. Every time Paul responded, he grew. In this context he specifies the Spirit taught him "to be content" in every circumstance, whether

---

44. Paul surely imbibed congregational and conversational teaching from the apostles and elders during the few weeks he was "with them coming in and going out in Jerusalem" (Acts 9:23), gleaning deep lessons, prophecies, and anecdotes from Christ's life, teaching, and ministry from these men who knew him on earth. Thus he increased his knowledge of Christ by receiving their ministry—though he denied they taught him the distinctive doctrines he ministered and asserted he was their equal in apostolic revelation (Gal. 1:15–20, 2:6).

45. It's likely that before his conversion Paul was exposed to or sat under Stoic teachers who held forth in Tarsus, where Paul spent part of his childhood and nearly a decade after his conversion (Acts 17:28–29). While as a Christian he didn't seek God's wisdom through Greco-Roman philosophers, or try to reconcile their views with that of Scripture (as Philo, Clement of Alexandria, Origen, and others mistakenly did), he nevertheless was acquainted with their views, if for no other reason than to become "all things to all men" when evangelizing those holding such philosophies (1 Cor. 9:19–22) or to adequately rebut heretics holding their views (Col. 2:3, 8–10).

desirable or deplorable (4:11–12), and assured him that if he would always be willing, Christ's strength would always be sufficient (4:13). Paul learned this and many other lessons very well. And very privately.

The original language emphasizes the secrecy of the Spirit's instruction. "Instructed" (4:12) is taken from a Greek word (*myēo*) meaning "initiated" in a secret teaching,[46] such as one taught in ancient mystery cults.[47] Paul uses it here to underscore the utterly confidential and non-public nature of the secret education given him. And received by him.

Paul's words, "I have learned [and now]...I know...I know" (4:11–12), also tell us he fully received and implemented the lessons the Spirit taught him. He understood, he surrendered, he practiced, and now these lessons were part of his character—those distinctive habitual thoughts, decisions, and actions that made him an amazingly Christ-filled man.

The same divine Teacher is our personal Tutor. He "opens" our inner ears to hear His voice like true disciples of Christ (Luke 24:45). He illuminates our minds with the meaning and application of texts as we prayerfully read or study Scripture. Like no human instructor, the Spirit knows precisely which biblical truths, principles, or lessons we need to "add" to our character at present (2 Pet. 1:5–8). He arranges circumstances that provide opportunities to obey these truths and brings them to

---

46. Jamieson, Fausset, and Brown, *Commentary Critical and Explanatory on the Whole Bible*, Phil. 4:12, note.
47. These mystery cults were ancient religious groups whose rites, teachings, and meetings were reserved for initiates and thus kept secret (a mystery) from the public. Two widely popular mystery cults in the Roman world were the cults of Mithras (Persian) and of Isis (Egyptian). Christians today, of course, should avoid secret societies (Freemasons, Shriners), however admirable their charities, especially those claiming to offer special spiritual or theological illumination not available outside their organizations (John 14:6; 8:31–32, 36; Col. 2:3).

mind spontaneously as we need them, confirming our obedience with peace and our disobedience with the absence of peace, joy, spiritual refreshment, biblical insight, and the sense of Christ's presence—until we self-examine, confess, and repent (1 John 1:9)! Thus besides teaching, He also trains us in God's ways of thinking and living, leading us ever further in spiritual maturity. As we cooperate, our knowledge of Christ and "ear" to hear what the Spirit is saying increase (Rev. 3:22).Without this intensely private instruction from our divine Life-Coach our knowledge of Jesus remains entirely academic, theoretic, cerebral, and exterior. We're left informed but unchanged, religious but unreal (2 Tim. 3:6–7). So here's a kingdom news flash…

We need divine instruction as well as human! "It is written in the prophets, 'And they shall all be taught of God'" (John 6:45, NAS; cf. Isa. 54:13). We need public ministry and private tutelage, interaction with teachers and the Teacher, obedience to preachers and the *Paraklētos*. Ruminate on this—and respect, receive, and respond to the private ministry of the Holy Spirit.

4:11–12 Total contentment. This is Paul's declaration of total contentment. He came to this not by a sudden divine experience but by a continuing inner education. One commentator notes, "Paul's spiritual contentment was not something he had immediately after he was saved. He had to go through many difficult experiences of life in order to learn how to be content."[48]

Indeed, the Holy Spirit kept working with him until he became restfully content "whatever" his lot (4:11), humiliating or exhilarating: "I know how to be abased and live humbly in straitened circumstances, and I know also how to enjoy plenty and live in abundance" (4:12, AMP). Most of us struggle with

---

48. Wiersbe, *The Bible Exposition Commentary*, Phil. 4:10–13, note.

hard circumstances, and some (stoical, ascetical Christians) with easy circumstances, but mature believers embrace both. For this we need the fruit of self-control (Gal. 5:22–23)—"I know in fact how to discipline myself in lowly circumstances. I know in fact how to conduct myself when I have more than enough" (Phil. 4:12, Wuest)—and for this fruit of the Spirit to flourish, we must learn to be refilled with the Spirit daily. Here's a tip.

To enjoy Paul's contentment, embrace his instructions in this context:

1. "Rejoice" in your close fellowship walk with Jesus "always" (4:4), giving thanks in "every" situation (1 Thess. 5:18; Eph. 5:20) and in "whatever" you do (Col. 3:17, niv). Why? "He hath said, I will never leave thee, nor forsake thee" (Heb. 13:5). Therefore you can be so deeply satisfied with Jesus—who is always with you—that no situation spoils your overcoming spirit.

2. Never worry but ever pray in faith with thanksgiving about every need (4:6–7). Then that disruptive inner Goliath, anxiety, can't spoil your contentment.

3. "Think on" spiritually edifying, morally right, and intellectually stimulating things to nourish, exercise, and guard your mind (4:8). We live largely in our thoughts; filling our minds with God thoughts keeps us content with God things (Isa. 26:3).

4. Never complain or covet (4:11, 17), instead offering "sacrifices" of thanksgiving and songs of

praise (Heb. 13:15; Acts 16:25). Paul, who taught us to always give thanks and never murmur (1 Thess. 5:18; 1 Cor. 10:10), and who realized murmuring unraveled even Job's amazing contentment (Job 3:1–2), conscientiously refused to murmur: "Not that I complain of want" (Phil. 4:11a, MOFFATT).

5. Remember and believe you can meet any challenge with God's grace (4:13; 2 Cor. 12:9–10).

6. When abased, remember that though your blessings are gone, they'll return one day and "flourish again," as Paul's did (Phil. 4:10).

7. When abounding, choose humility and moderation (gentleness, forbearance). Never turn to prideful boasting, willfulness, or self-reliance on your resources, strength, or wisdom (4:5; 1 Cor. 10:12).

Remember also, Christian contentment remains essentially a simple, determined choice to be satisfied enough with our worldly lot because we have Christ and the sweet inner benefits He gives, whatever our outward troubles or blessings. We'll never know this miraculous tranquility until we stop making selfish demands and seek only our King and His kingdom desires "first" daily (Matt. 6:33)—even if we never get what we want in this life!

Literally, *content* (Greek, *autarkēs*) means, "self-sufficient; sufficient in oneself."[49] The ancient Stoics and Cynics used this word

---

49. H. Liddell, *A Lexicon: Abridged From Liddell and Scott's Greek-English Lexicon* (Oak Harbor, WA: Logos Research Systems, Inc., 1996), s.v. *"autarkēs."*

to describe self-reliant ones who aspired to live independently of others' help.[50] Keener notes two historical facts:

1. Greek moralists, influenced by Stoic thought, praised those who could be content with little as well as with much. (Cynics went so far as to prove their contentment in little by making certain that was all they ever had.)

2. It was said that the wise man needed no one but himself and was completely independent.[51]

This first statement agrees with Philippians 4:11–13. The second, however, is proud Adamic nonsense. No human is created to be totally independent of God or people, and those claiming such only deceive themselves and forfeit the rich joys of divine or human fellowship. Satan repackaged and redistributed this lie among Christians beginning in the fourth and fifth centuries to promote (especially hermitic) monasticism as the superior way to spiritual maturity.

Paul uses *autarkēs* differently, to rejoice that he is "self-sufficient in Christ's sufficiency" (4:13, AMP; 2 Cor. 3:5), yet never so much that he has no need of other Christians. But truly, the more of Jesus' life, truth, and joy we possess, the less worldly possessions we need to be satisfied. Of all people Christians should be restfully content with a minimum of worldly things. Again, Paul sets God's standard: "If we have enough food and clothing, let us be content" (1 Tim. 6:8, NLT). Got food? Got clothes? Be content with that, since you always have Jesus to satisfy you (Heb.

---

50. Kittel, Friedrich, and Bromiley, *Theological Dictionary of the New Testament*, s.v. "*autarkēs*."
51. Keener, *The IVP Bible Background Commentary: New Testament*, Phil. 4:11–13, note.

13:5). End of conversation! That many today are rabid materialists proves how infrequently and inefficiently we satisfy our souls with Jesus, and that we're spiritually bankrupt (Rev. 3:17)—though not without hope of recovery (3:18–20)!

Paradoxically, Paul also learned to be "full" (satisfied) and "hungry" (seeking) simultaneously (Phil. 4:12, 18). His words have literal and figurative interpretations.

Literally, Paul experienced hunger: "I know how...to be hungry" (4:12). Surprisingly the great apostle occasionally experienced insufficient nourishment in his arduous travels and troubles (2 Cor. 11:27), while at other times feasting on excellent fare (Acts 16:15; 28:10). Yet—and this is the great lesson—neither experience moved him from his close walk and work with Jesus! Why did the all-sufficient God permit Paul's brief privation? Perhaps to enhance his compassion. We can't fully understand hunger unless we've been hungry.[52] Fasting and even dieting may give us hints, but they can't replicate involuntary food shortages. Have we learned, as Paul did, to not be offended with Christ even when we risk or experience temporary hunger? Many Christians learned about hunger in the Great Depression. Any significant disruption in our American power grid, transportation systems, or harvests could force us to relearn this humbling lesson.

---

52. Presently, of the world's 7.3 billion people, 791 million (13.5 percent) suffer some degree of hunger daily. How can the constantly well-fed fully understand the plight of the constantly hungry? It's not beyond the scope of possibility that God may let some of us taste their bitter cup—exposing us temporarily to undesirable, sporadic, or insufficient food supplies (Matt. 12:1, 2–3; Mark 11:12)—to fill us with compassion and urgency in helping the hungry (Mark 8:2–3; 2 Cor. 1:3–5). I neither predict nor favor but only suggest the possibility of this. For further information on current hunger statistics, see: http://www.worldhunger.org/articles/Learn/world%20hunger%20facts%202002.htm#Number_of_hungry_people_in_the_world (accessed April 1, 2015).

Figuratively Paul meant he had learned to be "full" (satisfied) with whatever material things he had (Phil. 4:18), yet always "hungry" for (unsatisfied in) the things of God—insatiable for more of Christ's sweet presence, illuminated Word, personal guidance, approval for service, ministry opportunities, compassionate power and gifts, and so forth. Also, he learned to be satisfied with what God had done in, for, and through him, yet always expected Him to do more (Ps. 81:10). Or, in the words of William Carey, "Expect great things from God; attempt great things for God!"[53]

Unlike Carey, who overcame tremendous adversities in India, if we won't be content, discontentment will breed instability and ultimately spiritual failure. Our circumstances will dictate our disposition and fruitfulness for Christ. Our emotions and labors will shift back and forth as our seasons of blessing and adversity change. We'll never maintain a steady good attitude or work (or ministry) output, but will be depressed by adversity and distracted by prosperity and not finish our course as faithfully and fruitfully as we should. Content believers, however, like Paul, will move steadily forward in devotion and duty daily "whatever" their state (Phil. 4:11; 1 Cor. 15:58).

So we must learn contentment wherever God puts us.[54] If not, we'll never enjoy His peace. And our discontentment—our dysfunction, and divine disapproval and disuse—will only increase. Henry said:

---

53. Mark Galli and Ted Olsen, *131 Christians Everyone Should Know* (Nashville, TN: B&H Publishing, 2000), 245.
54. There are four degrees of contentment: (1) in thriving success and prosperity, (2) in normalcy, (3) in adversity, and (4) in great adversity. Anyone can do the first, many people the second, fewer the third, and very few the last. But with God's grace, His Word, Christ's presence, and the Spirit's comforting guidance we can be among the very few who, never complaining, ever praying, and always thankful, remain heavenly minded and content in even the most hellish trials (Dan. 3:25–26; Mark 4:37–38a; Acts 12:6).

> What can a man desire more than enough?...A covetous worldling, if he has ever so much, would still have more; but a heavenly Christian, though he has little, has enough.[55]

Even the pagan philosopher Epicurus noted:

> Nothing is enough for the man to whom enough is too little....Do not spoil what you have by desiring what you have not.[56]

Thus Paul concludes, "Godliness with contentment" is "great profit" (1 Tim. 6:6, ISV) or "is itself great wealth" (NLT). Why? Those who seek material riches hope their wealth will bring contentment, so the contented Christian has in Christ what the discontented rich seek in materialism! That Christian, then, is "rich" whatever his net worth (Rev. 2:9), and the discontent Christian is "poor" even if his assets are substantial (3:17). Christ wants us all spiritually rich (Rev. 3:18). Wanna be rich?

Practice total contentment.

4:13 Perfect positivism. Paul asserted firmly that whatever challenge Christ set before him, he was equal to it in Him: "I am ready for anything and equal to anything through Him Who infuses inner strength into me; I am self-sufficient in Christ's sufficiency" (4:13, AMP). His positive attitude stands in sharp contrast to Moses' initial pessimism when God called him to lead the Exodus. Moses cited excuse after excuse and roused God's anger for his stubborn insistence that he couldn't do what God asked (Exod. 4:1–17). Why was Moses so negative and Paul so positive?

---

55. Henry, *Commentary in One Volume*, Phil. 4:18, note, 1867.
56. See http://quotationsbook.com/quote/140/ (accessed April 1, 2015).

Standing Fast!

The short answer is their focus. Paul focused on God's unfailing faithfulness and grace; Moses on his own human limitations, weaknesses, past failures, and inexperience. Let's look deeper.

In this context the "all things" Paul speaks of are undesirables, low places and tasks in which we're "abased" (Phil. 4:12) or mortified in the most despised conditions of life: poverty, hunger, persecution, tribulation, failure, and so forth. Paul's present condition underscored this. He had been a prisoner for approximately four years and was still unsure he would be released (2:23). Unaided, human stuff can't handle such unjust or cruel experiences very long without murmuring, rebelling, or running away. But "through Christ" within, we can. Paul learned this when praying for release from his thorn in the flesh. Christ assured him, whatever Paul's pains, griefs, burdens, or needs, "my grace is sufficient for thee" (2 Cor. 12:7–10). We too can handle "all things" adverse since the same Christ refills us with the same grace every day as we fellowship privately with Him (Isa. 40:28–31; Matt. 11:28–30). But grace does more.

"All things" also refers to desirables. The same grace that gets us through adversity sustains us in prosperity. And we need just as much of it there—the grace of humility, spiritual hunger, fear of God, wisdom to keep Christ "first" (Matt. 6:33), faithfulness to keep pursuing our calling, discernment to detect despiritualizing snares and distractions, strength of will to deny temptations—if we hope to stay on course. Why? Prosperity, success, ease, and popularity incline us to relax our spiritual concentration, live off our past accomplishments, and focus on enjoying ourselves. In such undisciplined moments we're tempted most strongly to pride, greed, sinful pleasures, worldly compromises, or other forms of putting self-will before Christ's will. Beware the many pitfalls of success!

Many noble individuals, powerful nations, the Roman church, and many Protestant denominations have fallen from high, not low places, stumbling while successful, not afflicted. They depended wholly on the Lord in their days of adversity because they had to! But when they became powerful, prosperous, and popular, they began relying on their wealth, influence, numbers, and other human means. David, Solomon, Uzziah, and Hezekiah were all in positions of strength and honor, not weakness and reproach, when lust, idolatry, pride, and ingratitude toppled them (2 Sam. 11:2–5; 1 Kings 11:9–11; Neh. 13:26; 2 Chron. 26:5, 15–16; 32:23–26). When prosperous, increasing in numbers, or growing in favor, we need to remember this and stay very humble, close, prayerful, watchful, and dutiful (Deut. 8:10–20). Better and wiser saints than us have suddenly tumbled down from Mount Blessings!

As a young man A. W. Tozer was wise beyond his years. When ordained to the ministry, he prayed the following:

> If, as sometimes it falleth out to Thy servants, I should have grateful gifts pressed upon me by Thy kindly people, stand by me then and save me from the blight that often follows. Teach me to use whatever I receive in such manner that will not injure my soul nor diminish my spiritual power.
>
> And if in Thy permissive providence honor should come to me from Thy church, let me not forget in that hour that I am unworthy of the least of Thy mercies, and that if men knew me as intimately as I know myself they

would withhold their honors or bestow them upon others more worthy to receive them.[57]

In this humble mind-set Tozer lived and labored persistently and productively. And positively! So should we.

While maintaining Tozer's humility, we need to frequently recall Paul's positivism. And believe it. And confess it confidently: "I—not just the great Apostle Paul, but I!—*can do* all things God sets before me, including walk and work closely with Jesus in prosperous seasons." While soaring on this rising thermal of God-confidence, we need one more small weight attached to our wings.

The "all things" Paul speaks of are in, not out, of God's will. Our unchecked positivism must be counterbalanced with the sweet advice of Jesus. The same One who assured us we can do all things through His sufficient grace added, "Without me ye can do nothing" (John 15:5), or "Apart from Me you can do nothing" (NAS). So here are our Christian capabilities: In God's will, everything! Out of it, nothing! It's that simple...and unchanging.[58] Our death with Christ means we're dead to the old life and everything outside of God's will. Even if a work or interest is fine for others to pursue, if Christ hasn't ordained it for us, He won't supply grace for it. The moment we step aside from His guidance or plan, we're on our own—and foolishly depending on the strength, wisdom, and graces of a dead man. And dead people can do "nothing." Oh, if we're stubborn and persistent, we can do something, but because it's outside God's will, whatever we build, He will ultimately destroy; whatever

---

57. A. W. Tozer, *The Best of A. W. Tozer* (Harrisonburg, PA: Christian Publications, 1978), 79.
58. God "does not grant us superhuman ability to accomplish anything we can imagine without regard to his interests." See *Life Application Study Bible*, Phil. 4:13, note, 2023.

we accomplish, He will ignore. So in the end, as Jesus warned, whatever we do without Him will come to "nothing."[59]

Notwithstanding this wise warning, Christians, like Paul, should be earth's most positive people. Whether you are or not depends on your response. When Christ providentially sets "all things" before you, will you...

Be content in whatever condition you're in? "I can do it!" Go through long seasons of humbling testing or grievous suffering? "I can do it!" Enjoy blessings, fulfillments, prosperity, popularity without being stumbled by them? "I can do it!" Accept challenging new positions, tasks, missions, ministries—without focusing on your limitations, weakness, and past failures, as Moses did? "I can do it!" Why be so positive? Jesus' grace will be sufficient! Yet you know your limitations. If it's out of God's will, it's out of your plans! You're not expending your energies, resources, and time on "nothing." Sound negative? No, it's all positive.

It's perfect positivism, a spiritually mature attitude perfectly balanced between unbridled optimism and unbelieving pessimism, neither too bold nor too timid. From now on think, live, and labor with perfect positivism.

4:14–19 A very giving church. Here Paul describes the Philippian church as being extraordinarily generous.

---

59. Solomon filled the temple courts with idolatrous altars, but God had them torn down. Jonah sailed to Tarshish, but God spoiled the voyage. Ahaz boarded up God's temple, but God prompted his son Hezekiah to restore and reopen it. Jehoshaphat made an alliance with wicked Ahab, but God broke it up. All these no doubt felt very positive about their divinely unauthorized pursuits while they temporarily looked successful. But God's eventual judgment proved that all along they were, well, a lot of nothing! Make your life and works count for something. Live very close to Christ (John 15:1–8), and "whatsoever he saith unto you, do it" (John 2:5).

Standing Fast!

They began giving to Paul's ministry when they first heard him preach and teach "in the beginning of the gospel [in Philippi]" (4:15). They continued supporting him when he left their region of northern Greece: "Ye did share...when I departed from Macedonia" (4:14–15). This was unusual, as Paul noted, "No [other] church shared with me...but ye only" (4:15). Even when he was ministering to other churches, they gave to him: "Even in Thessalonica ye sent...unto my necessity" (4:16). Now they've blessed him again, this time in his deep "affliction"—while a prisoner in Rome awaiting trial before the nefarious Nero (4:14)! Their gift has put him over the top financially, relieving all indebtedness and even giving him for the moment a surplus: "I have all, and abound" (4:18). Thus their charitable acts were outstanding.[60]

So were their motives. They didn't give to be known, awarded, enriched, or to blindly imitate or zealously compete with other churches—Paul explicitly says "no [other] church" was supporting his ministry when the Philippians began doing so (4:15). The only reason left, therefore, was to please Christ and forward His kingdom work through Paul. That's pure giving—and remarkably rare. And it didn't go unnoticed by heaven.

For this extraordinary giving, Paul writes an extraordinary assessment of the Philippians. He commends them for donating, "Ye have well done" (4:14). He recalls how persistent their giving was: "You sent me aid more than once when I was in need" (4:16, NIV). He says it was "fruit" (credit) on their heavenly "account" or statement of giving (4:17). It was also like

---

60. Paul boasted of the Philippians' generous giving (and the Thessalonicans' and Bereans') to the fund he was collecting from Gentile churches to deliver to the Jerusalem church, stating they gave out of "deep poverty" and insisted that he not refuse their donation due to their financial needs (2 Cor. 8:1–4). Where can we find churches today that, when in need themselves, continue giving to other churches and ministries?

the "sweet smell" (4:18) of a very pleasing offering in God's nostrils (hinting the Lord had revealed to Paul how pleased *He* was with the Philippians' giving). Then he bequeaths an extraordinary benefit.

Paul unequivocally guarantees their fullest support, material and spiritual—"my God shall supply all your need" (4:19)—a promise he makes so boldly to only one other church, the Corinthian assembly (2 Cor. 9:8). The wealth from which God will supply their provisions is inexhaustible, nothing less than "his riches in glory" (4:19; "the riches of his glory," Eph. 3:16)—or all the vast natural and spiritual resources of heaven available to Jesus now in His glorified condition. So now they were financially independent through their dependency on the unfathomable riches of Christ! Whether Rome's economy, Macedonia's fortunes, or Philippi's trade rose or fell, God would take care of the Philippians as faithfully as they had Paul. That's sweet. That's "rich" (Rev. 3:18). Thus Paul gives very full recognition to this very giving church. And he wasn't alone.

Since He inspired Paul, Christ also wanted to honor the Philippians.[61] Doesn't this tell us that we too can please Christ if we're very giving Christians and churches and our motives are pure? Let your giving be well done, and Christ's "well done" will follow in His time and way: "Well done, thou good and faithful servant…" (Matt. 25:21, 23).

4:15 Supporting other ministries. The Philippians' support of Paul's ministry fell outside the sphere of their own church or local needs—but within the scope of Christ's kingdom interests. Why? Paul's ministry was the real article, a true kingdom builder. Thus they faithfully sponsored him.

---

61. We know Christ is a keen observer and faithful rewarder of what and how we give to His work (Mark 12:41–44; Gal. 6:7; Heb. 11:6).

And set yet another example for us. Not only should we be generous churches, but we should also support other ministries (missionaries, tract societies, Christian periodicals, charities, Christian schools, and so forth) and ministers not directly linked to our assembly, church group, or city. If God has raised them to bless the church at large, they need not only our intercession but also our support. Such partnerships help enlarge our viewpoint. We start thinking universally rather than locally or provincially. Other churches can't be our guide here.

As Paul noted, *no* other churches did as the Philippians: "not one church helped out.... You were the only one" (4:15, THE MESSAGE). So they were willing to be different, if the Spirit so led. Are we? Will our leaders seek, trust, obey, and commune with Christ so closely that they respond unhesitatingly to vertical calls irrespective of horizontal confirmations (Acts 13:1–3)?

The timeliness of the Philippians' gift was especially sweet, since Paul was awaiting trial on charges of insurrection and preaching an illegal religion (Acts 24:5). As true partners in suffering, they "shared" Paul's "affliction" (Phil. 4:14) or "came alongside me in my troubles" (THE MESSAGE). Thus they lifted the spirits of a minister who had so often lifted theirs. Our support of other ministers, missionaries, churches, or charities is especially sweet to them when suffering and may relieve their burdens as crucially as their messages, missions, ministries, or gifts have relieved us: "The Lord has filled me with joy because you again showed interest in me" (4:10, GW). It would be wonderful for the heavenly record to show our gifts or deeds helped deliver some of God's choice servants in their cruelest moments (1 Sam. 21:1–6; 25:1–17, 18, 27, 35; 2 Sam. 17:27–29; 1 Kings 17:10–16; Jer. 38:6–13).

Therefore we do well as churches and individuals to partner with excellent ministries as the Spirit leads (Rev. 3:22). To do so, we should reprioritize our giving, spending less on superfluous programs of negligible benefit and mere Christian entertainment and more on ministries that are sustaining the body of Christ. When considering proposed offerings, ask: "Will this spending help committed Christians' spiritual or material needs? Will it strengthen or enlarge Christ's ministry among us by His Word, Spirit, and gifts? Will it produce eternal or temporal results? Is this the Spirit's leading for us or just a good idea posing as a God idea?"

If the work before you is indeed the Lord's, as you're able, follow the Philippians' lead. Give, commit, and be faithful to your commitment. Help "Paul" build Christ's kingdom!

4:17 *Not* desiring gifts. Paul also modeled the right attitude ministers should hold toward financial gifts.

The great apostle to the Gentiles determined to "be content" with "whatever" he had, always making do with his current budget (Phil. 4:11–12; 1 Tim. 6:8). Whether his income from ministry gifts and tent-making rose or fell, he refused to "set his heart upon" gain by coveting, trusting, or rejoicing in it (Ps. 62:10; Jer. 9:23–24). He shunned ministerial gimmicks and psychological manipulation, never saying or doing anything to subtly induce believers to give him money or property.[62] He praised the Philippians' charity because they were worthy, not to induce further giving: "Not because I desire a gift" (Phil. 4:17). When gifts came from God's people without strings

---

[62]. The collections he received from Gentile churches were love-gifts for the largely Jewish, often poor, Judean church intended solely to meet their material needs, honor the gospel's Jewish heritage (Rom. 9: 3–5; 15:25–27), and repair the troublesome Gentile-Jewish rift created in some churches by the Judaizers' heresy (1 Cor. 16:1–4; 2 Cor. 8:1–4).

attached, Paul accepted them freely in Christ's name, as he accepted the Philippians' gift from Epaphroditus (4:18). Even when poorer Christians gave sacrificial gifts, he accepted them freely, confident God would repay them (2 Cor. 8:1–4; Matt. 10:8b). But if gifts were offered in exchange for unrighteousness—special favors, unjust assistance, service outside God's call, etc.—or any discerned attempt to obligate him, I believe his response was a quick, polite "No, thank you." The result?

Satan couldn't move Paul. He couldn't bait him with financial inducements or bribes to act apart from God's will, way, or time. No rich elder could buy Paul or determine where, when, or how he ministered by offering large fees or other desirable ministry perks. Paul desired God, not gifts; His will, not wealth; spiritual, not metallic gold; heavenly, not earthly mansions. Paul had already been bought, and he knew it (1 Cor. 6:19–20). He was Christ's servant alone, under the Spirit's guidance always, at the service of the saints daily, and not for sale. The Good Shepherd provided all he needed, and he trusted Him implicitly—and did not want!

Thus Paul avoided the net that caught Judas, who for clinging to his avarice eventually turned to theft (John 12:4–6) and exchanged the gift of God for gifts from men (Matt. 26:15; 2 Cor. 9:15). He steered clear of the "way of Balaam...who loved the wages of unrighteousness" (2 Pet. 2:15; Num. 22:7, 18). His decision to not covet gifts didn't originate with him. It was God's wisdom frequently offered in Proverbs and Ecclesiastes, which Paul obviously studied assiduously: "A bribe corrupts the heart" (Eccles. 7:7, NAS; Prov. 15:27; 17:23; 29:4).

He also studied Jewish and Gentile history, current events, and his own experiences, noting how frequently and tragically greed had corrupted monarchs (1 Kings 21:1–16), princes

(Hosea 5:10), priests (Isa. 1:23), Pharisees (Luke 16:13–14), politicians (Acts 24:24–26)—and preachers (1 Tim. 6:3–5; 2 Tim. 4:10)! He remembered Israel's original judges were faithful men, above bribery, "hating covetousness" (Exod. 18:21–22). Thus he penned the famous epigram that, not money, but the "love of money is the [a] root of all evil" (1 Tim. 6:10), adding that, once yielded to, greed pulls its captives into a vicious whirlpool of self-opposing, heart-rending, life-ruining sin and confusion (6:9–10). By inspiration he further ordered that greed disqualify anyone seeking church leadership.[63] I wonder if he also knew how materialism was taking root in the Laodicean church, where he or his disciples surely ministered while he was based in Ephesus (Acts 19:10, 20, 26), and to whom he had written an epistle now lost (Col. 4:15–16)?

Regardless, Paul knew there were too many prophets for profit and imitating them would profit no one. Besides, he was owned and desired only his Master's profit. Minister, disciple of Christ, new convert to the faith, consider well Paul's model. Desire God, not gifts!

4:17 Our heavenly account. Paul wanted the Philippians to give generously so they would have abounding "fruit" on their "account" (4:17). Thus their church had a heavenly "account" with God, measuring their earthly "giving and receiving" (4:15).

"Account" (Greek, *logos*) is also translated "statement" and refers to a written document detailing one's financial standing

---

63. Ministerial boards should remember that, amid all qualifications for ministers and deacons, stands Paul's urgent decree that they be "not greedy of filthy lucre" (1 Tim. 3:3, 8; Titus 1:7). While we may not feel this mandate paramount, Paul did, giving Timothy a powerful second dose of anti-greed (1 Tim. 6:3–11) and pro-charity medicine (6:17–19).

with a bank, merchant, or other creditor.[64] Not only churches but also individual Christians have "giving accounts" or "statements of giving" in heaven much as we have checking, savings, credit card, and company accounts on earth.

Every gift we give willingly is "fruit" on our account: "Fruit which increases to your credit [the harvest of blessing that is accumulating to your account]" (4:17, AMP). As it accrues, this "fruit" produces a credit balance or profit. This profit is the secure, imperishable "treasure" Jesus and Paul exhorted us to lay up in heaven (Matt. 6:19–20; 1 Tim. 6:17–19). It brings us Christ's approval (2 Cor. 9:7b), rewards at our judgment, and supplies on earth as needed (Phil. 4:19). That is, if our credits exceed our debits.

Every financial account has not only credits but also debits, not only deposits but also withdrawals. So every time we give cheerfully to Christ, His ministers, churches, or the needy, our account is credited. Every time we receive Christ's monetary or material mercies in the form of gifts, donations, profits, salaries, or other grace-given support, our account is debited. Are we giving so steadily, generously, and joyfully that we have a credit balance on our heavenly account?[65] Is our church doing so? If we only receive and never give, it follows that our divine approval, ultimate rewards, and the current resupply of our earthly needs will be diminished. "He who soweth sparingly shall reap also sparingly" (2 Cor. 9:6); or, "The farmer who plants a few seeds will have a very small harvest" (GW); or, "A stingy planter gets a stingy crop" (THE MESSAGE).

---

64. Swanson, *Dictionary of Biblical Languages With Semantic Domains: Greek (New Testament)*, s.v. "*logos*."
65. In his sermon "The Use of Money" (c. 1744), John Wesley taught, "Gain all you can, save all you can, and give all you can." See this proverb briefly expounded at: http://www.umfmtc.org/john-wesley-on-stewardship.html (accessed April 1, 2015).

Our account includes not just financial giving but everything we say and do. Thus our giving will be just one part or chapter in the "books" of works written of our lives. When we're judged, these records will be used to decide our rewards in Christ's kingdom (2 Cor. 5:10; Dan. 7:10; Job 19:23–24; Ps. 56:8; Mal. 3:16).[66] On Philippians 4:17, one commentator notes:

> [This is] a clear reference to each man as having an account in heaven (v. 17; Ps. 144:3; Heb. 13:17; 1 Pet. 4:5). He is either storing up wrath by his deeds on record in heaven (Rom. 2:5) or he is storing up reward (Rom. 14:1–12; 1 Cor. 3:11–15; 2 Cor. 5:10; Gal. 3:6). Even every idle (useless) word men will give an account of (Mt. 12:36). Every cup of cold water given or refused and the minutest details of life as well as the major acts will be judged (Mt. 6:1–18; 10:41–42; 16:27; Lk. 6:23, 35; 1 Cor. 3:8–15; 9:17).[67]

Aware we will face this meticulous Messianic examination and accountability, Paul in this and other epistles urged believers to give (and obey) generously, like our Father, who "giveth us richly all things" (1 Tim. 6:17) and wants us to be "rich in good works," always "ready to distribute, willing to share" (6:18). Then we'll have a good heavenly account—and pleasant accounting! Also our large credit balance, accrued by wisely using this world's "money of unrighteousness" generously (Luke 16:9), will prepare us for any hard times we may yet face on earth, as "a good foundation against the time to come" (1 Tim. 6:19).

With their profitable heavenly account, the Philippians had a good foundation in place and were calmly assured Christ would

---

66. And, for the unsaved, these "books" determine their degrees of punishment in the lake of fire (Rev. 20:11–12).
67. *Dake's Annotated Reference Bible*, Phil. 4:14, note, 218.

meet "all their needs" until He took them home (Phil. 4:19). Does your heavenly "giving account" have a credit or debit balance? Today increase your credits, enlarge your profits, lay up heavenly treasure, build a sure foundation, and rest in Christ's approval and the assurance of His provision.

4:18 Giving—a New Testament sacrifice. While Jewish animal sacrifices are obsolete, sacrifices are not. As believer-priests serving in the spiritual temple of the church, every believer is duty bound to offer sacrifices to the Lord daily.

With this in mind, Paul described the Philippians' monetary gift as a New Testament sacrifice reminiscent of the sweet incense that accompanied Jewish burnt or thank offerings (Exod. 29:18) and assured them God was well pleased with it. It was "a lovely fragrance, a sacrifice that pleases the very heart of God" (4:18, PHILLIPS).[68] The special sweetness of their gift lay in its timeliness, as it lifted Paul's spirits when he was in deep trouble and some, perhaps many, Christians had cooled toward him. Today the Philippians' sacrifice represents churches' or individuals' love offerings given to ministers, churches, missionaries, or ministries for Christ's sake, especially when they're in special need. There are many kinds of New Testament sacrifices.

As faithful believer-priests, we should bring God all these offerings:

- A "LIVING SACRIFICE"—our yielded bodies and renewed minds abiding, obeying, and thus demonstrating God's will daily (Rom. 12:1–2)

---

68. The same is stated of Jesus' amazing self-sacrifice on the cross (Eph. 5:2) and implied of Mary of Bethany's sacrifice of costly spikenard (John 12:3; Mark 14:9).

- FINANCIAL OR MATERIAL GIFTS—as described above (Phil. 4:18; Acts 4:32–37; 1 Cor. 16:1–4; 2 Cor. 8:1–4; 9:7)

- A "SACRIFICE OF PRAISE"—whether simply giving thanks or singing songs of praise and worship for Christ's pleasure (Heb. 13:15; Ps. 100:4; 29:1–2; Eph. 5:19–20; Col. 3:16; 1 Thess. 5:18)[69]

- FAITHFUL SERVICE—"The sacrifice and service coming from your faith" (Phil. 2:17, NIV); or, "Your faith makes you offer your lives as a sacrifice in serving God" (NCV).

- GOOD DEEDS—whatever we do "heartily, as to the Lord" is an offering to Him (Col. 3:23); "Don't forget to do good things for others.... These are the kinds of sacrifices that please God" (Heb. 13:16, GW); or, paraphrased, "God takes particular pleasure in acts of worship—a different kind of 'sacrifice'—that take place in kitchen and workplace and on the streets" (THE MESSAGE).

- OBEDIENCE TO GOD—including anything done to comply with His Word, guidance, or correction, or to submit to His ordained authorities (John 14:15; Rom. 13:1–7; Eph. 5:22–24; 6:1–9; 1 Pet. 2:13–15)

---

69. Often the "sacrifice of praise" blesses the offerer as much as the Lord. One of the most powerful Christian writers of the twentieth century, A. W. Tozer, often began his sessions of prayer, study, and writing by softly singing hymns to God in his office. God's presence soon enveloped him, often bringing with it key ideas for articles and sermons. See Snyder, *In Pursuit of God: The Life of A. W. Tozer*, 135.

- CHRISTIAN FELLOWSHIP—communing with other believers in person or by various forms of communications (Heb. 13:16, KJV), especially when they're lonely or distressed (2 Tim. 1:16–18)

- THE FRUIT OF OUR MINISTRY—the converts or disciples we help lead, train, or recall to Christ as a way of thanking Him for His awesomely gracious salvation; Paul described himself as a "minister of Christ Jesus to the Gentiles [with] the priestly duty of proclaiming the gospel of God, so that the Gentiles might become an offering acceptable to God, sanctified by the Holy Spirit" (Rom. 15:16, NIV).

- INTERCESSION—our sacrifices of "prayer and supplication in the Spirit" offered daily for other souls (Eph. 6:18–19; Col. 4:12; 1 Thess. 5:17; 1 Pet. 2:5; 1 Tim. 2:1–3; Rev. 8:3–4)

- SUFFERINGS—all the "crosses" (lost relationships, possessions, aspirations; or griefs) we willingly carry or "thorns" (difficult people) we endure to do God's will or pursue His call on our life (Gen. 22:1–12; Mark 10:28–30; Luke 14:25–27; Matt. 10:34–39; Phil. 3:4–9)[70]

- MARTYRDOM—giving, in the words of Lincoln, the "last full measure of devotion" rather than

---

70. Expounding Mark 10:21, the late Assemblies of God Bible teacher Walter Beuttler declared, "No natural claim, no earthly possession, no kind of a relationship or attachment to things or persons can be allowed to stand between us and the call of God if we are indeed to 'follow Him.' Everything we are and possess and aspire to in the natural has to be subservient and subordinated to the claim of the Master, 'Take up thy cross and follow me.'"

deny our King or His truth or fail to complete His will; Paul likened his looming, potential execution to a "drink offering" (Phil. 2:17, NIV).

Are you a faithful or forgetful believer-priest? Study these sacrifices, and begin offering them daily in your bodily temple. Your Lord, who offered Himself to His Father for you, awaits your offerings to Him.

4:19 "All our needs" met! Paul confidently promised the Philippians, who had so faithfully met all his needs, that God would faithfully meet all their needs. Hudson Taylor said frequently, "When God's work is done in God's way for God's glory, it will not lack for God's supply."[71] How wonderful!

What a joyous privilege to have every earthly need met by our heavenly Shepherd from "his riches in glory" (4:19)—the limitless spiritual and material resources of heaven and earth now available to Christ in His glorified state (Matt. 28:18; Ps. 24:1; 50:12). This provision is comprehensive in scope. Christ provides *"all* our need," including all personal and situational necessities—material, spiritual, social, and emotional—all the time in all places and in all conditions. Specifically, Paul speaks of financial provision, since this was what the Philippians provided for him and what he obviously expects God to reciprocate to them.

Paul's phrase, "according to his riches in glory" (or, in another Pauline expression, "the riches of his glory," Eph. 3:16), implies that God's supply is glorious and regal, like the lavish gifts and favors typically given by monarchs or other royals. If our needs are met according to the limited resources of ordinary people, they'll barely be met. But if supplied "according to his

---

71. Wiersbe, *The Bible Exposition Commentary*, Phil. 4:18, note.

riches in glory," or according to the King of heaven's treasuries, our supply will be more than enough, a sufficiency plus extra thrown in for good measure. Why? This is how monarchs and Messiahs give, not skimpily but sumptuously, abundantly, overflowingly: "who giveth us *richly*" (1 Tim. 6:17; cf. 2 Chron. 25:9; 2 Cor. 9:8). The fabulous and numerous natural wonders, architectural splendors, and stunning riches of the golden city-state, New Jerusalem, will be Christ's regal gift to His royal bride-church (John 14:2–3; Rev. 21–22).[72]

Additionally, since Christ is the greatest King ("KING OF KINGS," Rev. 19:16) and gives generously from His inestimable riches, shouldn't we, His grace-begotten princes and princesses, also give generously, always confident our generous giving will be resupplied by our royal Husband-Lord and His royal Father?

Furthermore, let's remember Christ measures generosity proportionately, not numerically. Many rich people gave much to the temple treasury, but Jesus said the poor widow's "two mites" were of greater value than all their gifts because she donated all she had. So numerically their gifts were greater, but proportionately hers blessed Him more (Luke 21:1–4). If we're cut from the widow's cloth, and Philippian in spirit, we'll gauge our giving not by dollars but by its percentage of our discretionary income.[73]

We don't know what percentage the Philippians gave on average, but we know their donations were free, large, and steady. When teaching Philippians 4:19, therefore, we must point out how faithful they were. If we wish to own their promise, we must own their obedience. Non-givers are not

---

72. For more on royal gifts, see Genesis 12:16; 13:1–2; 41:42–43, 45; 1 Kings 10:13; Esther 1:7–8; 5:3; Matthew 2:11.
73. Yes, this challenges me as much as it does you!

here guaranteed divine provision—nor are they warned they'll be cut off. God mercifully often provides the needs of even His least-giving people and multitudes who are not and will never be His people (Matt. 5:44)! But this text assures those who give faithfully that God will provide "all" their needs. Why?

It's a matter of divine principle. Scripture asserts two key laws of giving: We reap *what* we sow (Gal. 6:7) and in the *measure* we sow it (2 Cor. 9:6, 8). The Philippians had given, and generously, supplying more than Paul needed. He had "all," was "full," and was "abound[ing]" (4:18). So Paul assured them they would reap what they sowed and in the measure they sowed it; God would resupply them, and generously! There's more.

These two principles also speak to us as recipients of blessings. When others freely bless us with financial resources, gifts, or other necessary supplies, we may freely receive them (Matt. 10:8b), even when our donors are needy themselves. Why? We know divine reciprocity will, it must, be released. God's principles are as immutable as He is. In His time and way He'll give back to our donors what they've given, and in the measure they've given (Luke 6:38; 1 Kings 17:10–16). Two key clarifications remain.

First, this faithful divine reprovision flows as we trust God, not our assets (mammon), and seek our King and His kingdom "first," not our worldly ends (Matt. 6:24–33). If we remain self-centered, money-loving, and unconcerned with Christ's will, we'll grieve Him and hinder His financial reciprocation even when we give. Why? Our heart isn't right. Yes, our devotion is more important to Jesus than our donations.

Second, in no way does Philippians 4:19 promise God will make us affluent. It pledges not prosperity but provision—simply that we will not lack life's necessities (Ps. 23:1). God may if He pleases prosper us financially to have more to share with His churches, ministries, ministers, missionaries, and the poor (Luke 8:1–3; Acts 16:14–15, 40), but that's not pledged here. To the contrary, the context implies mature Christians, like Paul, are "content" with "whatever" God provides (Phil. 4:11–12) and neither require nor desire excessive worldly wealth. They've found true, eternal, spiritual riches—in Christ's presence, truth, Spirit, and approval, and the loving fellowship of His people—and have lost interest in worldly affluence (1 Tim. 6:6–8; Rev. 3:18). They don't need a large stockpile of money or goods to rely on because they know and trust the unfailing Provider. They long for more of Jesus, not more money.[74] Like Paul, the Philippians were truly rich.

Are you rich in God, His truth, contentment, and the confidence that no matter what your condition, your fabulously wealthy King and Lord will amply supply your every human need?

4:20–23 Paul's excellent epilogue. In closing his Philippian letter, Paul cites several key topics. His epilogue is praiseful, preaching, personal, empowering, and prayerful.

His doxology praises the most worthy One: "Now unto God and our Father be glory forever" (4:20). Isn't this the ultimate final subject or last word anyway, glorifying God? We were born and reborn to this end. Thus Paul gives all credit for his endurance as a prisoner, his fruitful ministry

---

[74]. Two marks of spiritual maturity are increasing material contentment and insatiable spiritual hunger (Ps. 63:1–3; Heb. 13:5).

in Rome (Acts 28:30–31), including its highest circles (Phil. 4:22), and his inspiration for this letter, to "God...our Father" alone. Ultimately all people will audibly honor Him, even those eternally lost (2:10–11). Even Jesus will deliver up all His glorious power, honor, authority, and majesty to His Father (1 Cor. 15:24–28). Our praise of Him should be "constant and perpetual,"[75] since we'll be doing so "forever and ever" (Phil. 4:20).

Paul's doxology also reminds us of the comforting fact that "God"—the awesome Creator and Ruler of all things spiritual and material—is "our Father" (4:20). Though most precious to us, the fatherhood of God was a strange concept in the Roman world with all its distant, disinterested, capricious gods. Jesus repeatedly taught us to remember, pray to, and expect help from our warm, watchful, wondrously loving "Father in heaven" daily (Matt. 6:4, 6, 8–9, 14, 18, 32–33), who is "disposed to pity us and help us."[76]

Paul preached to the Philippians by ordering them to love all believers equally: "Greet *every* saint" (4:21), or "each of God's holy people—all who belong to Christ" (NLT). This reminds us that all Christians are important to God, not just those this world respects most (e.g., "Caesar's household," 4:22; cf. Col. 1:4). A large percentage of the Roman world was enslaved, and many Christians were slaves, as were many poor, women, children, and other socially marginalized people. So Paul reminds us that no Christian is to be lightly esteemed regardless of nationality, race, culture, age, or gender;[77] all are God's adopted

---

75. Henry, *Commentary in One Volume*, Phil. 4:20, note, 1868.
76. Ibid., Phil. 4:20, note, 1868.
77. But he didn't add "sexual preference." While anyone in the LBGT community may be saved if they repent and turn to Christ, none are acceptable in the holy Christian church while willfully continuing unholy, deviant sexual practices (Rom. 1:21–28; 1 Cor. 6:9–11; Eph. 5:3–12).

children, our spiritual siblings, members of Christ's body and bride, and distinguished citizens of heaven (3:20). Peter says the same (Acts 10:34–35), as does James, who forbids snobbery, reminding the poor that they're now honorable and beloved in Christ and the rich that their worldly privileges will pass (James 1:9–11; 2:1–9).

Paul issues three personal greetings from: (1) the Christians working and (possibly) living with him (4:21b), (2) the Roman Christians,[78] "all the saints [here in Rome] greet you" (4:22), (3) and especially "they that are of [associated with] Caesar's household" (4:22). The latter probably included some of Nero's servants and Praetorian guards and possibly some advisers or family members (1:12–13; Acts 28:16).

The Philippians surely found this last greeting empowering. It was no small thing that the gospel had invaded Caesar's palace:

> Even Caesar's slaves wielded more power and prestige than most well-off free persons; the Praetorian Guard itself held the prestige of the Roman military's elite, often rewarded by Caesar himself. Paul's greeting would impress his readers: his imprisonment has indeed advanced the gospel (1:12–13).[79]

---

78. The gospel arrived in Rome long before Paul, perhaps as soon as it took many of the proselytes and Jews of the Diaspora converted at Pentecost to return home (Acts 2:10, 5–11). Also Paul wrote his Roman epistle to the already well-established Roman church approximately three to five years before his arrival, commending their renowned faith (Rom. 1:8) and informing them he had been praying for and longing to visit them for some time (1:9–13).
79. Keener, *The IVP Bible Background Commentary: New Testament*, Phil. 4:22–23, note.

Knowing Paul's great humility, however, it's certain he didn't write this to boast on his ministry but rather to bolster the Philippians' faith in the sheer power of the God and gospel they had so totally embraced (Rom. 1:15–16). At a time when Christians were few, hated by Jews, grossly misunderstood by Romans, and widely ostracized or persecuted for being different, it was encouraging to know that Christ's Word was growing all over the Roman world (Acts 19:20). There weren't "many" high, noble, or otherwise influential Christians in the first century (1 Cor. 1:26), but there were some, and this encouraged all Christ's disciples that His kingdom was on the move. The downtrodden Jews were similarly encouraged and edified centuries earlier in the captivity and post-captivity periods when news spread of the amazing victories of faith won by their own—Daniel, his three friends, Mordecai, Esther, Nehemiah, and others (Esther 8:15–17; 9:2–4; 10:3; Dan. 3:29–30; 5:29; 6:25–27).

These three warm, personal greetings remind us of the importance of fellowship. From the beginning fellowship has been a key part of Christian life (Acts 2:42, 44–47), and something Paul deeply valued (Phil. 1:3–5), and encouraged (2:1–4). We should treasure brotherly fellowship and pursue it regularly. When for Christ's sake we're wounded with rejection or worn with the rigors of severe adversities, the sweet communion of our spiritual siblings is a powerful and priceless healing balm (Gal. 2:9; Col. 4:10–11; 1 John 1:3, 7).

Paul closed this epistle like his others, prayerfully, asking for God's "grace" to continue with the Philippians (Phil. 4:23). This ministered still more blessing to them, since Paul's powerful prayers surely brought a fresh release of God's Spirit, favor, and blessing upon them. It was also a necessary reminder to them,

Standing Fast!

and us, that we're not only saved by grace, but we also live by grace. Every moment of every day every believer is sustained by the wondrously abundant unmerited favor of Jesus Christ and the divine life, strength, provisions, and abilities imparted to us by that grace. Amen, so be it!

Thus Paul closes his excellent epistle with an excellent epilogue.

SELECT BIBLIOGRAPHY OF SOURCES CITED

Carson, D. A., R. T. France, J. A. Motyer, and G. J. Wenham, editors. *New Bible Commentary: 21st Century Edition*, 4th edition. Leicester, England; Downers Grove, IL: Inter-Varsity Press, 1994.

Chambers, G. *Oswald Chambers: His Life and Works*. London: Marshall, Morgan, & Scott, 1959.

Chambers, Oswald. *My Utmost for His Highest*. New York: Dodd, Mead, & Company, 1935.

Dake, Finnis Jennings. *Dake's Annotated Reference Bible*. Lawrenceville, GA: Dake Bible Sales, Inc., 1963.

Galli, Mark, and Ted Olsen. *131 Christians Everyone Should Know*. Nashville: B&H Publishing, 2000.

Harris, R. L., G. L. Archer Jr., and B. K. Waltke, editors. *Theological Wordbook of the Old Testament*, electronic edition. Chicago: Moody Press, 1999.

Hayford, Jack W., general editor. *The Spirit-Filled Life Bible*. Nashville: Thomas Nelson Publishers, 1991.

Henry, Matthew. *Commentary in One Volume*. Grand Rapids, MI; Zondervan Publishing, 1961.

Jamieson, R., A. R. Fausset, and D. Brown. *Commentary Critical and Explanatory on the Whole Bible*. Oak Harbor, WA: Logos Research Systems, Inc., 1997.

Keener, C. S. *The IVP Bible Background Commentary: New Testament*. Downers Grove, IL: InterVarsity Press, 1993.

Kittel, G., G. Friedrich, and G. W. Bromiley. *Theological Dictionary of the New Testament*, electronic edition. Grand Rapids, MI: W. B. Eerdmans, 1985.

Lambert, D. W. *Oswald Chambers: An Unbribed Soul*. Fort Washington, PA: Christian Literature Campaign, 1968.

Life Application Study Bible. Wheaton, IL: Tyndale House, 2004.

Liddell, H. *A Lexicon: Abridged From Liddell and Scott's Greek-English Lexicon*. Oak Harbor, WA: Logos Research Systems, Inc., 1996.

Louw, J. P. and E. A. Nida. *Greek-English Lexicon of the New Testament: Based on Semantic Domains*, electronic edition of the second edition. New York: United Bible Societies, 1996.

Mueller, George. *Answers to Prayer*. Chicago: Moody Press, 1984.

Myers, A. C. *The Eerdmans Bible Dictionary*. Grand Rapids, MI: Eerdmans, 1987.

Nuzum, Mrs. C. *The Life of Faith*. Springfield, MO: Gospel Publishing House, 1956.

Pfeiffer, Charles F., Howard F. Vos, and John Rea. *The Wycliffe Bible Encyclopedia*, volume 2. Chicago: Moody Press, 1975.

Robertson, A. *Word Pictures in the New Testament*. Nashville: Broadman Press, 1933.

Rogers, Nigel and Hazel Dodge,. *Roman Empire*. New York: Metro Books, 2011.

Sauer, Christof and Thomas Schirrmacher. "Father, Forgive Them." *Christian History Magazine*, issue 109: Eyewitnesses to the Modern Age of Persecution. Worchester, PA: Christian History Institute, 2014.

Smith, S. and J. Cornwall. *The Exhaustive Dictionary of Bible Names*. North Brunswick, NJ: Bridge Logos Publishers, 1998.

Snyder, James L. *In Pursuit of God: The Life of A. W. Tozer*. Camp Hill, PA: Christian Publications, 1991.

Spicq, C. and J. D. Ernest. *Theological Lexicon of the New Testament*. Peabody, MA: Hendrickson Publishers, 1994.

Strong, J. *A Concise Dictionary of the Words in the Greek Testament and The Hebrew Bible*. Bellingham, WA: Logos Bible Software, 2009.

———. *Enhanced Strong's Lexicon*. Bellingham, WA: Logos Bible Software, 2001.

Swanson, J. *Dictionary of Biblical Languages With Semantic Domains: Greek (New Testament*, electronic edition. Oak Harbor: Logos Research Systems, Inc., 1997.

Tan, P. L. *Encyclopedia of 7700 Illustrations: Signs of the Times*, electronic edition. Garland, TX: Bible Communications, Inc., 1996.

Thomas, R. L. *New American Standard Hebrew-Aramaic and Greek Dictionaries*, updated edition. Anaheim: Foundation Publications, Inc., 1998.

Tozer, A. W. *Of God and Men*. Harrisburg, PA: Christian Publications, 1960.

———. *The Best of A.W. Tozer.* Harrisonburg, PA: Christian Publications, 1978.

Verploegh, Harry. *Oswald Chambers: The Best From All His Books.* Nashville: Thomas Nelson Publishers, 1987.

Walvoord, J. F., R. B. Zuck, and Dallas Theological Seminary. *The Bible Knowledge Commentary: An Exposition of the Scriptures.* Wheaton, IL: Victor Books, 1985.

Wesley, Luke. *Stories From China: Fried Rice for the Soul.* Waynesboro, GA: Authentic Media, 2005.

Weymouth, Richard F. *New Testament in Modern Speech.* Grand Rapids, MI: Kregel Publications, 1978.

Wiersbe, W. W. *The Bible Exposition Commentary.* Wheaton, IL: Victor Books, 1996.

Wuest, K. S. *The New Testament: An Expanded Translation.* Grand Rapids, MI: Eerdmans, 1961.

CONTACT THE AUTHOR

Greg Hinnant Ministries
P. O. Box 788
High Point, NC 27261

Telephone:
(336) 882-1645

E-mail:
rghministries@aol.com

Website:
greghinnantministries.org

OTHER BOOKS BY THE AUTHOR

Walking in His Ways

Walking on Water

DanielNotes:
An Inspirational Commentary on the Book of Daniel

Precious Pearls From the Proverbs

Word Portraits:
Five Illustrations of the Mature Christian

Gold Tried in the Fire:
Tested Truths for Trying Times

Spiritual Truths for Overcoming Adversity:
Life-Changing Biblical Insights on Christian Difficulties

Not by Bread Alone:
Daily Devotions for Disciples, Volume One

Sweeter Than Honey:
Daily Devotions for Disciples, Volume Two

Water From the Rock:
Daily Devotions for Disciples, Volume Three

Key New Testament Passages on Divorce and Remarriage